POCKET ME(

Mercedes-Ber
Series 163 (1997
Series 164 (2005 ~~ ~~~~)
2.7, 3.0, 4.0 Litre CDI
5-cyl., 6-cyl. and 8 cyl.

COVERING:
GENERAL INFORMATION, DIMENSIONS, WEIGHTS, CAPACITIES, GENERAL, SERVICING NOTES	4
DIESEL ENGINES	12
LUBRICATION SYSTEM	79
COOLING SYSTEM	85
DIESEL FUEL INJECTION SYSTEM	96
CLUTCH	109
MANUAL TRANSMISSION/TRANSFER CASE	114
PROPELLER SHAFT	117
FRONT AXLE AND FRONT SUSPENSION	118
REAR AXLE AND REAR SUSPENSION	130
STEERING	137
BRAKE SYSTEM	141
ELECRICAL SYSTEM	156
AUTOMATIC TRANSMISSION	162
EXHAUST SYSTEM	166
SERVICING AND MAINTENANCE	168
FAULT FINDING SECTION	171
WIRING DIAGRAMS	176

BY PETER RUSSEK

ORDER NO.: 323

Published by
Peter Russek Publications Ltd.
3rd Floor, Block C,
Commercial Square,
High Wycombe, Bucks, HP11 2RH
Tel.: High Wycombe (01494) 440829
(01494) 526882
Fax: (01494) 473980
E-mail: russek@globalnet.co.uk
www.russek-manuals.co.uk

ISBN. NO. 1-898780-32-3

**WITH FAULT FINDING SECTION
AT END OF MANUAL**

No part of this publication may be reproduced, stored in a retrieval system or transmitted in any form, electronic, mechanical, photocopying, recording, translating or other means without prior permission by the author.

The publisher would like to thank Daimler Chrysler U.K. Ltd. for their invaluable support in producing this manual.

No liability can be accepted for any inaccuracies or Omissions in this workshop manual, although every possible care has been taken to make it as complete and accurate as possible Every care has also been taken to prevent personal injury or damage to equipment when working on the vehicle We have tried to cover all models produced to the day of publication, but are unable to refer to all modifications and changes for certain markets or updating of models.

PREFACE

Small though this Workshop Manual is in size, it lacks no detail in covering most of the servicing and repair of the Mercedes-Benz vehicles, known as "ML-Class", but built in two series. Originally the vehicles were introduced as series „163", manufactured until the end of approx. 2004. The new series "164" was introduced during 2005. The various models are listed in Section 0 under "Introduction".

Brief, easy-to-follow instructions are given, free from all necessary complications and repetitions, yet containing all the required technical detail and information, and many diagrams and illustrations.

Compiled and illustrated by experts, this manual provides a concise source of helpful information, all of which has been cross-checked for accuracy to the manufacturer's official service and repair procedures, but many instructions have derived from actual practice to facilitate your work. Where special tools are required, these are identified in the text if absolutely necessary and we do not hesitate to advise you if we feel that the operation cannot be properly undertaken without the use of such tools.

The readers own judgement must ultimately decide just what work he will feel able to undertake, but there is no doubt, that with this manual to assist him, there will be many more occasions where the delay, inconvenience and the cost of having the van off the road can be avoided or minimised.

The manual is called "Pocket Mechanic" and is produced in a handy glove pocket size with the aim that it should be kept in the vehicle whilst you are travelling. Many garage mechanics themselves use these publications in their work and if you have the manual with you in the car you will have an invaluable source of reference which will quickly repay its modest initial cost.

Finally – We do not claim that we know everything. If you have any suggestions to facilitate certain operations, please do not hesitate to pass them onto us, so other fellow motorists can benefit later on.

0. INTRODUCTION

Our "Pocket Mechanics" are based on easy-to-follow step-by-step instructions and advice, which enables you to carry out many, jobs yourself. Moreover, now you have the means to avoid these frustrating delays and inconveniences which so often result from not knowing the right approach to carry out repairs which are often of a comparatively simple nature.

Whilst special tools are required to carry out certain operations, we show you in this manual the essential design and construction of such equipment, whenever possible, to enable you in many cases to improvise or use alternative tools. Experience shows that it is advantageous to use only genuine parts since these give you the assurance of a first class job. You will find that many parts are identical in the various makes covered, but our advice is to find out before purchasing new parts - **Always buy your spare parts from an officially appointed dealer.**

0.0. General Information

Four-cylinder, six-cylinder and eight-cylinder petrol engines and five- and six-cylinder diesel engines are fitted to ML vehicles. Only diesel models are covered in the manual:

Models 1998 to 1999

ML 230, four-cylinder: Four-cylinder engine, 2295 c.c., with 16 valves with a performance of 150 B.H.P (110 kW) at 3800 rpm. Engine type "111"977 is fitted. Model identification 163.136. The vehicle is available with manual transmission (717.461) or automatic transmission (722.660).

ML 320, 3.2 litre six-cylinder: V6 engine with 18 valves, 3199 c.c., with a performance of 219 B.H.P (160 kW) at 5600 rpm. Engine type "112.942". Model identification 163.154. The vehicle is fitted with an automatic transmission (722.662).

ML430, 4.3 litre, eight-cylinder: V8 engine with 24 valves, 4266 c.c., with a performance of 271 B.H.P (199 kW) at 5500 rpm. Engine type "113.942". Model identification 163.172. The vehicle is fitted with an automatic transmission (722.663).

Models 2000 to 2001

Models ML230, ML320 and ML 430 were sold with the engines listed above to the end of 2000. The ML230 was discontinued for 2001. Additional:

ML270 CDI, 2.7 litre, five-cylinder: Five-cylinder diesel engine with direct injection (CDI) with a performance of 163 B.H.P. (120 kW) at 4200 rpm. Fitted with the engine uses in other MB models, as for example in the Sprinter (612.942). Model identification 163.113. The vehicle is fitted with a six-speed manual transmission 716.644 or 717.461) or an automatic transmission (722.661).

Models 2002 to 2003

ML 320, 3.2 litre six-cylinder: V6 engine with 18 valves, 3199 c.c., with a performance of 219 B.H.P (160 kW) at 5600 rpm. Engine type "112.942". Model identification 163.154. The vehicle is fitted with an automatic transmission (722.662).

ML 500, 5.0 litre eight-cylinder: V8 engine with 24 valves, with a performance of 292 B.H.P. (215 kW) at 5600 rpm. Engine type "113.965". Model identification 163.175. The vehicle is fitted with an automatic transmission (722.660).

ML270 CDI, 2.7 litre, five-cylinder: Five-cylinder: As fitted to 2000 and 2001 models.

ML400 CDI, 4.0 litre, eight-cylinder: V8 engine with 32 valves, with a performance of 250 B.H.P. (185 kW) at 4000 rpm. Engine type "628.963". Model identification 163.965. The vehicle is fitted with an automatic transmission (722.666 or 722.773).

Models 2002 to 2004

ML 350, 3.7 litre six-cylinder: V6 engine with 18 valves, with a performance of 234 B.H.P. (172 kW) at 3000 rpm. Engine type "112.970". Model identification 163.157. The vehicle is fitted with an automatic transmission (722.662).

ML 500, 5.0 litre eight-cylinder: V8 engine with 24 valves, with a performance of 292 B.H.P. (215 kW) at 5600 rpm. Engine type "113.965". Model identification 163.175. The vehicle is fitted with an automatic transmission (722.660).

ML270 CDI, 2.7 litre, five-cylinder: Five-cylinder: As fitted to 2000 and 2001 models.

ML400 CDI, 4.0 litre, eight-cylinder: As fitted to 2003 and 2004 models.

Models 2005 to 2006

This sees the introduction of the new model series "164".

ML 350, 3.5 litre six-cylinder: V6 engine with 24 valves, with a performance of 272 B.H.P. (200 kW) at 6000 rpm. Engine type "272.967". Model identification 164.186. The vehicle is fitted with an automatic transmission (722.906 or 722.944).

ML 500, 5.0 litre eight-cylinder: V8 engine with 24 valves, with a performance of 306 B.H.P. (225 kW) at 5600 rpm. Engine type "113.964". Model identification 164.175. The vehicle is fitted with an automatic transmission (722.901).

ML280 CDI, 3.0 litre, six-cylinder: V6 diesel engine with 24 valves with direct injection (CDI) with a performance of 190 B.H.P. (140 kW) at 3800 rpm. Engine type 642.940. Model identification 164.186. The vehicle is fitted with an automatic transmission (722.902).

ML320 CDI, 3.0 litre, six-cylinder: V6 diesel engine with 24 valves with direct injection (CDI) with a performance of 224 B.H.P. (165 kW) at 3800 rpm. Engine type 642.940. Model identification 164.122. The vehicle is fitted with an automatic transmission (722.906 or 722.644).

The advantages of a multi-valve technology

One of the basis problems of a four stroke engine is the filling of the cylinders during the induction stroke with the necessary amount of the fuel/air mixture. The problem is increased with increasing engine speed, as the opening period of the valves is shortened. Technicians refer to filling loss. To compensate the valve diameters are selected as large as possible so that more fuel/air mixture can enter, but the disadvantage is, of course, the larger diameter of the compression chamber.

This is the main reason for the introduction of the multi-valve technology. Three or four valve heads make up a lager opening area than two large valve heads and the size of the compression chamber can remain the same.

The advantages of the four valves can therefore given as follows:

- Four valves enable larger opening diameters for inlet and exhaust gases. This helps the engine performance and the fuel consumption. This is one of the reasons that an engine with four valves per cylinder has a better consumption than a valve with two valves.
- Engines with three/four valves per cylinder have smaller valves and thereby less weight to be moved. A quicker response of the valve gear is therefore possible. One more advantage of this construction that valve springs with a lower pressure is necessary to close the valves.
- Smaller valves are able to cool down quicker during the closing period.
- Engines with three/four valves per cylinder also enable to obtain a higher compression ratio.
- The spark plugs can be centred in the compression chamber to provide the best possible igniting of the fuel/air mixture.

The vehicles covered in this manual are fitted with a five- or six-speed manual transmission or 5- or 7-speed automatic transmission.

The vehicles have a double wishbone front suspension with torsion bars and telescopic shock absorbers and a stabiliser bar in the case of model series "163" to the end of 2004. The torsion bars were replaced by coil springs on model series "164" with the introduction of model year 2005. .

The independent rear suspension comprises double wishbones, coil springs and a stabiliser bar in the case of model series "163". With the introduction of model series "164" the rear suspension has been changed and now consists of a four-suspension arm suspension with coil springs. The stabiliser bar has been retained.

Disc brakes on all four wheels, with dual-line brake system and brake servo is fitted. The handbrake acts on the rear wheels.

A rack and pinion steering with servo-assistance is fitted.

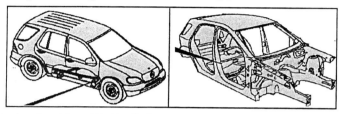

Fig. 0.1 – Location of the vehicle identification number. On the L.H. side for model series 163, on the R.H. side for model series 164 (from 2005).

0.1. Vehicle Identification

The type identification plate is located at the R.H. side at the position shown in Fig. 01, in the case of models 163 on the L.H. side and models 164 on the R.H. side. All vehicle identification numbers start and end with the Mercedes star and has 19 numbers Fig. 0.2 shows an example of an identification number. The number refers to the world manufacturing code (2 to 4), model designation (t to 10), steering (11), manufacturing plant (12) and the production number (13 to 18).

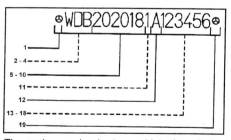

Fig. 0.2 – Vehicle identification number (shown on a different model). Numbers (1) and (19) show the Mercedes star. The remaining numbers are explained in the text.

Any other type identification plates will be given in the Owners Manual, for example chassis number, permissible maximum weight and the permissible axle load on front and rear axle, paint code, etc.

The engine number is stamped into the cylinder block on the side of the starter motor, immediately below the intake tube.

The code numbers and letters must always be quoted when parts are ordered. Copy the numbers on a piece of paper and take it to your parts supplier. You will save yourself and your parts department delays and prevents you from ordering the wrong parts.

0.2. General Servicing Notes

The servicing and overhaul instructions in this Workshop Manual are laid out in an easy-to-follow step-by-step fashion and no difficulty should be encountered, If the text and diagrams are followed carefully and methodically. The "Technical Data" sections form an important part of the repair procedures and should always be referred to during work on the vehicle.

In order that we can include as much data as possible, you will find that we do not generally repeat in the text the values already given under the technical data headings. Again, to make the best use of the space available, we do not repeat at each operation the more obvious steps necessary - we feel it to be far more helpful to concentrate on the difficult or awkward procedures in greater detail. However, we summarise below a few of the more important procedures and draw your attention to various points of general interest that apply to all operations.

Always use the torque settings given in the various main sections of the manual. These are grouped together in separate sub-sections for convenient reference.

Bolts and nuts should be assembled in a clean and very lightly oiled condition and faces and threads should always be inspected to make sure that they are free from damage burrs or scoring. DO NOT degrease bolts or nuts.

All joint washers, gaskets, tabs and lock washers, split pins and "O" rings must be replaced on assembly. Seals will, in the majority of cases, also need to be replaced, if the shaft and seal have been separated. Always lubricate the lip of the seal before assembly and take care that the seal lip is facing the correct direction.

References to the left-hand and right-hand sides are always to be taken as if the observer is at the rear of the vehicle, facing forwards, unless otherwise stated.

Always make sure that the vehicle is adequately supported, and on firm ground, before commencing any work on the underside of the car. A small jack or a make shift prop can be highly dangerous and proper axle stands are an essential requirement for your own safety.

Dirt, grease and mineral oil will rapidly destroy the seals of the hydraulic system and even the smallest amounts must be prevented from entering the system or coming into contact with the components. Use clean brake fluid or one of the proprietary cleaners to wash the hydraulic system parts. An acceptable alternative cleaner is methylated spirit, but it this is used, it should not be allowed to remain in contact with the rubber parts for longer than necessary. It is also important that all traces of the fluid should be removed from the system before final assembly.

Always use genuine manufacturer's spares and replacements for the best results.

Since the manufacturer uses metric units when building the cars it is recommended that, these are used for all precise units. Inch conversions are given in most cases but these are not necessarily precise conversions, being rounded off for the unimportant values.

Removal and installation instructions, in this Workshop Manual, cover the steps to take away or put back the unit or part in question. Other instructions, usually headed "Servicing", will cover the dismantling and repair of the unit once it has been stripped from the vehicle it is pointed out that the major instructions cover a complete overhaul of all parts but, obviously, this will not always be either necessary and should not be carried out needlessly.

There are a number of variations in unit parts on the range of vehicles covered in this Workshop Manual. We strongly recommend that you take care to identify the precise model, and the year of manufacture, before obtaining any spares or replacement parts.

Std.: To indicate sizes and limits of components as supplied by the manufacturer. Also to indicate the production tolerances of new unused parts.

O/S   Paris supplied as Oversize or Undersize or recommended limits for such parts, to enable them to be used with worn or re-machined mating parts.
U/S   O/S indicates a part that is larger than Std. size U/S may indicate a bore of a bushing or female part that is smaller than Std.
Max.: Where given against a clearance or dimension indicates the maximum allowable If in excess of the value given it is recommended that the appropriate part is fitted.
TIR: Indicates the Total Indicator Reading as shown by a dial indicator (dial gauge).
TDC: Top Dead Centre (No. 1 piston on firing stroke).
MP: Multi-Purpose grease.

0.3. Dimensions and Weights (typical)

Overall length – ML 230, ML 320, ML 430 , ML 270 CDI – 1998/2001: ....4590 mm
Overall length – ML 320, ML 500, ML 270 CDI – 2002 : ....4535 mm
Overall length – ML 350, ML 500, ML 270 CDI, 400 CDI – 2003/2004 : ....4640 mm
Overall length – ML 350, ML 500, ML 280 CDI, 320 CDI – 2005/2006 : ....4578 mm
Overall width – ML 230, ML 320, ML 430 , ML 270 CDI – 1998/2001:...........1830 mm
Overall width – ML 320, ML 500, ML 270 CDI – 2002 : ....1850 mm
Overall width – ML 350, ML 500, ML 270 CDI, 400 CDI – 2003/2004 :..........1840 mm
Overall width – ML 350, ML 500, ML 280 CDI, 320 CDI – 2005/2006 :..........1910 mm
Overall height – ML 230, ML 320, ML 430 , ML 270 CDI – 1998/2001: ....1780 mm
Overall height – ML 320, ML 500, ML 270 CDI, 400 CDI – 2002 : ....1840 mm
Overall height – ML 350, ML 500, ML 270 CDI, 400 CDI – 2003/2004 : ....1840 mm
Overall height – ML 350, ML 500, ML 280 CDI, 320 CDI – 2005/2006 : ....1815 mm
Wheelbase – ML 230, ML 320, ML 430 , ML 270 CDI – 1998/2002:..............2820 mm
Wheelbase – ML 350, ML 500, ML 270 CDI, 400 CDI – 2003/2004:..............2820 mm
Wheelbase – ML 350, ML 500, ML 280 CDI, 320 CDI – 2005/2006 : ....2915 mm
Front track – ML 230, ML 320, ML 430 , ML 270 CDI – 1998/2001: ....1560 mm
Front track – ML 320, ML 500, ML 270 CDI – 2002 : ....1555 mm
Front track – ML 350, ML 500, ML 270 CDI, 400 CDI – 2003/2004 : ....1555 mm
Front track – ML 350, ML 500, ML 280 CDI, 320 CDI – 2005/2006 : ....1630 mm
Rear – ML 230, ML 320, ML 430 , ML 270 CDI – 1998/2001:........................1560 mm
Rear track – ML 320, ML 500, ML 270 CDI – 2002 : ....1555 mm
Rear track – ML 350, ML 500, ML 270 CDI, 400 CDI – 2003/2004 : ....1555 mm
Rear track – ML 350, ML 500, ML 280 CDI, 320 CDI – 2005/2006 : ....1630 mm
Kerb weight .... Refer to Owners manual

0.4. Capacities

Engines:
- Oil and filter change – 2.3 litre four-cylinder (111 engine): ....5.9 litres
- Oil and filter change – 3.2 litre V6 (112 engine):...7.5 litres
- Oil and filter change – 4.3 litre V8 (113 engine):...9.5 litres
- Oil and filter change – 5.0 litre V8 (113 engine):...8.0 litres
- Oil and filter change – 3.5 litre V6 (272 engine):...7.5 litres
- Oil and filter change – 2.7/3.0/4.0 litre CDI diesel engines: Refer to Owners manual
- Difference between Max/Min:..2.0 litres
Cooling system: .... Refer to Section "Cooling System"
Transmissions:...See Section 3.0

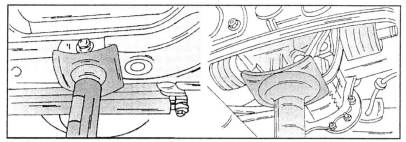

Fig. 0.3 – Jacking up the front end of the vehicle. The L.H. view shows where the jack is placed underneath the front crossmember. The R.H. view shows the jacking up of the rear of the vehicle. The jack is placed underneath the centre piece of the rear axle.

0.5. Jacking up the Vehicle

To prevent damage to the underside of the vehicle, apply a jack or chassis stands only to the points specified below:

Fig. 0.4 – Jacking up one side of the vehicle. Place the jack (2) underneath the side of the body as shown. Chassis stands (1) are placed at the position shown.

The front end of the vehicle should be lifted up by placing a jack underneath the transverse crossmember (cross bridge) for the front axle carrier as shown in Fig. 0.3, taking care not to damage the undercover for the engine compartment. To lift the rear end of the vehicle, place the jack underneath the rear cross bridge for the rear axle carrier, similar as shown as shown in Fig. 0.3 on the R.H. side. Make sure the jack is sufficient to take the weight of the vehicle. The vehicle can also be jacked up on one side. In this case place the jack underneath the hard rubber inserts near the wheels, as shown in Fig. 0.4 on one side of the vehicle. Never place a jack underneath the oil sump or the gearbox to lift the vehicle.

Fig. 0.5 – Three-legged chassis stands are the safest method to support the vehicle when work has to be carried out on the underside of the vehicle.

Chassis stands should only be placed on the L.H. and R.H. sides under the side of the body without damage to the paint work. Use chassis stands of the construction shown in Fig. 0.5, should be used, but again make sure that they are strong enough to carry the weight of the vehicle. Make sure the vehicle cannot slip off the stands.

Before lifting the front of the vehicle engage first or reverse gear when a manual transmission is fitted or place the gear selector lever into the "P" (park) position when an automatic transmission is fitted. Use suitable chocks and secure the front wheels when the rear end of the vehicle is jacked up.

Always make sure that the ground on which the vehicle is to be jacked up is solid enough to carry the weight of the vehicle.

Note: *It is always difficult to raise a vehicle first on one side and then on the other. Take care that the vehicle cannot tip-over when the first side is lifted. Ask a helper to support the vehicle from the other side. Never work underneath the vehicle without adequate support.*

0.6. Recommended Tools

To carry out some of the operations described in the manual we will need some of the tools listed below:

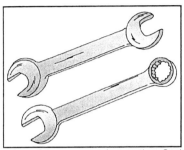

Fig. 0.6 – A double open-ended spanner in the upper view and an open-ended/ring spanner in the lower view. Always make sure that the spanner size is suitable for the nut or bolt to be removed and tightened.

As basic equipment in your tool box you will need a set of open-ended spanners (wrenches) to reach most of the nuts and bolts. A set of ring spanners is also of advantage. To keep the costs as low as possible we recommend a set of combined spanners, open-ended on one side and a ring spanner on the other side. Fig. 0.6 shows a view of the spanners in question. Sockets are also a useful addition to your tool set.

Fig. 0.7 – A graduated disc is used to "angle-tighten" nuts and bolts. "Torx" head bolts are shown on the R.H. side.

A set of cross-head screwdrivers, pliers and hammers or mallets may also be essential. You will find that many bolts now have a "Torx" head. In case you have never seen a "Torx" head bolt, refer to Fig. 0.7. A socket set with special "Torx" head inserts is used to slacken and tighten these screws. The size of the bolts are specified by the letter "T" before the across-flat size.

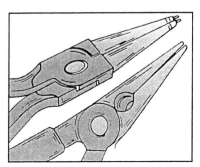

Fig. 0.8 – Circlip pliers are shown in the upper view. The type shown in suitable for outside circlips. The lower view shows a pair of pointed pliers.

Circlip pliers may also be needed for certain operations. Two types of circlip pliers are available, one type for external circlips, one type for internal circlips. The ends of the pliers can either be straight or angled. Fig. 0.8 shows a view of the circlip pliers. Apart from the circlip pliers you may also need the pliers shown in Fig. 0.9, i.e. side cutters, combination pliers and water pump pliers.

Fig. 0.9 – Assortment of pliers suitable for many operations.
1 Side cutter
2 Combination pliers
3 Water pump pliers

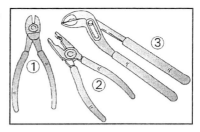

Every part of the vehicle is tightened to a certain torque value and you will therefore need a torque wrench which can be adjusted to a certain torque setting. In this connection we will also mention a graduated disc, shown in Fig. 0.7, as many parts of the vehicle must be angle-tightened after having been tightened to a specific torque. As some of the angles are not straight-forward (for example 30 or 60 degrees), you will either have to estimate the angle or use the disc.

Finally you may consider the tool equipment shown in Fig. 0.10 which will be necessary from time to time, mainly if you intend to carry out most maintenance and repair jobs yourself.

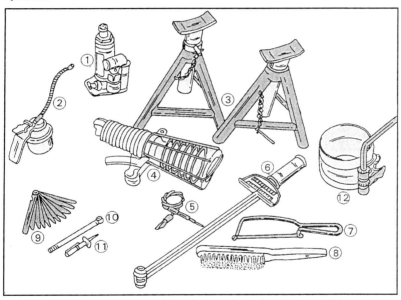

Fig. 0.10 – Recommended tools to service and repair your vehicle.

1 Hydraulic jack
2 Oil can
3 Chassis stands
4 Electric hand lamp
5 Test lamp (12 volts)
6 Torque wrench
7 Small hand saw
8 Wire brush
9 Feeler gauges
10 Tyre pressure gauge
11 Tyre profile depth checker
12 Piston ring clamp band

0.7. Before you start

Before you carry out any operations on your vehicle it may be of advantage to read the following notes to prevent injuries and damage to the vehicle:

- Never carry out operations underneath the vehicle when the front or rear is only supported on the jack. Always place chassis stands in position (refer to next section). If no chassis stands are available and if the wheels are removed place on wheel on top of the other one and place them under the side of the vehicle where you work. If the jack fails the vehicle will drop onto the two wheels, preventing injury.
- Never slacken or tighten the axle shaft nuts or wheel bolts when the vehicle in resting on chassis stands.
- Never open the cooling system when the engine is hot. Sometimes it may, however, be necessary. In this case place a thick rag around the cap and open it very slowly until all steam has been released.
- Never allow brake fluid or anti-freeze to come in contact with painted areas.
- Never inhale brake shoe or brake pad dust. If compressed air is available, blow off the dust whilst turning the head away. A mask should be worn for reasons of safety.
- Remove oil or grease patches from the floor before you or other people slip on it.
- Do not work on the vehicle wearing a shirt with long sleeves. Rings and watches should be removed before carrying out any work.
- If possible never work by yourself. If unavoidable ask a friend or a member of the family to have a quick look to check that's everything is OK.
- Never hurry up your work. Many wheel bolts have been left untightened to get the vehicle quickly back on the road.
- Never smoke near the vehicle or allow persons with a cigarette near you. A fire extinguisher should be handy, just in case.
- Never place a hand lamp directly onto the engine to obtain a better view. Even though that the metal cage will avoid direct heat it is far better if you attach such a lamp to the open engine bonnet.
- Never drain the engine oil when the engine is hot. Drained engine oil must be disposed of in accordance with local regulation.
- Never place a jack underneath the oil sump or the gearbox to lift the vehicle.

1 DIESEL ENGINES

1.0. Technical Data

Fitted Engines:
- ML 270 CDI (163 series):   612 (612.963)
- ML 400 CDI (163 series):   628 (628.963)
- ML 280 CDI, ML 320 CD (164 series): 642 (643.940)

Number of Cylinders:
- 612 engine: Five
- 642 engine: Six (V)
- 628 engine: Eight (V)

Arrangement of cylinders:
- 612 engine: In-line
- 628 engine: 75° V
- 642 engine: 72° V

Camshafts:
- 612 engine: Two overhead camshafts (chain)
- 628 engine: 2 x 1 overhead camshaft (chain)
- 642 engine: 2 x 2 overhead camshafts (chain)

Arrangement of valves: Overhead
Cylinder bore – 612 engine: 88.00 mm
Cylinder bore – 628 engine: 86.00 mm
Cylinder bore – 642 engine: 83.00 mm
Piston stroke – 612 engine: 88.4 mm
Piston stroke – 628 engine: 86.0 mm
Piston stroke – 642 engine: 92.0 mm

Capacity:
- 612 engine: 2688 c.c.
- 628/642 engines: 3996/2987 c.c.

Compression Ratio:
- 612 engine: 18.0 : 1
- 628/642 engines: 18.0 : 1

Max. kW/B.H.P. (DIN):
- 612 engine, ML 270 CDI: 120 kW (163 BHP) at 4200 rpm
- 628 engine, ML 400 CDI: 184 kW (250 BHP) at 4000 rpm
- 642 engine, ML 280 CDI: 140 kW (190 BHP) at 3800 rpm
- 642 engine, ML 320 CDI: 165 kW (224 BHP) at 3800 rpm

Max. Torque:
- 612 engine, ML 270 CDI: 370 Nm (266 ft.lb.) at 1800 rpm
- 628 engine, ML 400 CDI: 560 Nm (271 ft.lb.) at 1700 rpm
- 642 engine, ML 280 CDI: 440 Nm (317 ft.lb.) at 1400 rpm
- 642 engine, ML 320 CDI: 510 Nm (367 ft.lb.) at 1600 rpm

Crankshaft bearings: 6 (5-cyl.), 4 (V6), 5 (V8) friction bearings
Cooling system: Thermo system with water pump, thermostat, cooling fan with fluid clutch, tube-type radiator
Lubrication: Pressure-feed lubrication with gear-type oil pump, driven with chain from crankshaft. With full-flow and by-pass oil filter
Air cleaner: Dry paper element air cleaner
Injection system: Common rail injection system (CDI)

General Information
The engines fitted to the ML vehicles in the series 163 and 164 are different in many ways. The following information will tell you something about the new engines of type "612" (five-cylinder) and types "628" (V8) in model series 163 and "642" (six-cylinder V6). The information are given in general for all engines. V6 engines have 24 valves, the V8 engine has 32 valves and the four-cylinder engine has 20 valves.
- The 2.7 litre engine (engine type 612.963) fitted to the end of production of series 163 in ML 270 CDI vehicles is no longer fitted to series 164. Introduced for model year 2000 and discontinued during 2004.
- The cylinder head, as already mentioned, has four valves per cylinder (either 20 valves in the case of a four-cylinder 612 engine, 24 valves in the case of a six-

cylinder or 32 in the case of the V8. The cylinder head is made of light alloy metal. The valve seats, made of hardened steel, are pressed into the cylinder head. The valves are „gliding" in brass valve guides and are arranged as „overhead" valves, i.e. they are inserted vertically, valve head down, into the combustion chambers.
- Identical engines are fitted to ML 280 and ML 320 models (engine type 642.940) in model series 164, but have a different performance.
- Two camshafts or four camshafts are fitted, depending on the engine. The bearings for the camshafts are not machined directly into the cylinder head.
- The valve tappets are inserted between camshafts and valve ends. The cams push against the ends of the tappets to operate the valves. The tappets are known as bucket tappets.

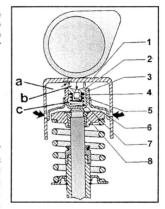

Fig. 1.1 – The operation of the hydraulic tappets. The oil enters via the bore (1) in the tappet into the valve tappet chamber (a), then into the smaller chamber (b) and then via the ball valve into the working chamber (c). The remaining parts are given below.
1 Valve tappet
2 Thrust pin
3 Retaining ring
4 Pressure spring
5 Ball guide
6 Ball
7 Gall guide
8 Guide sleeve

- The adjustment of the valves is no longer necessary on these engines. Hydraulic compensating elements are fitted which will ensure the correct valve clearance at all times. The function of the hydraulic valve clearance compensating elements is to eliminate valve clearance, i.e. the dimensional changes in the valve train (valve lash) due to heat expansion and wear are compensated by the elements. The rocker arm is in constant contact with the cam. The compensating elements cannot be repaired, but can be checked for correct functioning as described below. Fig. 1.1 shows sectional views of a valve with clearance compensation. We will give a short description of the operation. All references refer to Fig. 1.1.

The hydraulic valve compensating element are fitted into the rocker levers and operate the valves directly via a ball socket:
- The thrust pin with oil supply chamber and the return bores and the ball valve (check valve). The ball valve separates the supply chamber from the work chamber.
- The guide sleeve with the work chamber (c), the thrust spring (4) and the closing cap.

When the engine is stopped and the tappet is held under load from the cam, the element can completely retract. The oil displaced from the work chamber (c) flows through an annular gap, i.e. the clearance between the guide sleeve and the thrust pin to the oil supply chamber (b).

When the cam lobe has moved past the valve tappet, the thrust pin will be without load. The thrust spring (4) forces the thrust pin upwards until the valve tappet rests against the cam.

The vacuum resulting from the upward movement of the thrust pin in the work chamber (c) opens the ball valve and the oil can flow from the supply chamber into the work chamber. The ball valve closes when the valve tappet presses against the cam and puts the thrust pin under load. The oil in the work chamber acts as a "hydraulic rigid connection" and opens the valve in question.

When the engine is running and depending on the engine speed and the cam position, the thrust pin is only pushed down slightly.

The oil contained in the oil supply chamber is sufficient to fill the work chamber under all operating conditions of the engine. Oil or leak oil which is not required, as well as air are able to escape via the annular gap between the washer and the rocker lever. The oil ejected from the work chamber flows via the annular gap between the guide sleeve and the thrust pin and the two return bores into the oil supply chamber.

Important Notes when working on the Engine

Before any work is carried out in the engine compartment note the following points, mainly when the engine is running:

- The engine is fitted with electronic components with a very high voltage. For this reason never touch any electrical/electronic elements when the engine is running or when the engine is being started.
- Never touch any of the electronic elements with the ignition key in position „2" and the engine is cranked over by hand.
- Persons with pace maker should not carry out any operations on the on the electronic ignition system.

1.1. Engine – Removal and Installation

The removal of the engine requires a suitable lifting hoist or hand crane to lift the power unit out of the vehicle. The engine is removed from the vehicle as a complete unit after the parts shown in Figs. 1.2 and 1.3 are removed from the vehicle. The engine is a heavy unit and the hoist or crane must be strong enough to take the weight of the assembly, remembering that the weight is more than 200 lbs. The following description is a general guide line, as we cannot refer to every possible variation and/or equipment that may be fitted to your vehicle. If an air conditioning system is fitted, it is not possible to remove the engine under DIY conditions, unless you have the system discharged and after completion of the installation re-charged at a Mercedes Dealer or a workshop dealing with A/C systems. The following instructions refer to the 2.7 litre "612" engine. Any differences for the remaining engines will be given further on in the description.

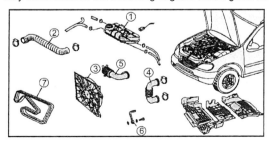

Fig. 1.2 – Details for the removal and installation of the engine (612 engine shown). Disconnect or remove the items as described.
1. Coolant expansion tank
2. Coolant hose
3. Electric fan
4. Air intake hose
5. Air intake scoop
6. Power steering fluid line
7. Poly V-belt

Figs. 1.2 and 1.3 show details of the items to be removed or disconnected. The following removal instructions will also give your information to refit a certain part or unit or the applicable tightening torque of bolts and/or nuts. All self-locking nuts and bolts must be replaced during installation. The numbers given in the description refer to Figs. 1.2 and 1.3 as applicable.

- Open the engine bonnet and place it in an upright position (vertical).

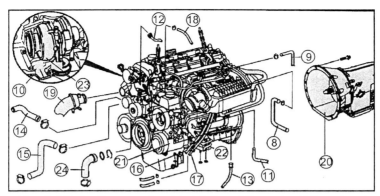

Fig. 1.3 – Details for the removal and installation of the engine (612 engine shown). Disconnect or remove the items as described. The numbers are continued from Fig. 1.2.

- 8 Fuel feed or pre-heater unit/ fuel pre-heating system
- 9 Fuel return flow to tank
- 10 Vacuum hose to turbocharger
- 11 Vacuum hose to mixing housing
- 12 Vacuum line to vacuum pump
- 13 Fluid line
- 14 Coolant hose to pump
- 15 Coolant hose to pump
- 16 Coolant hose to fuel cooler
- 17 Coolant hose to low temperature cooler
- 18 Coolant hose to fuel cooler
- 19 Charge air pipe
- 20 Transmission
- 21 A/C compressor
- 22 Front engine mount
- 23 Turbocharger
- 24 Charge air pipe to mixing chamber

- Jack up and support the vehicle as required when operations are carried out from below.
- Disconnect the battery.
- Remove the trim panels from the cylinder head as described later on for the 612 engine.
- Remove the bottom section of the sound-proofing capsule.
- Drain the cooling system as described in section "Cooling System" and remove the coolant expansion chamber (1) in Fig. 1.2. Detach the coolant hose (2) between thermostat housing and radiator.
- Remove the intake air hose (4) and the intake air scoop (5).
- Remove the electric fan ("Cooling System").
- Remove the Poly V-belt as described for this engine in section "Cooling System".
- Drain the fluid out of the steering fluid reservoir. A hand pump can be used to suck out the fluid. The power steering pipe (6) can now be disconnected from the radiator (tightened to 3.0 kgm /22 ft.lb.). Sealing rings are fitted on both sides of the banjo bolts and must be replaced. A second line connected to the steering pump is shown with (13) in Fig. 1.3 and must also be disconnected. Close the open ends of the pipes in suitable manner to prevent entry of dirt.
- Disconnect the vacuum hose to the vacuum control unit of the turbo charger (10), the vacuum hose to the mixing chamber (11) and the vacuum line to the vacuum pump (12).
- Disconnect the charge air pipe (19) at the turbo charger (23) and the hose (24) from the mixing chamber. A 6 mm or 7 mm hexagon socket will be required.
- Disconnect the two hoses (14) and (15) from the coolant pump, the coolant hose (16) from the fuel cooler, the coolant hose (17) from the low temperature cooler and the coolant hose (18) from the thermostat housing. The condition of the hoses and hose clamps must be checked before the parts are re-used.

- Disconnect the fuel feed to the pre-heater/fuel pre-heating system (8). The hose should be pinched together with a suitable clamp to avoid loss of fuel. The fuel return hose (9) to the fuel cooler must be disconnected and also clamped.
- Disconnect the wiring harness from the engine. Make each connection to facilitate the re-connection. Place the harness over the engine.
- Remove the charge air pipe (19) between turbo charger and charge air cooler and the mixing chamber (24). The support for the charge air distribution pipe is tightened to 2.0 kgm (14.5 ft.lb.).
- Disconnect the connector plug from the compressor and remove the compressor from its mountings. Attach the compressor with a piece of wire, with all lines connected. Tighten the compressor with 2.0 kgm (14.5 ft.lb.) to the timing cover.
- The engine must now be lifted with a suitable hand crane or hoist and ropes or chains attached to the engine lifting eyes. Carefully lift the engine without damaging the injection pipes. The workshop inserts a guard plate between the engine and the radiator/condenser to protect the items. If possible prepare a metal/aluminium plate to cover the width of the radiator and insert it. This will prevent any damage.
- Remove the bolts securing the transmission support to the transmission. The bolts are tightened to 4.0 kgm (29 ft.lb.) during installation.
- Place a mobile jack with a suitable protective plate underneath the transmission until just under tension and unscrew the bolts securing the transmission to the engine. The transmission-to-engine bolts are tightened to 4.0 kgm (29 ft.lb.).
- The spring connection between the primary catalytic converter and the catalytic converter must now be released. To do this press the spring discs together, using a pair of water pump pliers and pry off the steel tongue with a screwdriver. During installation the disc springs are pressed together with the pliers until the steel tongues snap in position.
- Unscrew the front engine mounts (22) from the vehicle frame. The engine mounts remain on the engine. Raise engine and remove it.

The installation of the engine is a reversal of the removal procedure, noting the various points already given during the removal procedure. Fuel connections and the cooling system must be checked for leaks after installation. Also note the additional points:
- Check the engine mountings, the oil and the fuel pipes for damage and replace as necessary.
- Check and if necessary correct the oil level in engine and transmission. If the engine has been drained fill it with the recommended oil.
- Before filling the cooling system make sure that all drain points have been closed.
- All bolts and nuts must be tightened to the necessary torque setting.
- After starting the engine and allowing it to warm up, check the cooling system for leaks. Drive the vehicle a few miles to check for exhaust pipe rattle.

Note: There is no need to remove the engine and the transmission when the engine mountings or the rear crossmember must be removed or replaced.

642 engine in models 280CDI and 320 CDI (model series 164)
Although the removal and installation is similar as described for the previous engine it will be necessary to remove the transmission together with the torque converter to take out the engine. The following is a summary of the necessary operations, but the work is rather complicated.
- Open the engine bonnet and place it in an upright position (vertical).
- Disconnect the battery.

17

- Remove the trim panels from the cylinder head as described later on for this engine.
- Remove both air cleaner housings, i.e. the L.H. one and the R.H. one.
- Jack up and support the vehicle as required when operations are carried out from below.
- Remove the bottom section of the sound-proofing capsule.
- Drain the cooling system from the radiator as described in section "Cooling System".
- Locate the charge air cooler and disconnect the charge air hoses. One is connected upstream of the air cooler and the other one downstream of the cooler. Check the condition of the hose clamp before installation.
- Disconnect a vacuum line for the brake servo unit from the fitting of the vacuum pump. To disconnect, press both clamps together and pull out the vacuum line.
- Locate the thermostat housing and disconnect two coolant hoses. Check the condition of hoses and hose clamps before re-using the parts.
- At the bottom of the oil sump locate a bracket securing the power steering fluid pipe. Tighten the bracket bolt to 1.0 kgm (7.2 ft.lb.) during installation. The fluid reservoir for the power steering must be emptied of fluid, using a hand pump, similar as a brake fluid reservoir is drained, as described in the brake section.
- On the power steering pump remove a banjo bolt securing the pressure line to the pump. Close the open end in suitable manner. The banjo bolt is tightened to 4.5 kgm (32.5 ft.lb.) during installation. Also disconnect the hydraulic hose from the steering fluid reservoir. Again seal off the hose end.
- Remove the Poly V-belt as described for this engine.
- Near the bracket for the power steering pipe at the bottom of the oil sump you will find two coolant hoses. Disconnect them. A further coolant hose is connected to the heat exchanger on the engine bulkhead (firewall), which must also be disconnected. Check the condition of hoses and hose clamps before re-using the parts.
- The upper crossmember, i.e. the radiator crossmember must be removed. *Note that the instructions also apply to petrol models ML350 and ML500.* First pull the sealing strip across the crossmember upwards and remove it. Locate the securing bolts on the L.H. and R.H. sides and remove them. One bolt is located at the lower end. At the inside of the radiator withdraw the connector plugs (left and right), remove two retaining clips and undo two visible bolts at the lower end. Looking at the front and at the centre of the crossmember you will see a square plate. At the lower end remove two expansion rivets. Raise the crossmember slightly and unclip the bonnet release cable from the R.H. bonnet latch from three retaining clamps. The crossmember can now be lifted out. All removed bolts are tightened to 1.0 kgm (7.2 ft.lb.).
- Remove the electric fan as described in section "Cooling System" for the 642 engine.
- Disconnect the wiring harness from the engine. Make each connection to facilitate the re-connection. Place the harness over the engine.
- Remove the complete exhaust system.
- Remove the complete transmission together with the torque converter.
- Remove the A/C compressor from the timing cover after removal of the securing bolts. A connector plug must be withdrawn, do not disconnect any pipes/hoses. The compressor is tied to the bottom of the engine compartment, lines connected. Tighten the bolts to 2.0 kgm (14.5 ft.lb.).
- Disconnect the fuel lines from the fuel pipes. Escaping fuel must be collected in a suitable container – Attention: Working on fuel items could mean risk of fire – Take

care. The disconnected fuel lines are attached with a cable tie to the exhaust manifold.
- Remove the bolts securing the front engine mountings to the front axle carrier. Tighten the bolts to 5.3 kgm (38 ft.lb.) during installation.
- The engine must now be lifted with a suitable hand crane or hoist and ropes or chains attached to the engine lifting eyes. Carefully lift the engine without damaging any of the parts. The workshop inserts a guard plate between the engine and the radiator/condenser to protect the items. If possible prepare a metal/aluminium plate to cover the width of the radiator and insert it. This will prevent any damage. The engine is lifted out in a horizontal position towards the front.

The installation of the engine is a reversal of the removal procedure, noting the various points already given during the removal procedure. Fuel connections and the cooling system must be checked for leaks after installation. The points given for the previous engine also apply to this engine.

628 engine in model ML400CDI (model series 163)

As the vehicle is fitted with air conditioning system as standard and the air conditioning system must be discharged to remove the engine we cannot describe the removal and installation as only a workshop dealing with A/C systems will be able to carry out the operation. The following operations are therefore only valid if you can take the vehicle to a workshop dealing with A/C systems. Have the system discharged and after installation of the engine re-charged. Provided that this is possible proceed as follows. We would like to point out that both headlamps must be removed, amongst other operations:

- Disconnect the battery.
- Pull the engine cover upwards, away from the engine.
- Remove the upper radiator crossmember by referring to Fig. 1.4. To do this, remove the two headlamps (5 and 6) as described in the electrical section, Remove the bolts (2) at the positions shown. The engine bonnet control cable (3) is disconnected from the engine bonnet lock (4). The crossmember (1) can now be removed.

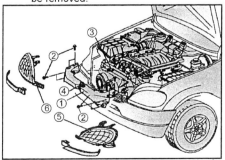

Fig. 1.4 – Details for the removal of the front end crossmember. The numbers are referred to in the text.

- Remove the washer fluid reservoir and the complete air cleaner.
- Empty the fluid reservoir for the power steering, using a hand pump and then remove the reservoir from the retaining plate of the intake air distribution tube.
- Jack up the front end of the vehicle and remove the L.H. front wheel. This is necessary to remove the front wing liner inside the wheel housing.
- Separate the refrigerant line of the evaporator coolant compressor in the L.H. wheel house – Remember !!! The A/C system must be discharged. Also in the L.H. wheel house disconnect the fuel lines. *Careful when working with fuel.* The two hoses must be pinched off with suitable clamps before they are disconnected. Allow fuel to run into a suitable container. Close the open ends in suitable manner.

Fig. 1.5 – Parts to be removed during the removal of the 628 engine (ML 400 CDI).

1   Radiator
2   Oil line, transmission cooling
3   Oil line, transmission cooling
4   Coolant return hose
5   Coolant bleed hose
6   Coolant feed hose
7   Oil line, steering cooling
8   Oil line, steering cooling
9   L.H. turbo charger air hose
10 R.H. turbo charger air hose
11 Charge air cooler
12 Charge air hose

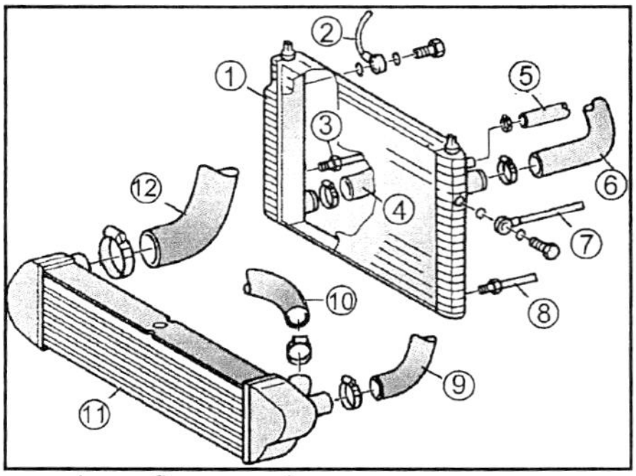

- Remove the bottom section of the sound-proofing capsule.
- Drain the cooling system as described later on – engine cold.
- For the next operations you can refer to Fig. 1.5. Disconnect the charge air hose of the L.H. turbo charger (9), the charge air hose from the R.H. turbo charger (10) and the charge air hose (12) from the charge air cooler.
- Unscrew the mounting clamps for the primary catalytic converters from the L.H. and R.H. turbo chargers.
- Remove the bolts securing the transmission bell housing to the engine. The lower bolts are only slackened at this stage. Bolts are tightened to 4.0 kgm (29 ft.lb.) during installation, but note that the bracket for the oil filler pipe and the exhaust brackets are tightened together with the bolts.
- Remove the nuts securing the L.H. and R.H. engine mountings.
- Remove the access cover for the torque converter on the crankcase and unscrew the torque converter from the driven plate. 6 bolts are used and the crankshaft must be rotated to gain access to all bolts. The crankshaft must be prevented from rotating. Bolts are tightened evenly to 4.2 kgm (30 ft.lb.) during installation.
- Refer to Fig. 1.6 and unclip the R.H. drain hose (4) and the L.H. drain hose (5) on the L.H. and R.H. sides of the transmission.

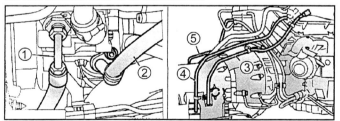

Fig. 1.6 – Some hoses and pipes to be disconnected.
1 Pressure line for power steering pump   4 R.H. drain hose
2 Refrigerant hose for compressor   5 L.H. drain hose
3 Transmission oil filler pipe

- Disconnect the coolant vent hose (5) in Fig. 1.5 and the coolant feed hose (6) from the radiator. Also in Fig. 1.5 disconnect the oil cooling hoses (2) and (3) from the radiator. Escaping oil must be collected. Use new sealing rings during installation. Tighten the union nut to 1.8 kgm (13 ft.lb.).
- Disconnect the fluid line for the steering oil cooling (7) and (8) in Fig. 1.5 at the radiator. Tighten the banjo bolt to 3.0 kgm (22 ft.lb.).

- Remove the electric fan.
- Three hoses must be disconnected from the low temperature cooler. These are shown in Fig. 1.7 and are the hose (1) for the lower temperature cooler, hose (2) for the heater return and hose (3) again to the lower temperature cooler.

Fig. 1.7 – Location of the three hoses mentioned above.

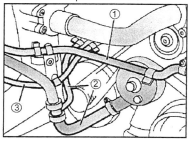

- Locate and disconnect the connector plug from the L.H. and R.H. hot film air mass meter at the front of the engine and the intake air distribution tube with the air filter intake hose.
- Remove the coolant expansion tank from the bulkhead.
- Remove the hot water circulation pump from the battery shield and place it to one side with the cooling hoses connected.
- Unscrew the transmission oil filler pipe (3) in Fig. 1.6 from the cylinder head cover. Standing in front of the engine compartment, on the R.H. side disconnect a vacuum hose. This is connected to the inlet port shut-off switchover valve. A second vacuum line is connected to the brake servo unit which must also be disconnected. Also disconnect the coolant vent hose from the housing for the fuse and relay module.
- Disconnect the refrigerant hose (2) in Fig. 1.6 from the compressor and the power steering pump pressure pipe (1) from the power steering pump. Tighten the hose connection (2) to 2.0 kgm (14.5 ft.lb.) and the union nut of pipe (1) to 4.5 kgm (32.5 ft.lb.) during installation.
- Engine compartment, top right, detach the throttle control cable from the position sensor and detach the position sensor from the bulkhead.
- Disconnect the engine wiring harness. Locate all connections and mark them accordingly.
- The engine must now be lifted away from the engine mounts, but observe the space between the engine and the bulkhead. Remove the two lower engine-to-transmission bolts still in position and then lift the engine towards the front until it is free of the transmission

The installation of the engine is a reversal of the removal procedure, noting the various points already given during the removal procedure. Fuel connections and the cooling system must be checked for leaks after installation. The points given for the previous engine also apply to this engine. *Take the vehicle to the workshop to have the A/C system charged.*

1.2 Engine - Dismantling

Before commencing dismantling of the engine, all exterior surfaces should be cleaned, as far as possible, to remove dirt or grease. Plug the engine openings with clean cloth first to prevent any foreign matter entering the cavities and openings. Detailed information on engine dismantling and assembly is given in the sections dealing with servicing and overhaul (sections commencing at 1.4.) and these should be followed for each of the sub-assemblies or units to be dealt with.
Follow the general dismantling instructions given below.
- Dismantling must be carried out in an orderly fashion to ensure that parts, such as valves, pistons, bearing caps, shells, tappets and so on, are replaced in the same

positions as they occupied originally. Mark them clearly, but take care not to scratch or stamp on any rotating or bearing surfaces. A good way to keep the valves in order is by piercing them through an upside-down cardboard box and writing the number against each valve. Segregate together the tappets, the springs and retainers with collets for each valve, if possible in small plastic bags for each individual valve.
- If a proper engine dismantling stand is not available, it will be useful to make up wooden support blocks to allow access to both the top and bottom faces of the engine. The cylinder head, once removed from the block, should be supported by a metal strap, screwed to the manifold face and secured by two nuts onto the manifold studs.

1.3   Engine - Assembling

The assembly of the engine is described in the following section for the component parts in question.

1.4.   Engine - Overhaul

1.4.0.   Cylinder Head and Valves – Technical Data

The following values are mostly given for the 612.963 engine as fitted to model ML 270 CD of series 163. Values for the other engines are similar but not identical and are either not available or too comprehensive to list. We therefore recommend to contact you dealer for any important value you may need. We strongly recommend to follow the recommendation in section 1.4.0.3., "Cylinder Head Overhaul".

Cylinder Head:

Cylinder head height:	126.85 - 127.15 mm
Max. Distortion of Cylinder Head Faces:	
- Longitudinal direction:	0.08 mm
- Across the face:	0.00 mm
Max. deviation of faces between upper and lower sealing faces (parallel to each other):	0.10 mm

Depth of valve head faces and cylinder head sealing face:
- Inlet valves: +0.17 to 0.23 mm
- Exhaust valves: +0.12 to 0.28 mm
- With re-cut valve seats: 1.0 mm – all valves

Valves

Valve Head Diameter:
- Inlet valves – 612 engine: 30.10 – 30.30 mm
- Inlet valves – 642 engine: 25.30 – 25.50 mm
- Exhaust valves – 612 engine: 28.30 – 28.50 mm
- Exhaust valves – 642 engine: 28.40 – 28.60 mm

Valve seat angle: 45° + 15'

Valve Stem Diameter:
- Inlet valves – 612 engine: 6.960 – 6.975 mm
- Inlet valves – 642 engine: 5.945 – 5.975 mm
- Exhaust valves – 612 engine: 6.955 – 6.990 mm
- Exhaust valves – 642 engine: 5.960 – 5.975 mm

Valve Length:
- Inlet valves - 612 engine: 104.70 – 104.90 mm

- Inlet valves - 642 engine: 102.10 – 102.50 mm
- Exhaust valves – 612 engine: 104.50 – 104.90 mm
- Exhaust valves – 642 engine: 102.10 – 102.50 mm

Valve Seat Width:
- Inlet/exhaust valves: 1.7 – 1.9 mm

Valve Identification: Check with parts list

Valve Seats
Valve seat width – Inlet/exhaust valves: 1.7 – 1.9 mm
Valve seat angles: 45° - 15'
Upper correction angle: 15°
Lower correction angle: 60°

Valve Timing   **612 Engine**
Inlet valves open: 19° after TDC
Inlet valves close: 7° after BTDC
Exhaust valves open: 9° before BTDC
Exhaust valves close: 22° before TDC

Cylinder Head on R.H. side: **642 Engine**
Inlet valves open: 19.6° after TDC
Inlet valves close: 5.6° after BTDC
Exhaust valves open: 17.9° before BTDC
Exhaust valves close: 27.9° before TDC
Cylinder Head on R.H. side:
Inlet valves open: 21.5° after TDC
Inlet valves close: 3.7° after BTDC
Exhaust valves open: 16.0° before BTDC
Exhaust valves close: 26.0° before TDC

Cylinder Head on L.H. side: **642 Engine**
Inlet valves open: 20.7° after TDC
Inlet valves close: 4.5° after BTDC
Exhaust valves open: 16.8° before BTDC
Exhaust valves close: 26.8° before TDC
Cylinder Head on L.H. side:
Inlet valves open: 21.5° after TDC
Inlet valves close: 3.7° after BTDC
Exhaust valves open: 16.0° before BTDC
Exhaust valves close: 26.0° before TDC

Cylinder Head on R.H. side: **628 Engine**
Inlet valves open: 18° after TDC
Inlet valves close: 6° after BTDC
Exhaust valves open: 11° before BTDC
Exhaust valves close: 23° before TDC

Cylinder Head on L.H. side: **628 Engine**
Inlet valves open: 18° after TDC
Inlet valves close: 6° after BTDC
Exhaust valves open: 11° before BTDC
Exhaust valves close: 28° before TDC

Valve seat basic bore in cylinder head (for reference only) – 612 engine:
- Inlet valves – Std.: 40.000 – 40.016 mm
- Exhaust valves – Std.: 37.000 – 37.016 mm

Valve seat height, all valves: 6.97 – 7.00 mm
Upper edge of valve seat rings to cylinder head face:
- Inlet valves: 2.37 – 2.25 mm
- Exhaust valves: 2.44 – 2.25 mm

Valve Springs (612 engine)
Colour code: yellow-green or purple-green
Outer diameter: 33.20 mm
Wire diameter: 4.25 mm
Free length: 50.80 mm
Length under load of 72 to 77 kg: 27.00 mm
- Wear limit: 27.00 mm at 65 kg

Valve Guides
Inlet valve Guides:
- Outer diameter – Std.: 14.044 – 14.051 mm
- Outer diameter – Repair size: 14.214 – 14.222 mm
- Inner diameter – 612 engine: 7.000 – 7.015 mm
- Inner diameter – 642 engine: 6.000 – 6.015 mm

Basic bore in cylinder head:
- Std.: 14.030 – 14.035 mm
- Repair size: 14.198 – 14.203 mm

Exhaust Valve Guides:
- Outer diameter – Std.: 14.044 – 14.051 mm
- Outer diameter – Repair size: 14.214 – 14.222 mm
- Inner diameter – 612 engine: 7.000 – 7.015 mm
- Inner diameter – 642 engine: 6.000 – 6.015 mm

Basic bore in cylinder head:
- Std.: 14.030 – 14.035 mm
- Repair size: 14.198 – 14.203 mm

Interference fit of valve guides – All guides:
- Std.: 0.009 – 0.021 mm
- Repair size: 0.011 – 0.024 mm

Camshaft
Camshaft Bearings:
Journal diameter: Not available
Camshaft Bearing Clearance:
- New condition: 0.050 – 0.091 mm
- Wear limit: 0.11 mm
Camshaft End Float:
- New condition: 0.07 – 0.15 mm
- Wear limit: 0.18 mm

1.4.0.1. Cylinder Head – Working on the Cylinder Head

The following information should be noted when work is carried out on a cylinder head:

- The cylinder head is made of light-alloy. Engine coolant, engine oil, the air required to ignite the fuel and the exhaust gases are directed through the cylinder head. Glow plugs, injectors and valve tappets are fitted to the cylinder head. Also in the cylinder heads you will find the camshafts.
- The exhaust manifold and the inlet manifold are bolted to the outside of the head. The fuel enters the head on one side and exits on the other side.
- The cylinder head is fitted with various sender units, sensors and switching valves, responsible for certain functions of the temperature control.
- As the cylinder head is made of light alloy, it is prone to distortion if, for example, the order of slackening or tightening of the cylinder head bolts is not observed. For the same reason never remove the cylinder head from a hot engine.
- A cylinder head cannot be checked in fitted position. Sometimes the cylinder head gasket will "blow", allowing air into the cooling system. A quick check is possible after opening the coolant reservoir cap (engine fairly cold). Allow the engine to warm-up and observe the coolant. Visible air bubbles point in most cases to a "blown" gasket. Further evidence is white exhaust smoke, oil in the coolant or coolant in the engine oil. The latter can be checked at the oil dipstick. A white, grey emulsion on the dipstick is more or less a confirmation of a damaged cylinder gasket.
- If you are convinced that water has entered the engine and you want to get home or to the nearest garage, unscrew the injectors and crank the engine with the starter motor for a while to eject the water. Refit the injectors, start the engine and drive to your destination without switching off the engine. This is the only method to avoid serious engine damage (bent connecting rods for example).

The cylinder head must only be removed when the engine is cold. New cylinder head gaskets are wrapped in plastic und must only be unwrapped just before the gasket is fitted. The cylinder head can be removed with the engine fitted and these operations are described below, but note that operations may vary, depending on the equipment fitted. Many secondary operations are necessary before the actual cylinder head can be removed. The following description refers therefore in detail to the various jobs on different engines.

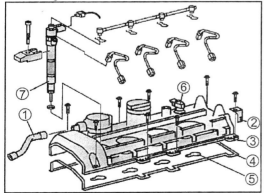

Fig. 1.8 – Details for the removal and installation of the cylinder head cover. Shown in this case is a four-cylinder engine. The numbers are explained in the text. One more injector is fitted to the 2.7 litre engine.

612 Engine – Cylinder Head Cover – Removal and Installation

Fig. 1.8 shows the parts fitted to the top of the cylinder head cover, but depending on the engine you will find different parts, i.e. the illustration shows the parts as fitted to an engine with four cylinders. Some of the individual operations are also described on the next pages. This will enable you to remove parts from the cylinder head when necessary.

- Disconnect the battery earth cable.

- Remove the trim panels above the cylinder head cover as described below.
- Detach the air cleaner housing from the cylinder head cover.
- Disconnect the hose (1) for the crankcase ventilation.
- Disconnect the electrical connector plug from the Hall sensor (6).
- Detach the electrical connector plug at the shut-off valve and place the line that is positioned over the cylinder head cover to one side.
- Detach the engine wiring harness from the bracket (2), if this is fitted.
- Undo the cable duct for the engine wiring harness to the cylinder head cover (3). Place the duct for the wiring harness to one side.
- Remove the fuel injectors (7) as described below.
- Remove the cylinder head cover (3)

The installation is a reversal of the removal procedure. The following points must be observed:

- Fit the cylinder head cover. Check the gaskets (4) and (5) in Fig. 1.8 and replace them if damaged. Do not tighten the cover bolts fully as the injectors are aligned by means of the cylinder head cover.
- Fit all injectors and the tensioning brackets (see also further on) and tighten them in the following order: 3-4-5-2-1. The bolts securing the cylinder head cover are now tightened to 0.9 kgm (7 ft.lb.).
- Push the cable plugs over the connections, install the cable duct with the engine wiring harness to the cylinder head cover and tighten the bolt.
- Push the cable plug over the camshaft position/Hall sensor (6).
- Re-connect the crankcase ventilation hose to the cylinder head cover.
- Install the trim panel to the cylinder head cover as described below under separate headings.
- All other operations are now carried out in reverse order.

Trim Panel of Cylinder Head Cover – Removal and Installation

The part in question is shown in Fig. 1.9. Different versions are shown. One of them is fitted. Remove as follows:

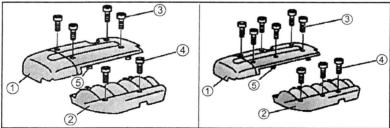

Fig. 1.9 – Removal of the trim panel above the cylinder head cover. The panel (2) for the charge air distribution pipe has a cut-out on the 2.7 litre (612) engine. The numbers are referred to below.

- Remove the bolts (3) and (4). Note the tightening torque. All bolts are tightened to 1.0 kgm (7.5 ft.lb.
- Pull out the panel (2) of the charge air distribution pipe and place it to one side. During installation insert the plates of the panel (2) into the rubber mounts (5).
- Take the trim panel (1) off the cylinder head cover. During installation make sure that none of the lines/pipes are trapped.

The installation is a reversal of the removal procedure, noting the points already given above.

Injection Pipes of Common Rail injection – Removal and Installation

- Detach the coolant expansion tank (reservoir) without disconnecting any of the hoses and place the reservoir over the engine.
- Remove the trim panel of the cylinder head cover.
- Slacken the union nuts at the end of the pipes on the injectors and the injection rail. The hexagons on the injectors must be held in position with an open-ended spanner. Remove the pipes and plug the open ends in suitable manner.

The installation is a reversal of the removal procedure. To ensure a stress free fitting of the pipes slacken the injection rail and connect the pipes at each end. Tighten the union nuts (hexagons held with the open-ended spanner) to 2.3 kgm (16.5 ft.lb.). Make sure that the pipes are properly installed and re-tighten the injection rail.

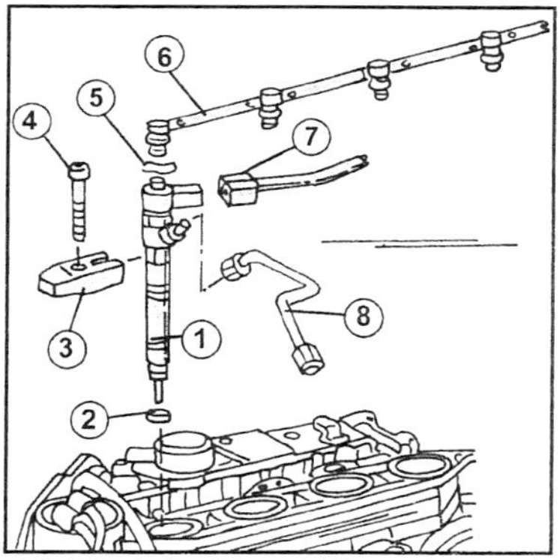

Fig. 1.10 – Removal and installation of injection pipes. The numbers are referred to in the text.

Injector – Removal and Installation

Fig. 1.10 shows the arrangement of the injectors together with the injection pipe and the leak off pipe. A clamp piece with a stretch bolts secures each injector to the cylinder head. It is possible that the injectors have a tight fit. If this is the case you may need a claw-type puller to pull them out of the cylinder head.

- Detach the coolant expansion tank (reservoir) without disconnecting any of the hoses and place the reservoir over the engine.
- Remove the two trim panels shown in Fig. 1.8. The bolts (3) and (4) are tightened to 1.0 kgm (7.5 ft.lb.).
- Withdraw the connector plugs (7) from the side of each injector (1).
- Remove the locking clips (5) at the connections of the leak-off pipe (6) lift off the pipe and place it to one side.
- Remove the injection pipes (8) as already described earlier on.
- Unscrew the stretch bolt (4) from each injector. The bolts must always be replaced during installation of the injectors.
- Take off the clamp pieces (3) and pull out the injectors, if necessary using the extractor mentioned above.

The installation is a reversal of the removal procedure. If new injectors are fitted quote the engine type and engine number as not all 612 engines have the same injectors. The seal (2) must always be replaced. Tighten the bolts (4) to 0.7 kgm (5 ft.lb.) and then by a further quarter of a turn.

Charge air distribution pipe – Removal and installation

The 612 engine is fitted with the charge air distribution pipe. Fig. 1.11 shows the items to be removed and disconnected, as is the case, to remove the pipe (1) as follows:

- Drain the cooling system as described in section "Cooling System".
- Remove the trim panels of the cylinder head cover as described above.
- Disconnect the engine wiring harness at the vehicle side.

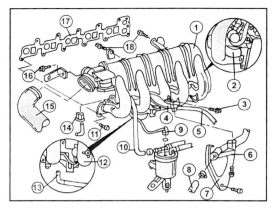

Fig. 1.11 – Details for the removal and installation of the charge air distribution pipe – 612 engine. The numbers are referred to in the text.

- Disconnect the charge air hose (15) at the mixing chamber with the exhaust gas circulation. Also withdraw the cable plug (14) at approx. the same position.
- Unscrew the bolt (3).
- Detach the coolant hose (8) at the intermediate piece (6).
- Detach the fuel hoses (9) and (10) from the fuel filter connections. The hose clamp of hose (10) may have to be replaced. Fuel may run out of hose (9). Also replace the seal of the latter hose and make sure it locks in position during installation.
- Remove the support (7) with the bracket (6) from the distribution pipe and the crankcase. Tighten the support to the distribution pipe to 1.4 kgm (11 ft.lb.) and to the crankcase to 2.0 kgm (14.5 ft.lb.).
- Remove the bolts (18) and take off the bracket (16).
- Disconnect the vacuum hose (13) from the vacuum unit (12) and the coolant hose (2) from the charge air distribution pipe (1) and unscrew the bolts (11) securing the distribution pipe to the cylinder head. Withdraw the pipe away from the cylinder head, lift it upwards and take it out. The engine wiring harness (5) and the fuel lines (9) and (10) must be guided through the openings in the charge air pipe during removal.

The installation is a reversal of the removal procedure. When fitting the pipe to the cylinder head prepare two M7 studs by cutting a slot in their ends and screw them into the head. Place the gasket and the distribution pipe in position and tighten the pipe provisionally with the bolts. Remove the two studs with a screwdriver (reason for the slots in the stud ends) and fit the remaining bolts instead. Tighten all bolts evenly all round to 1.6 kgm (11.5 ft.lb.). The torque for the support is already given above.

Front Cover of Cylinder head – Removal and Installation – 612 engine

The following operations must be carried out before the front cover can be removed.

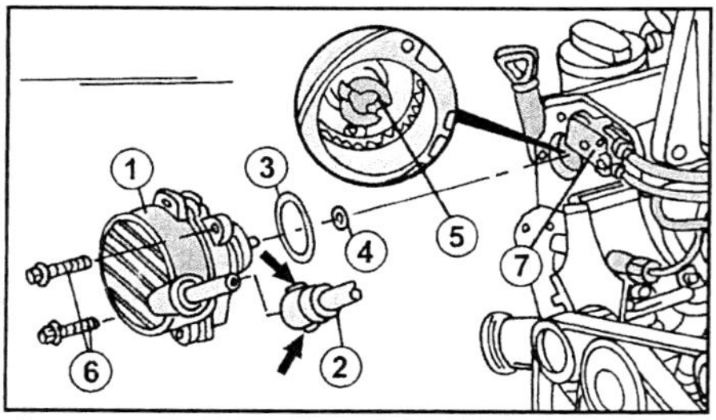

Fig. 1.12 – Details of the removal and installation of the vacuum pump. The numbers are referred to below.

Vacuum Pump – Removal and Installation – 612 engine

- Remove the cylinder head cover as already described.
- Remove the vacuum pump by referring to Fig. 1.12. First disconnect the vacuum line (2) from the pump (1). Compress the two catches shown by the arrows and at the same time pull off the pipe connector.

- Remove the oil dipstick guide tube from the cylinder head.
- Remove the bolts (6) securing the pump (1) and withdrawn the pump towards the front. During installation insert the driver at the rear of the pump into the driver slot in the end of the exhaust camshaft (5). The sealing rings (3) and (4) must be replaced, the surfaces of pump and cylinder head must be clean.
- The installation is a reversal of the removal procedure. Tighten the bolts (6) to 1.4 kgm (10 ft.lb.).

Fig. 1.13 – Removal and installation of the pre-delivery pump. Its fitting position is shown in Fig. 1.12 with (7).

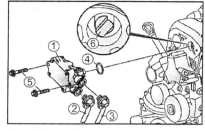

- Remove the oil dipstick guide tube from the cylinder head.
- Remove the bolts (6) securing the pump (1) and withdrawn the pump towards the front. During installation insert the driver at the rear of the pump into the driver slot in the end of the exhaust camshaft (5). The sealing rings (3) and (4) must be replaced, the surfaces of pump and cylinder head must be clean.
- The installation is a reversal of the removal procedure. Tighten the bolts (6) to 1.4 kgm (10 ft.lb.).

Pre-Delivery Pump – Removal and installation – 612 engine

The fitted position of the pump is shown with (7) in Fig. 1.12 and can be removed after the vacuum pump has been removed as described above. Then disconnect the two fuel lines (2) and (3) from the pump (1) and unscrew the bolts (5) in Fig. 1.13. Remove the pump. The poly V-belt should be protected with a thick rag as fuel will run out. During installation replace the sealing ring (4). Make sure that the sealing surfaces are clean. Ensure that the driver of the pump enters the driver (6) at the end of the inlet camshaft. Tighten the bolts (5) to 0.9 kgm (7 ft.lb.).

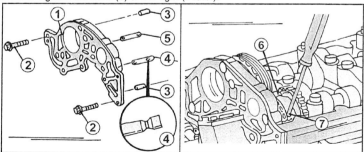

Fig. 1.14 – Details of the removal and installation of the front cover on the cylinder head. The numbers are referred to below.

Chain Tensioner – Removal and Installation – 612 engine

The chain tensioner is located on the outside of the cylinder head as shown later on in the section dealing with the timing mechanism. From the outside only the head of a hexagonal bolt is visible, with a sealing washer below. To remove the tensioner unscrew the "bolt". Replace the sealing ring during installation. To facilitate the installation turn the crankshaft slightly in the direction of rotation. This will slacken the tension of the timing chain near the tensioning rail. The tensioner is tightened to 8.0 kgm (58 ft.lb.).

Front Cover of Cylinder Head – Removal and installation
Fig. 1.14 shows the attachment of the cover in the L.H. view. With the cylinder head cover, chain tensioner and pre-delivery pump removed, first remove the bolts (2) securing the cover (1). The bolts are tightened to 1.4 kgm (10 ft.lb.) during installation. Using a screwdriver as shown in the R.H. view lift the locking pawl (6) of the guide rail (7) upwards and off the dowel pin with the notch (4).
Pull the front cover forwards and off the cylinder head.

During installation clean the faces of cover and cylinder head and coat the sealing face of the cover with "Loctite" sealing compound (width of 1.5 mm). The cover must be fitted within 10 minutes after the application of then sealing compound. Place the cover over the dowels (3), (4) and (5) and push it against the cylinder head face and tighten the bolts (2) to the torque given above.

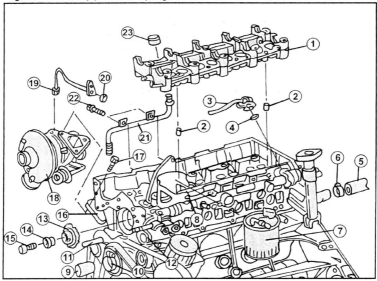

Fig. 1.15 – Details for the removal and installation of the cylinder head.

1 Camshaft housing	9 Coolant hose	17 Screw
2 Fitting sleeve	10 Hose clamp	18 Turbocharger
3 Fuel pipe	11 Coolant hose	19 Oil feed pipe
4 Sealing ring	12 Hose clamp	20 Sealing ring
5 Coolant hose	13 Drive gear	21 Coolant pipe
6 Hose clamp	14 Bush	22 Screw
7 Fuel filter	15 Screw	23 Hydraulic valve
8 Screw	16 Exhaust manifold	clearance element

1.4.0.2. Cylinder Head – Removal and Installation – ML 270 CDI

The camshaft sprockets must be locked against rotation when the head is removed. We therefore recommend to read the instructions before you attempt the removal. Fig.

1.15 shows on the example of the similar four-cylinder engine (611) the parts to be disconnected and/or removed. Similar operations are carried out on the 612 engine. Again we describe all necessary operations under separate headings.
- Disconnect the battery earth cable.
- Remove the bottom section of the sound-proofing panel.
- Drain the cooling system as described in section "Cooling System".
- Remove the trim panels from the cylinder head cover as described.
- Remove the air cleaner housing. Also disconnect the coolant hoses from the thermostat housing and the converter from the turbo charger.
- Detach the air intake hose from the end of the turbo charger (18). Also disconnect a vacuum hose from the turbo charger vacuum unit at the bottom of the turbo charger.
- Remove all injectors and the cylinder head cover as already described.

Removal and Installation of Camshafts

The details of the camshafts are shown in Fig. 1.16, but again in the case of a 4-cyl. engine. One more bearing journal is fitted in the case of the 5-cyl. engine. Note the identification of the camshafts, which will be explained later on.

Fig.1.16 – The camshafts. The arrows in the circle show where the alignment of the camshaft on the bearing cap is checked. The numbers are referred to in the text.

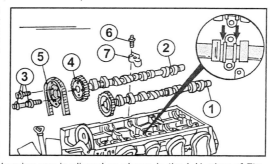

- Position the No. 1 piston to the top dead centre position. To do this rotate the crankshaft in clockwise direction – never backwards – until the markings in the camshaft and camshaft bearing cap is aligned as shown in the L.H. view of Fig. 1.16. Do not rotate the camshaft(s) to obtain the setting. The "OT" (TDC) mark in the vibration damper must be in line with the mark in the damper pulley.

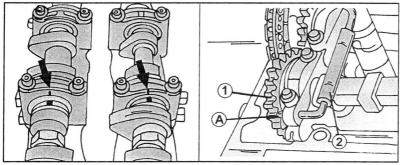

Fig. 1.17 – With No. 1 piston at top dead centre the marks in camshafts and camshaft bearing caps must be aligned as shown. The R.H. view shows where the retaining pin (2) is inserted into the bore (A) of the inlet camshaft sprocket (1). See also Fig. 1.18.

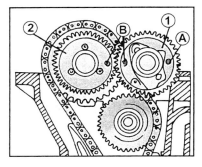

Fig. 1.18 – View of the inlet camshaft sprocket (1) and the exhaust camshaft sprocket (2). The retaining pin in Fig. 1.17 is inserted into bore (A). The marks (B) must be opposite each other.

- Lock the inlet camshaft (1) in Fig. 1.16 against rotation. The workshop uses a retaining tool, shown on the R.H. side of Fig. 1.17 which is inserted from the rear of the No. 1 bearing cap into the bore "A" in the inlet camshaft sprocket, as shown in Fig. 1.18. The markings (B) in the two sprockets must be opposite each other as shown in the same illustration.

- Remove chain tensioner and the front cylinder head cover as already described (see also Fig. 1.14). Then unscrew the driver out of the inlet camshaft and take off the slide rail. Details of the operation are also given in the section dealing with the timing mechanism.

- Remove the sprocket (5) in Fig. 1.16 from the exhaust camshaft (2) together with the timing chain after removal of bolts (3). If necessary use an open-ended spanner and prevent the camshaft from rotating by applying the spanner to a hexagon on the camshaft.

- Remove the camshaft bearing caps (7). Slacken the "Torx" head bolts (6) securing the bearing caps (7) evenly in steps of one turn until the pressure onto the bearings is released. The bearing caps are marked as shown in Fig. 1.19. Remove the caps and lift out the camshafts (1) and (2).

- Remove the hydraulic valve clearance and compensating elements (23) in Fig. 1.15 and lift off the camshaft bearing housing (1). The dowel pins (2) must engage when the housing is fitted.

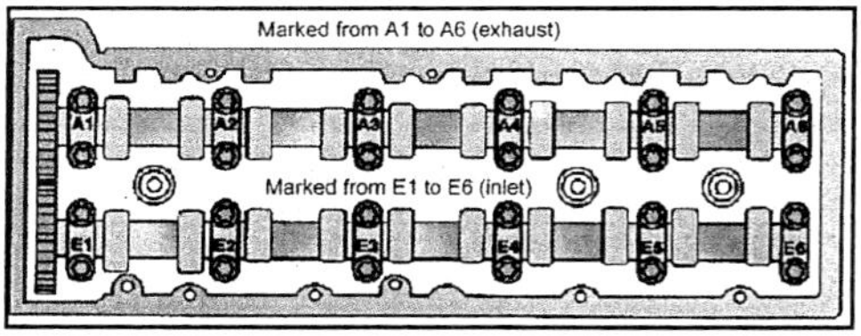

Fig. 1.19 – The camshaft bearing caps are marked from 1 to 6. Caps must not be inter-changed during installation.

The installation of the camshafts is carried out as follows:

- Place the camshaft housing (1) in Fig. 1.15 over the dowel pins (2) and tap the housing in position, using a rubber mallet.

- Lubricate the hydraulic valve clearance and compensating elements with engine oil, place the camshafts into their bearing bores and rotate the shafts until the alignment shown in Fig. 1.16 is obtained (arrows). The shafts must now be rotated until the two bores (B) in the sprockets in Fig. 1.18 are opposite each other and the marks shown by the arrows in the L.H. view of Fig. 1.17 are in line. Remember, if new camshafts are fitted quote the engine type and the model year.

- Place the bearing caps in Fig. 1.16 in accordance the their numbers in Fig. 1.19 and tap them in position with a mallet. Fit the bolts (6) and tighten them in several stages by one turn each, using a "Torx" head socket and a torque wrench until all bolts are tightened to 0.9 kgm (7 ft.lb.). Finally check once more that all bearing caps are fitted in accordance with their numbers in Fig. 1.19.

- Fit the exhaust camshaft sprocket (5) to the shaft (2) with the timing chain around the sprocket, making sure the dowel pin (4) engages. Insert the bolts (3) – always new bolts must be used – and tighten them evenly to 1.8 kgm (13 ft.lb.).

- Fit the glide rail and the driver to the inlet camshaft, the front cover to the cylinder head and the cylinder head cover as described earlier on.

Fig. 1.20 – Removal and installation of the cylinder head. The numbers are referred to below.

Final Removal of Cylinder Head

The following operations are now carried out by referring to Fig. 1.15.
- Remove the bolt (15), withdraw the bush (14) and take off the high pressure pump drive gear (13).
- Disconnect the engine wiring harness on the engine side.
- Detach the charge air distribution pipe as already described. To remove the bottom part remove the bolts and place it to one side with the engine wiring harness connected.
- Detach the oil feed pipe (19) at the cylinder head and at the turbocharger (18). The seal (20) must always be replaced. When fitting tighten the pipe at the turbocharger to 1.8 kgm (13 ft.lb.) and at the cylinder head to 0.9 kgm (7 ft.lb.).
- Disconnect the turbocharger (18) from the exhaust manifold (16). Tighten the connection during installation to 3.0 kgm (22 ft.lb.).
- Disconnect the coolant pipe (21) at the cylinder head and push it to one side with the coolant lines connected.
- Disconnect the coolant hoses (9) and (11) from the thermostat housing.
- Slacken the bolt (8) at the bracket of the fuel filter, take out the fuel filter (7) and place it to one side with the fuel lines connected.
- Disconnect the fuel line (3) at the rear of the fuel rail and unclip it at the front from the attachment. The sealing ring (4) must always be replaced.
- Slacken the hose clamp (6) and disconnect the coolant hose (5) at the rear.

The following operations are now carried out by referring to Fig. 1.20:
- Slacken the cylinder head bolts from the timing cover and then slacken the bolts (1) in stages from the outside towards the inside in several stages, until they all slack and can be removed without force.
- Lift the cylinder head from the cylinder block and take off the cylinder head gasket (3). The head is located on the dowel sleeves (4), i.e. must be removed in an upward direction. Chain can be attached to the lifting eyes as shown in the illustration to facilitate the removal.

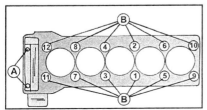

Fig. 1.21 – Tightening sequence for the cylinder head.

The installation of the cylinder head is carried out as follows, taking into account some of the points already mentioned during removal.
- Measure the length of each cylinder head bolt between the end of the thread to the underside of the bolt head. The standard length is 102 mm. Any bolt longer than 104 mm must be replaced.

33

- Coat the bolt thread and the underside of the bolt heads with engine oil. The bores in the cylinder block must be free of oil.
- Place a new cylinder head gasket (3) in Fig. 1.20 in position over dowels (4).
- Place the cylinder head (2) in position and tap it down with a mallet. Insert the cylinder head bolts and tighten them hand-tight.

The bolts are now tightened in the following order. Fig. 1.21 shows the tightening sequence for the engine. Bolts (A) are Allen-head bolts (M8 thread), bolts (b) have a "Torx" head and a suitable socket is required. Bolts (A) secure the cylinder head to the timing cover. Tighten the bolts as follows:
- Tighten the bolts (B) to 6.0 kgm (43 ft.lb.) in the order shown.
- Tighten bolts (A) to 2.0 kgm (14.5 ft.lb.).
- Tighten bolts (B) a further 90° in the order shown and re-check the torque of bolts (A) once more.
- Tighten the bolts (B) again a further 90° in the order shown.

A re-tightening of the cylinder head bolts is not necessary.
- All other operations are carried out in reverse order.

1.4.4.3. Cylinder Head – Removal and Installation – ML 280/320 CDI

642 engine in model series 164

Important: Note that not all engines have the same cylinder head gasket, as 642 engines are fitted with or without vacuum pump. Always quote the model and engine type when a new gasket is required.

The following operations are necessary before the final removal of the cylinder head after the battery has been disconnected and the cooling system drained. The L.H. and R.H. cylinder heads can be removed separately. We would like to point out that the removal and installation is a complicated operation – you have been warned. The difficult task is to find the items mentioned in the description

Charge Air Distribution Pipe – Removal and Installation

Fig. 1.22 and Fig. 1.23 show the items to be removed on the engine. the cooling system must be drained. Also disconnect the coolant pipe from the thermostat housing, remove the mixing chamber and the turbo charger, the oil feed fitting from the turbo charger and the L.H. fuel distributor rail. Fig. 1.24 shows the shape of the pipe.

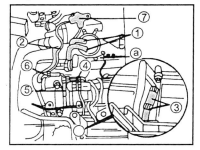

Fig. 1.22 – Details for the removal and installation of the charge air distribution pipe.
1 Fuel lines
2 Leak-off line
3 Fuel lines
4 Rail leak off line
5 Fuel pipe
6 Fuel supply line
7 Distributor leak-off line
a Connection lead

• Refer to Fig. 1.22 and unscrew the union nut to disconnect the pipe (a). Seal off the pipe end to prevent entry of dirt.

- Disconnect the fuel line (1) from the fuel filter and the leak oil line (2) from the fuel line. The fuel lines (3) must also be disconnected – Attention you are working with fuel.
- Pull out the fuel supply line (6) for the high pressure pump.
- Unscrew the bolts securing the coolant pipe (5) and remove the fuel pipes.

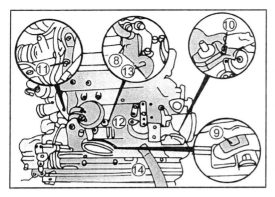

Fig. 1.23 – Removal of the charge air distribution pipe. The numbers are referred to in the text.

- Remove the fuel filter with the cage, fitted to the charge air distribution pipe (tightened to 1.2 kgm/9 ft.lb.).
- Disconnect the engine wiring harness at position (12) in Fig. 1.23.
- On the L.H. cylinder only remove the glow plug coupling and the coupling for the injectors.
- Remove the coupling (8) from the engine intake port shut off motor and the coupling (10). The latter is connected to the exhaust back pressure sensor.

Fig. 1.24 – The location and tightening sequence for the charge air distribution pipe.

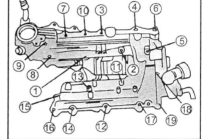

- Remove the L.H. exhaust gas recirculation positioner, shown with (14).
- Remove the bottom bolt (11) on the thermostat housing. Place the engine wiring harness (12) to one side, out of the way.
- Unscrew the bolts securing the charge air distribution pipe. Fig. 1.24 shows the location of the bolts. Note that the bolts must be tightened in the order shown. During installation tighten all bolts to 1.6 kgm (11.5 ft.lb.) and then bolts 1 to 11 again to the same torque.
- Remove the charge air distribution pipe. The seal must be replaced.

Installation is a reversal of the removal procedure, noting the point already given above.

Removal and Installation of Cylinder Head Covers

With the battery disconnected and the bonnet open, proceed as follows, as described under the individual headings. Note that different operations are necessary for the L.H. and R.H. cylinder head cover. We must point out that an impact extractor and a extractor bolt is required to remove the cylinder head covers.

Removal and Installation of Engine Intake Air Duct

- Refer to Fig. 1.25 and remove the engine suction air duct downstream of the air filter. The air duct is shown with (1) in the illustration. To do this, first remove the R.H. air filter housing (2).
- Locate the electrical connectors plug from on the L.H. hot film mass air meter (7) and the R.H. mass air meter (8). A further connector must be withdrawn from the vent line heater element (6).
- Disconnect the hose (3) from the crankcase ventilation system at the so-called cyclone separator.

35

- Slacken the hose clamp (4) at the turbo charger and a further hose clamp (5) at the air cleaner housing (2) on the L.H. side.
- Withdraw the air intake duct (1) forwards, away from the air cleaner.

The installation is a reversal of the removal procedure, but note: The rubber seal on the air intake duct must be replaced if a new heater element (6) is fitted.

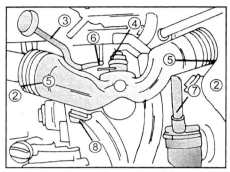

Fig. 1.25 – Details for the removal of the intake air duct. The numbers are referred to in the text.

Removal and Installation of Engine Charge Air Channel

This is item (9) in Fig. 1.25 and must be removed from the turbo charger. The duct is secured at the upper end by means of a bolt. Remove the bolt and take out the duct. The bolt is tightened to 1.2 kgm (9 ft.lb.) during installation

- Remove the exhaust gas re-circulation positioner.
- Remove the injectors and the injector rail as described later on.
- On the L.H. side of the cylinder head cover remove the fluid reservoir for the power steering. Locate the fuel line at one end of the L.H cylinder head cover and disconnect it. The fuel line must be removed with the flexible feed and return hose so that the fluid reservoir can be moved.
- On the L.H. cylinder head cover remove a bracket securing a vacuum line. Tighten the bracket to 0.9 kgm (7 ft.lb.). Also remove the bolts securing the L.H. cylinder head cover. Note that M6 x 20 mm bolts are tightened to 0.4 kgm, M6 x 35 mm bolts to 0.9 kgm.
- Remove the L.H. cylinder head cover. The tools shown in Fig. 1.26 are now required to remove the cover.

The R.H. cylinder head cover is now removed as follows:
- Remove the vacuum pump and the cyclone separator. The latter is located in the centre of the cover. On the outside of the cover you will find two fittings for the oil separator which must be removed. The "O" sealing ring and the radial shaft sealing ring must be replaced.
- In the centre of the cover detach the electrical connector from the camshaft Hall sensor.
- Remove the bolts securing the cylinder head cover, again using the special tools shown in Fig. 1.26. The tightening torques are identical to the values given for the L.H. cover.

Fig. 1.26 – Impact extractor (116 5898 20 33 00) on the left and the threaded pin (102 589 00 34 00) on the right, required to remove the cylinder head covers and the slide tail pins.

The installation is a reversal of the removal procedure, noting the point given above.

Proceed as follows with the removal of the cylinder head:
- Remove the oil filter housing (section "Lubrication System").

- Remove the camshaft sprockets and the camshafts as described in the section dealing with the timing mechanism.
- Remove the heat shield above the exhaust manifolds.
- Remove the side rail pins from the end of the cylinder head, again described in the section dealing with the timing mechanism. The special tools shown in Fig. 1.26 (impact extractor and bolt) must be used. Three pins must be removed, seen from the front end two on the right and one on the left.

Final Removal and Installation of the Cylinder Head

- Slacken the cylinder head bolts (2) in Fig. 1.27 from the timing cover and then slacken the bolts (1) in stages in reverse order to the sequence given in the illustration.

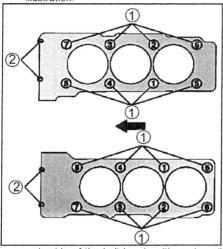

Fig. 1.27 – Tighten the cylinder head bolts (1) in the sequence shown. Bolts (2) secure the head to the timing side.

- Lift the cylinder heads from the cylinder block and take off the cylinder head gasket. Chain can be attached to the lifting eyes to facilitate the removal. The exhaust manifold must be removed if a new cylinder head must be fitted.

The installation of the cylinder head is carried out as follows, taking into account some of the points already mentioned during removal.

- Measure the length of each cylinder head M12 bolt between the end of the thread to the underside of the bolt head. The standard length is 205 mm. Any bolt longer than 207 mm must be replaced.
- Coat the bolt thread and the underside of the bolt heads with engine oil. The bores in the cylinder block must be free of oil.
- Place a new cylinder head gasket in position over dowels.
- Place the cylinder head in position and tap it down with a mallet. Insert the cylinder head bolts and tighten them hand-tight.

The bolts are now tightened in the following order. Fig. 1.27 shows the tightening sequence for the engine. Bolts (2) are Allen-head bolts (M8 thread), bolts (1) have a "Torx" head and a suitable socket is required. Bolts (2) secure the cylinder head to the crankcase. Tighten the bolts as follows, noting that the cylinder head bolts are tightened in 5 stages:

- Tighten the bolts (1) to 1.0 kgm (7.2 ft.lb.) in the order shown and then again to 6.0 kgm (43.5 ft.lb.) – Stage 1 and 2.
- Tighten bolts (2) to 2.0 kgm (14.5 ft.lb.).
- Tighten bolts (1) a further 90° in the order shown (stage 3) and re-check the torque of bolts (2) once more.
- Tighten the bolts (1) again a further 90° in the order shown (stage 4) and then a further 90° (stage 5). Finally re-check the torque of bolts (2).

A re-tightening of the cylinder head bolts is not necessary.

- All other operations are carried out in reverse order.

1.4.4.4. Cylinder Head – Removal and Installation – ML 400 CDI

Again several operations are necessary before the actual removal of the R.H. or L.H. cylinder head can take place. The description refers to the individual operations when necessary.
- Carry out the preliminary operations described for the previous engines regards battery, cooling system, etc.
- *Remove the exhaust gas re-circulation cooler* together with the exhaust gas re-circulation positioner on the left and right. The item has the shape shown in Fig. 1.28 and is located in the centre of the cylinder head. First remove the charge air distribution pipe.

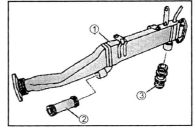

Fig. 1.28 – The exhaust gas re-circulation cooler.
1   Re-circulation cooler
2   Fitting
3   Fitting

- Locate the two coolant hoses and unplug two electrical connectors.
- Open a bracket and take out the two refrigerant lines. Do not press the two lines too far to one side in order to prevent damage.
- Locate and disconnect all coolant lines/hoses, connected to the exhaust gas re-circulation positioner at the left and right and from the cooler.
- Remove the four bolts securing the two exhaust gas re-circulation positioners to the cylinder head.
- The cooler can now be removed. First pull it towards the rear and towards the top and then towards the rear to free it from the connections (2) and (3) in Fig. 1.28.

The installation is a reversal of the removal procedure. Tighten the two bolts to 1.5 kgm (11 ft.lb.). The sealing rings at connections (2) and (3) must be replaced.

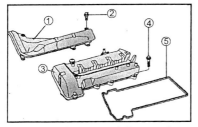

Fig. 1.29 – Parts fitted to a cylinder head cover.
1   Covering panel
2   Securing bolt
3   Cylinder head cover
4   Cover securing bolt, 0.9 kgm
5   Cover gasket

- *Remove the L.H. and R.H. Cylinder Head Cover:* It is assumed that the cylinder head cover is removed without any additional operations. Fig. 1.29 shows the items to be removed. Remove the covers as follows:
- *Remove the intake air distribution pipe (2).* This is the part visible in the centre of the engine, next to the power steering fluid reservoir (3), after the engine cover has been pulled upward from the engine. Refer to Fig. 1.30 for details. The text describes the complete removal.
- Detach the steering fluid reservoir with the connected fluid lines from the mounting plate of the intake air distribution pipe (2) and place it to one side.
- Detach the intake hose (1) from the air cleaner and the charge air hoses (4) and (7) from the charge air pipes (5) and (6) on the L.H. and R.H. side.
- Disconnect the connector plugs (8) and (9) from the hot film mass air flow sensors at the positions shown.

Fig. 1.30 – Details for the removal of the intake air distribution pipe. The numbers are referred to in the text.

- Detach the intake air distribution pipe (2) with the retaining plate together with the charge air lines (4) and (7) as one assembly. For a successful removal unscrew the bolt on the right front of the retaining plate last, because the space between the hot film mass air flow sensor (8) and the bolt on the right front of the retaining plate is too small. Lift the pipe as you remove it. After removal place a piece of cloth over the open tubes (5) and (6),

Continue as follows with the removal of the cylinder head covers:
- Remove the L.H. charge air intake pipe from the cylinder head cover and press to one side. This is the pipe connected to the black tube. Also disconnect it from the turbo charger.
- Remove the trim panel (1) in Fig. 1.29
- Locate and disconnect the connector plug from the camshaft Hall sensor if the R.H. cylinder head cover is removed.
- Remove the injectors as described in section "Diesel Injection".
- Disconnect the small drain hose from the L.H. and R.H. cylinder covers and unscrew the fuel feed line and fuel return line from the cover. Three bolts secure the fuel lines (around where the small drain hose was disconnected). Press the fuel lines on the L.H. cover to one side.
- In the area of the black filler cap remove a bracket with the inlet port shut-off switch-over valve when the L.H. cylinder head cover is removed.
- The cylinder head cover can now be unscrewed.

The installation is a reversal of the removal procedure, noting the following points:
- The cylinder head cover gasket (5) in Fig. 1.29 must always be replaced.
- Tighten the bolts (4) in Fig. 1.29 to 0.9 kgm after the injectors have been fitted.
- Refit the fuel lines and tighten the bolts, re-connect the rear drain hose (both covers), refit the mounting bracket with the shut-off switch-over valve in the case of the L.H. cover and mount the charge air intake pipe onto the cylinder head cover and turbo charger (0.9 kgm).

The R.H. cylinder head is now removed as follows:
- *Remove the R.H. charge air distribution pipe:* This is the large duct connected to the black hose at the upper end. The inner panel inside the R.H. front wing must be removed to gain access. Detach the intake air distribution pipe and detach the plug from the boost pressure sensor. Remove two bolts from the cylinder head cover and take off the cover of the injectors. After one of the hose clamps is slackened at one end of the distribution pipe, the pipe can be withdrawn. Remove the clamp with the easier access. The installation is a reversal.
- *Remove the bottom charge air pipe:* Fig. 1.31 shows where the pipe is located. Remove the bottom section of the sound-proofing panel to work from below

(vehicle on chassis stands). Not an easy operation. Installation is carried out in reverse order.

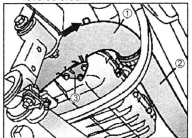

Fig. 1.31 – Details for the removal of the bottom charge air pipe on the R.H. side.

- Detach the protective caps from the starter motor terminal, disconnect the cables and remove the starter motor bolts. Leave the starter motor in position for the time being. The bolts are tightened to 4.2 kgm (30 ft.lb.). The small terminal nut is tightened to 0.6 kgm, the large one to 1.4 kgm.
- Loosen the transmission oil lines in the area of the charge air pipe. Near the starter motor remove the upper bolt securing the connecting link at the intake flange of the turbo charger and the lower bolt of the link at the charge air pipe.
- Refer to Fig. 1.31 and detach the charge air hose (2) from the charge air pipe (1).
- Remove the brackets (3) from the oil sump bottom section and from the intake pipe (1).
- At the position shown by the arrow unscrew the upper bracket of the charge air pipe from the crankcase.
- Press the starter motor and the transmission oil lines to the side and detach the charge air pipe from the intake flange of the turbo charger. To remove the pipe, direct it towards the front and take it out of the engine compartment from the side towards the rear. The pipe sealing ring must be replaced.

Proceed as follows:

- Remove the intermediate gear for the high pressure pump and the camshaft housing as described under separate headings.
- Fully slacken the R.H. side three-way catalytic converter and push it towards the rear.
- Locate an electrical connector plug at the turbo charger and withdraw it. Also disconnect the oil return line from the turbo charger. The gasket and sealing ring must be replaced. The return line is tightened to 0.9 kgm (7 ft.lb.).
- Remove the bracket securing the turbo charger. During installation tighten the bolts to 3.0 kgm (22 ft.lb.).

Fig. 1.32 – Details for the removal of the bottom charge air pipe on the L.H. side.

The L.H. cylinder head is now removed as follows:

- *Remove the L.H. charge air intake pipe* in a similar manner as described for the R.H. pipe, this time removing the panel inside the L.H. wing. After removal of the intake air distribution pipe remove the bolts from the coolant flange and a single bolt from the cylinder head cover.

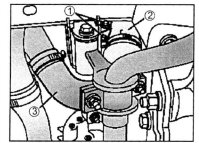

Remove the hose clamp at the lower end and remove the pipe. Install in reverse order.

- *Remove the L.H. bottom charge air pipe:* Fig. 1.32 shows where the pipe is located. Remove the bottom section of the sound-proofing panel to work from below (vehicle on chassis stands). Panel inside front wing already removed.

- Remove the charge air hose (3) and unscrew the bolts (1).
- On the turbo charger remove the upper bolt securing the connecting link at the intake flange of the turbo charger and the lower bolt of the link at the charge air pipe (2).
- Detach the charge air pipe (2) from the intake flange of the turbo charger. To remove the pipe, take it out of the engine compartment towards the bottom.
- Fully slacken the L.H. side three-way catalytic converter and push it towards the rear.
- Locate an electrical connector plug at the turbo charger and withdraw it. Also disconnect the oil return line from the turbo charger. The gasket and sealing ring must be replaced. The return line is tightened to 0.9 kgm (7 ft.lb.).
- Remove the bracket securing the L.H. turbo charger. During installation tighten the bolts to 3.0 kgm (22 ft.lb.).
- Remove the oil filter housing.
- Mark the camshaft timing gear relative to the timing chain and remove the timing gear from the exhaust camshaft. Pay attention to the dowel pin. Tie the timing chain to the timing sprocket and remove the gearwheel with the chain.
- Remove the L.H. camshaft housing as described later on and remove the slide rail pins (refer to "Timing Mechanism"). The slide rails must be tied together.

Final Removal and Installation of both Cylinder Heads
- Unplug the glow plug connector plugs.
- Slacken the cylinder head bolts (2) in Fig. 1.33 from the timing cover and then slacken the bolts (1) in stages in reverse order to the sequence given in the illustration.

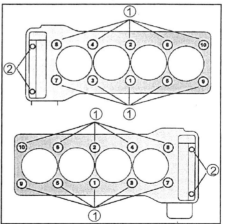

Fig. 1.33 – Tighten the cylinder head bolts (1) in the sequence shown. Bolts (2) secure the head to the timing side.

- Lift the cylinder heads from the cylinder block and take off the cylinder head gasket. Chain can be attached to the lifting eyes to facilitate the removal.

The installation of the cylinder head is carried out as follows, taking into account some of the points already mentioned during removal.

- Measure the length of each cylinder head M12 bolt between the end of the thread to the underside of the bolt head. The standard length is 201.5 mm. Any bolt longer than 203 mm must be replaced.
- Coat the bolt thread and the underside of the bolt heads with engine oil. The bores in the cylinder block must be free of oil.
- Place a new cylinder head gasket in position over dowels.
- Place the cylinder head in position and tap it down with a mallet. Insert the cylinder head bolts and tighten them hand-tight.

41

The bolts are now tightened in the following order. Fig. 1.33 shows the tightening sequence for the engine. Bolts (2) are Allen-head bolts (M8 thread), bolts (1) have a "Torx" head and a suitable socket is required. Bolts (2) secure the cylinder head to the crankcase. Tighten the bolts as follows, noting that the cylinder head bolts are tightened in 5 stages:

- Tighten the bolts (1) to 2.0 kgm (14.5 ft.lb.) in the order shown and then again to 6.0 kgm (43.5 ft.lb.) – Stage 1 and 2.
- Tighten bolts (2) to 2.0 kgm (14.5 ft.lb.).
- Tighten bolts (1) a further 90° in the order shown (stage 3) and re-check the torque of bolts (2) once more.
- Tighten the bolts (1) again a further 90° in the order shown (stage 4) and then a further 90° (stage 5). Finally re-check the torque of bolts (2).

A re-tightening of the cylinder head bolts is not necessary.

- All other operations are carried out in reverse order, noting tightening torque values already given during the removal instructions.

1.4.0.5. Cylinder Head – Dismantling

The following text assumes that the cylinder head is to be replaced. If for example only the valves require attention, ignore the additional operations. Fig. 1.34 shows the V6 engine to give you an inside view of its construction. The cylinder head must, of course, be removed. Similar valve parts are fitted to the other engines, as you can see in Fig. 1.35.

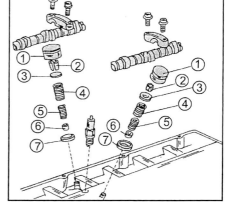

Fig. 1.34 – Exploded view of the valve gear of a six-cylinder. Other engines are similar.
1 Valve tappets
2 Valve cotter halves
3 Upper valve spring seat
4 Outer valve spring
5 Inner valve spring
6 Valve stem seal
7 Valve seat insert

- Remove the thermo switch, sender units, etc. from the cylinder head and unscrew the exhaust manifold. Also unscrew the glow plugs. Also remove all other parts from the head as applicable. Not all cylinder head are fitted with identical parts.
- Remove the camshafts as described under a separate heading.
- A valve spring compressor is required to remove the valves. Fig. 1.36 shows such a compressor. Different types are available, must it must be possible to compress the springs. Valves are held in position by means of valve cotter halves. Compress the springs and remove the valve cotter halves (2) with a pair of pointed pliers or a small magnet (1).
- If a valve spring compressor is not available, it is possible to use a short piece of tube to remove the valve cotter halves. To do this, place the tube over the upper valve spring collar and hit the tube with a blow of a hammer. The valve cotter halves will collect in the inside of the tube and the components can be removed.

The valve head must be supported from the other side of the cylinder head. Keep the hammer in close contact with the tube to prevent the cotter halves from flying out.

Fig. 1.35 – Valves removed from the cylinder head (V6).
1 Valve cotter halves
2 Upper valve spring cup
3 Valve spring
4 Valve stem seal
5 Lower valve spring retainer
6 Cylinder head bolts
7 Cylinder head
8 Valve

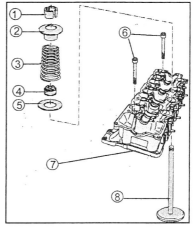

- Remove the camshafts as described under a separate heading.
- Remove the valve spring collar and the valve spring. The valve springs (one spring or two springs per valve) are identified with a paint spot and only a spring with a paint spot of the same colour must be fitted. Remove the valves one after the other and keep them in their numbered order, writing the number in front of each valve.

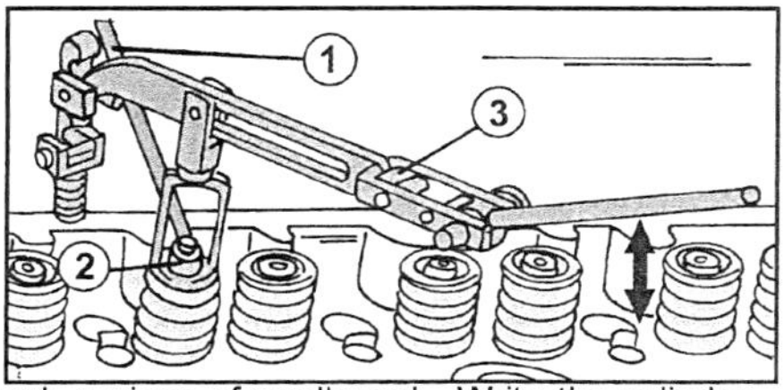

Fig. 1.36 – Removal of valves with a valve lifter (3). The valve cotter halves (2) can be removed with a small magnet (1.

- Remove valve stem oil seals (1) in the L.H. view of Fig. 1.37 carefully with a screwdriver or a pair of pliers (2).
- Remove the valves one after the other out of the valve guides and pierce them in their fitted order through a piece of cardboard. Write the cylinder number against each valve if they are to be re-used.

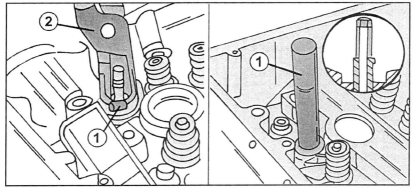

Fig. 1.37 – Removal of valve stem oil seals on the left.. Use a pair of pliers (2) to remove the seal (1). The R.H. view shows the installation of a seal with the piece of tube (1).

43

1.4.0.6. Cylinder Head - Overhaul

We do not recommend the overhaul of the cylinder head. Instead take the head (or heads) to an engine shop to have it professionally overhauled, ready for installation. Below you will find a few useful hints before you decide to have the head overhauled. The cylinder head must be thoroughly cleaned and remains of old gasket material removed. The checks and inspections are to be carried out as required. Operations are similar on all engines.

Valve Springs: If the engine has a high mileage, always replace the valve springs as a set. To check a valve spring, place the old spring and a new spring end to end over a long bolt (with washer under bolt head) and fit a nut (again with a washer). Tighten the nut until the springs are under tension and measure the length of the two springs. If the old spring is shorter by more than 10%, replace the complete spring set.

The springs must not be distorted. A spring placed with its flat coil on a surface must not deviate at the top by more than 2 mm (0.08 in.).

Valve Guides:
Clean the inside of the guides by pulling a petrol-soaked cloth through the guides. Valve stems can be cleaned best by means of a rotating wire brush. Measure the inside diameter of the guides. As an inside micrometer is necessary for this operation, which is not always available, you can insert the valve into its guide and withdraw it until the valve head is approx. level with the cylinder head face. Rock the valve to and fro and check for play. Although no exact values are available, it can be assumed that the play should not exceed 1.0 - 1.2 mm (0.04 -0.047 in.). Mercedes workshops use gauges to check the guides for wear.

Before a valve guide is replaced, check the general condition of the cylinder head and then decide if you have the guides replaced.

Valves must always be replaced if new valve guides are fitted. The valve seats must be re-cut when a guide has been replaced. If it is obvious that seats cannot be re-ground in the present condition, new valve seat inserts must be fitted. Again this is an operation for a specialist and the work should be carried out in a workshop.

Valve Seats: If the camshaft bearings are excessively worn, fit a new or exchange cylinder head. In this case there is no need to renovate the valve seats.

Check all valve seats for signs of pitting or wear. Slight indentations can be removed with a 45° cutter. If this operation is carried out properly, there should be no need to grind-in the valves. Use correction cutters to bring the valve seating area into the centre of the valve seat. Make sure that the valve seat width, given in Section 1.4.0.0. is obtained. This again is achieved by using cutters of different angles (for example 15°and 60°). Valve seat inserts can be fitted to the cylinder head. Replacement of valve seat inserts will require that the old seat insert is removed by machining. The machining must not damage the bottom face of the head recess. As this is a critical operation,- we advise you to bring the cylinder head to your Mercedes Dealer or an engine shop who has the necessary equipment and experience to do the job. It may be possible to obtain a reconditioned cylinder head in exchange for the old one to avoid time delay. In this case remove all ancillary parts from the old head and refit them to the new head.

Valves can be ground into their seats in the conventional manner. To do this, coat the valve seat with lapping compound and use a suction tool, as shown in Fig. 1.38. Move the valve backwards and forwards. Ever so often, lift the suction tool, move it forward by ¼ of a turn, and continue grinding. Work the seat until an uninterrupted ring is visible around the face of the valve. After grinding-in, clean the cylinder head, and even more important the inside of the valve guide bores thoroughly. Any lapping paste inside the cylinder head will accelerate the wear of the new parts.

Use a pencil and mark across the valve seat closely spaced. Drop the valve into the respective valve guide and turn the valve by 90°, using the suction tool, applying slight pressure to the tool. Remove the valve and if the pencil marks have been removed from the entire circumference. The gap created will indicate the width of the valve seat and can be measured with a ruler or caliper. Otherwise repeat the grinding until this is the case.

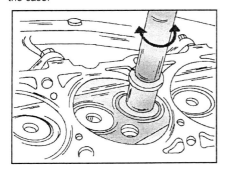

Fig. 1.38 – Grinding-in of valves.

Valves: The exhaust valves must not be discarded as ordinary scrap metal. They are filled with sodium, as is the case with other Mercedes engines. Never use such a valve as a drift – it may be tempting. Valves can be cleaned best with a rotating wire brush.

Check the valve stem diameters and in this connection the inside diameters of the valve guides. If there is a deviation from the nominal values, it may be necessary to replace the valve guides (see above). Also check the end of the valve stems. There should be no visible wear in this area.

Sometimes it is only required to replace the exhaust valves, if these for example are burnt out at their valve head edges.

Cylinder Head: Thoroughly clean the cylinder head and cylinder block surfaces of old gasket material and check the faces for distortion. To do this, place a steel ruler with a sharp edge over the cylinder head face and measure the gap between ruler and face with feeler gauges. Checks must be carried out in longitudinal and diagonal direction and across the face. If a feeler gauge of more than 0.10 mm (0.004 in.) can be inserted, when the ruler is placed along or across the cylinder head, have the cylinder head face re-ground.

Camshaft: See separate heading.

1.4.0.7. Cylinder Head - Assembly

The assembly of the cylinder head is a reversal of the dismantling procedure. Note the following points:

- Lubricate the valve stems with engine oil and insert the valves into the correct valve guides.
- Valve stem seals must be suitable for the engine in question. Make sure to order the correct seals. The repair kit contains fitting sleeves and these must be used to fit the seals (see last Section).
- The sleeves are fitted over the valve stem before the seal is pushed in position
- Fit the valve spring and valve spring collar over the valve and use the valve lifter to compress the spring. Insert the valve cotter halves and release the valve spring lifter. Make sure that the cotter halves are in position by tapping the end of the valve stem with a plastic mallet. Place a rag over the valve end - just in case.

- Fit the camshaft(s) as described later on and carry out all other operations in reverse order to the dismantling procedure.

1.4.0.8. Hydraulic Valve Clearance Compensation

The function of the hydraulic valve clearance compensating elements is to eliminate valve clearance, i.e. the dimensional changes in the valve train (valve lash) due to heat expansion and wear are compensated by the elements. The rocker arm is in constant contact with the cam. The compensating elements cannot be repaired, but can be checked for correct functioning as described below. Fig. 1.1 shows a sectional view of a valve with clearance compensation. You will also find a short description of the operation on the same page.

If the tappets are removed, note the following points:
- Always keep the tappets in an upright position, i.e. the open side towards the top.
- After removal of a tappet (see below), mark the cylinder number and the compensating element in suitable manner. Always fit original parts in their same locations.

Checking a hydraulic compensating element: As the elements are in continuous contact with the camshaft, you will rarely hear noises from the area of the hydraulic elements. If noises can be heard, check the elements as follows:
- Start the engine and run it approx. 5 minutes al 3000 rpm.
- Remove the cylinder head cover.
- Rotate the crankshaft until the cam for the tappet to be checked is pointing vertically towards the top.
- Use a drift and push the tappet towards the inside, or try to move the tappet with the fingers.
- If the tappet cannot be depressed or excessive clearance can be felt between the tappet and the back of the cam, replace the tappet. The tappet is supplied together with the hydraulic compensating element. Mercedes workshops can reset the tappet to its original position, but this operation is beyond the scope of the home mechanic.

Tappet Removal and Installation:
- Remove the camshafts as described later on.
- Use a suction tool to remove the tappets. Mark them, if they are to be refitted.
- Fit the tappets into their original bores, if re-used. Refit the camshaft as described and carry out all other operations in reverse order to the removal procedure.
- Fit the tappets into their original bores, if re-used. Refit the camshaft or the camshafts as described and carry out all other operations in reverse order to the removal procedure.

1.4.1. PISTON AND CONNECTING RODS

1.4.1.0. Technical Data

All dimensions are given in metric units.

Pistons
Available pistons:................................. Standard and oversize (depending on engine)
Piston Running Clearance :
- Standard (new) – 612 engine:.. 0.025 – 0.035 mm
- Standard (new) – other engines: .... 0.04 mm

- Wear limit: .... 0.08 mm
Max. weight difference of pistons in
  one engine: .... 4 grams (wear limit 10 grams)

Running clearance of piston pins :
- In connecting rod small end: .... 0.007 – 0.017 mm
- In Piston: .... 0.002 – 0.011 mm

Piston Ring Gaps (612 and 628 engine) – ML 270CDI and ML 400 CDI:
- Upper piston rings: .... 0.40 – 0.55 mm (wear limit 1.00 mm)
- Centre rings: .... 0.25 – 0.50 mm (wear limit 0.80 mm)
- Lower rings: .... 0.20 – 0.40 mm (wear limit 0.80 mm)

Piston Ring Gaps (642 engine) – ML 280 CDI/ML 320 CDI:
- Upper piston rings: .... 0.20 – 0.55 mm (wear limit 1.00 mm)
- Centre rings: .... 0.25 – 0.50 mm (wear limit 0.80 mm)
- Lower rings: .... 0.20 – 0.40 mm (wear limit 0.80 mm)

Side Clearance of Piston Rings in Piston (612, 628 and 642 engines):
- Groove 1: .... 0.12 – 0.16 mm
- Groove 2: .... 0.065 – 0.011 mm
- Groove 3: .... 0.03 – 0.07 mm

Connecting rod bearing details: .... See under "Crankshaft"

1.4.1.1. Piston and Connecting Rods – Removal

Pistons and connecting rods are pushed out towards the top of the cylinder bores, using a hammer handle alter connecting rod bearing caps and shells have been removed. The engine must be removed to remove the connecting rod piston assemblies. The operations are not the same on all engines and will be summarised under separate headings below. If the pistons require replacement we suggest to have the work carried out in an engine shop.

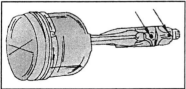

Fig. 1.39 – Big end bearing caps and connecting rods must be marked at opposite points as shown before removal.

Three piston rings are fitted to each piston. The two upper rings are the compression rings, i.e. they prevent the pressure above the piston crown to return to the crankcase. The lower ring is the oil scraper ring. Its function is to remove excessive oil from the cylinder bore, thereby preventing the entry of oil into the combustion chamber. The three rings are not the same in shape. The upper ring has a rectangular section, the centre ring has a chamfer on the inside and the lower ring is chrome-plated on its outside. Only the correct fitting of the piston rings will assure the proper operation of the piston sealing. Before removal of the assemblies note the following points:
- Pistons and cylinder bores are graded in three diameter classes within specified tolerance groups and marked with the letters or numbers. The class number is stamped into the upper face of the cylinder block, next to the particular cylinder bore. If the cylinder block has been re-bored, you will receive the block with the correct pistons.
- Mark each piston and the connecting rod before removal with the cylinder number. This can be carried out by writing the cylinder number with paint onto the

piston crown. Also mark an arrow, facing towards the front of the engine (the arrow in the piston crown will be covered by the carbon deposits). When removing the connecting rod, note the correct installation of the big end bearing cap. immediately after removal mark the connecting rod and the big end bearing cap on the same side. This is best done with a centre punch (cylinder No. 1 one punch mark, etc., see Fig. 1.39).

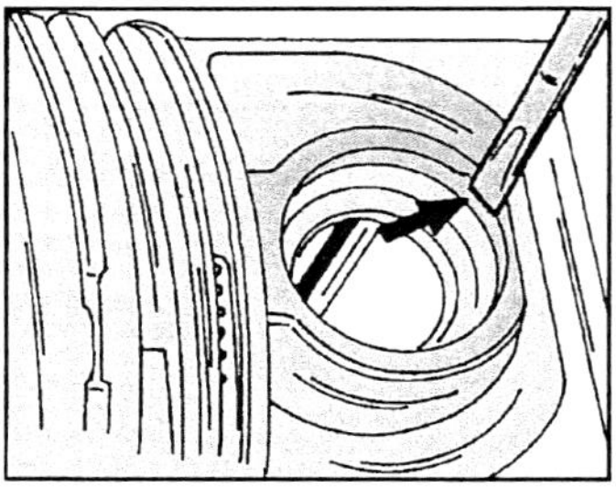

Fig. 1.40 - Cut-out in the piston pin bore allows to insert a screwdriver blade to remove the piston pin securing ring.

- Mark the big end bearing shells with the cylinder number.
- Big end bearing journals can be re-ground to four undersizes (in steps of 0.25 mm between sizes). Corresponding bearing shells are available.
- Remove the bearing caps and the shells and push the assemblies out of the cylinder bore. Any carbon deposits on the upper edge of the bores can be carefully removed with a scraper.
- Remove the piston pin snap rings. A notch in the piston pin bore enables a pointed drift to be inserted, as shown in Fig. 1.40, to remove the rings.

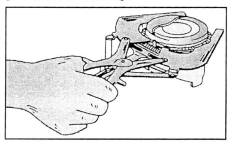

Fig. 1.41 – Removal or installation of piston rings.

- Press the piston pins out of the pistons. If necessary heat the piston in boiling water.
- Remove the piston rings one after the other from the pistons, using a piston ring pliers if possible (Fig. 1.41). If the rings are to be re-used, mark them in accordance with their pistons and position.

After the engine has been removed carry out the following operations to remove the pistons as described above:

612 Engine (ML 270 CDI)
Remove the cylinder head, the oil sump and the oil pump. The operations can now be carried out in accordance with Fig. 1.42 on the next page.

642 Engine (ML 280 CDI, ML 320 CDI)
The most complicated operations on the series. The engine must be removed together with the front axle carrier, the transmission must be removed together with the torque converter and the engine must be detached from the front axle carrier. Then remove the cylinder head, the oil sump and the oil pump. Mark the L.H. and the R.H. pistons and the cylinder bores in suitable manner. Do not interchange pistons from left to right or visa versa if the same pistons are fitted. Remove the piston(s) as described above, but again make sure that L.H. and R.H. connecting rods are marked accordingly.

628 Engine (ML 400 CDI)
Before the piston(s) can be removed as described above remove the following component parts of the engine, with the engine removed.

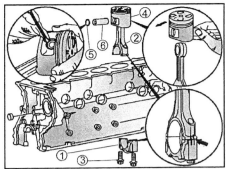

Fig. 1.42 – Details for the removal of pistons in the case of a 612 engine.
1 Big end bearing cap
2 Connecting rod
3 Bearing cap bolts
4 Piston
5 Piston pin securing ring
6 Piston pin

The most complicated operation is perhaps the removal of the bottom part of the crankcase, considering that 42 bolts are used. Additionally bolts have a diameter of 6 mm, 8 mm and 11 mm (M6, M8 and M11) and a different length. Is is therefore important that the numbered order of the bolts in Fig. 1.43 during the removal and Figs. 1.51 and 1.52 during installation are followed.

Fig. 1.43 – Slacken the bolts securing the lower crankcase in the order shown. Note the different diameter and length of the bolts.
1 to 10 = M11 x 115 mm
11 to 20 = M11 x 137 mm
21 to 23 = M6 x 90 mm
25 to 27 = M6 x 90 mm
31 to 40 = M6 x 90 mm
29 = M6 x 90 mm
24, 26, 28 = M6 x 80 mm
30 = M6 x 45 mm
41, 42 = M8 x 45 mm

- Mount the engine into an assembly stand and remove the cylinder head or cylinder heads.
- Remove the oil sump as described later on "Lubrication System").
- Remove the bracket of the A/C compressor together with the compressor.
- Remove the driven plate from one side of the engine. Also on this side of the engine remove the rear end cover. The pulley with the vibration damper must be removed from the opposite side of the engine, followed by the front end cover of the engine.
- Remove the lower bolts on the side of the oil sump from the engine support at the lower section of the crankcase. Top and bottom part of the crankcase are connected by the engine support.
- Remove the bottom part of the crankcase. The bolts (Torx head) are slackened in the order shown in Fig. 1.43. Carefully follow the numbering, starting at bolt "42".
- The piston or pistons can now be removed as described for the other engines.

1.4.1.2. Measuring the Cylinder Bores

An inside caliper is necessary to measure the diameter of the cylinder bores. We strongly recommend to have the bores measured in an engine shop. If the cylinder block must be re-bored, the shop will also replace the pistons.

1.4.1.3. Checking Pistons and Connecting Rods

All parts should be thoroughly inspected. Signs of seizure, grooves or excessive wear requires the part to be replaced. Check the pistons and connecting rods as follows:

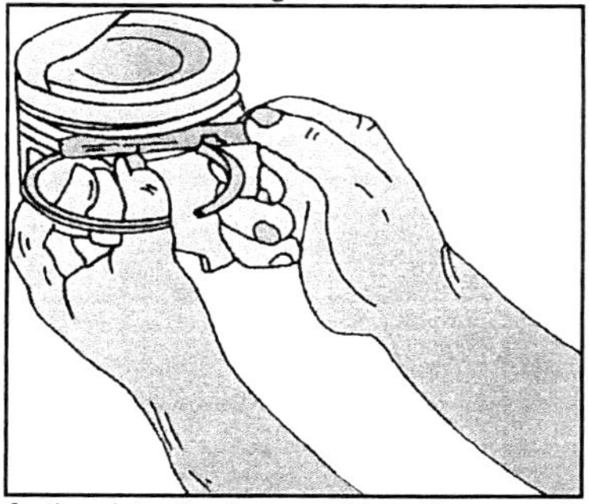

Fig. 1.44 – Checking the side clearance of the piston rings in the grooves of the piston.

- Check the side clearance of each piston ring in its groove by inserting the ring together with a feeler gauge, as shown in Fig. 1.44. The grooves must be thoroughly cleaned before the check. If the wear limit exceed the values in the technical data is reached, either the rings or the piston are worn.
- Check the piston ring gap by inserting the ring from the bottom into the cylinder bore. Use a piston and carefully push the piston ring approx. 1 in. further into the bore. This will square it up. Insert a feeler gauge between the two piston ring ends to check the ring gap, as shown in Fig. 1.45. Refer to Section 1.4.1.0. for the wear limits. Rings must be replaced, if these are exceeded. New rings should also be checked in the manner described.

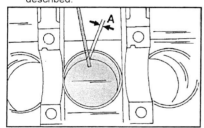

Fig. 1.45 – Checking the piston ring gaps, using a feeler gauge. The gap "A" must be measured.

- Piston pins and small end bushes must be checked for wear or seizure. One individual connecting rod can be replaced, provided that a rod of the same weight group is fitted. Connecting rods are marked with either one or two punch marks (arrow, Fig. 1.46), indicating the weight category, and only a rod with the same mark must be fitted.
- Connecting rod bolts must have a certain length. Just in case they have stretched previously we recommend to replace the bolts.

Fig. 1.46 – The arrow shows the weight category marking of the connecting rods.

- Connecting rods should be checked for bend or twist, particularly when the engine has covered a high mileage. A special jig is necessary for this operation and the job should be carried out by an engine shop.

The following information concern the connecting rods:

- Connecting rods which were overheated due to bearing failure (bluish colour) must not be refitted.
- Connecting and bearing caps are matched to each other and must be fitted accordingly.

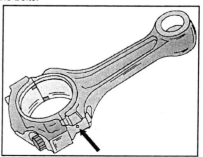

- New connecting rods are supplied together with the small end bearing bush and can be fitted as supplied.
- If the piston pin has excessive clearance in the small end bush, a new bush must be fitted. Again this is best left to an engine shop, as the bush must be reamed out to the correct diameter to obtain the correct running clearance for the piston pin.

1.4.1.4. Piston and Connecting Rods - Assembly

If new pistons are fitted, check the piston crown markings to ensure the correct pistons are fitted. if the original pistons are fitted, arrange them in accordance with the cylinder number markings.
- If connecting rods have been replaced check the bottom of the big end bearing caps. Either one or two punch marks are stamped into the centre of the cap, as shown in Fig. 1.46.
- Insert the connecting rod into the piston and align the two bores. Make sure that the arrow in the piston crown is facing the front of the engine.
- Generously lubricate the piston pin with engine oil and insert it into the piston and connecting rod, using thumb pressure only. Never heat the piston to fit the piston pin. Fit the circlips to both sides of the piston, making sure of their engagement around the groove.
- Using a pair of piston ring pliers (Fig. 1.41), fit the piston rings from the top of the piston, starting with the bottom ring. The two compression rings could be mixed up. Under no circumstances mix-up the upper and lower compression rings.

1.4.1.5. Pistons and Connecting Rods – Installation

- Generously lubricate the cylinder bores with oil. Markings on connecting rods and bearing caps must be opposite each other. The arrows in the piston crowns must face towards the front of the engine.

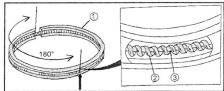

Fig. 1.47 – Correct installation of the multi-part oil control ring (applies to all engines).
1 Chamfered piston ring with spring insert
2 Round spring
3 Spring insert

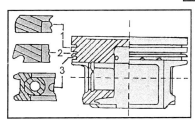

Fig. 1.48 – Sectional view of the pistons and piston rings (all engines).
1 Upper compression ring
2 Second compression ring
3 Multi-part oil control ring

- Arrange the piston rings at equal spacing of 120° around the circumference of the piston skirt and use a piston ring compressor to push the rings into their grooves. Check that all rings are fully pushed in. Check that the marking "Top" or the name of the manufacturer can be read from above after installation. Arrange the multi-part oil control ring (scraper ring) so that the spring ends are offset by 180°. Study Fig. 1.47 before further assembly. Fig. 1.48 shows the section of the piston rings, again as fitted to all engines. Make sure that all rings are fitted as shown.

- Rotate the crankshaft until two of the crankpins are at the bottom.
- Place a piston ring compressor around the piston rings as shown in Fig. 1.49 and push the piston from above into the cylinder bore as shown in the illustration. The cylinder block can be placed on its side to guide the connecting rod. The big end bearing shell should be in the big end bearing.

Fig. 1.49 – Fitting a piston with a piston ring compressor. Push the piston into the bore with a hammer handle.

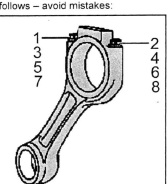

- Insert the second bearing shell into the connecting rod bearing cap, with the locating tab and fit the assembly over the connecting rod. Check that connecting rod/cap marks are facing each other.
- Coat the contact areas for the cap bolts with engine oil and fit and tighten the bolts as follows:
- *In the case of an 612 and 628 engine (ML 270 CDI and ML 400 CDI)* to 0.5 kgm (3.5 ft.lb.) and then again to 2.5 kgm (18 ft.lb.) in several stages. From this position tighten each bolt by a further 90 ° (1/4 of a turn) without using the torque wrench. It is assumed that the stretch bolts have been replaced.
- *In the case of a 642 engine (ML 280/ML 320 CDI)* complete different tightening instructions apply. The bolts are tightened in 8 stages, which are referred to by Mercedes-Benz as "short arm stage" and "long arm stage". Fig. 1.50 shows a connecting rod with the explanation of the tightening procedure. The numbers refer to the stages of tightening. Proceed as follows – avoid mistakes:

Fig. 1.50 – Tightening the connecting rod bearing caps of a 642 engine. The numbers refer to the stages of tightening.

- Tighten the bolt – short arm stage (1) to 1.5 kgm (11 ft.lb.).
- Tighten the bolt – long arm stage (2) to 2.0 kgm (14.5 ft.lb.).
- Tighten the bolt - short arm stage (3) to 3.0 kgm (22 ft.lb.).
- Tighten the bolt – long arm stage (4) to 4.0 kgm (29 ft.lb.).
- Tighten the bolt - short arm stage (5) to 4.0 kgm (29 ft.lb.) and from the final position a further 90° (quarter of a turn).
- Tighten the bolt – long arm stage (6) by a further 90°.
- Tighten the bolt – short arm stage (7) by a further 90°.
- Tighten the bolt – long arm stage (8) by a further 90°.

- Rotate the crankshaft until the remaining crankpins are at bottom dead centre and fit the two other piston/connecting rod assemblies in the same manner.
- Check the pistons and connecting rods once more for correct installation and that each piston is fitted to its original bore, if the same parts are refitted.
- Check the pistons and connecting rods once more for correct installation and that each piston is fitted to its original bore, if the same parts are refitted.
- With a feeler gauge measure the side clearance of each big end bearing cap on the crankpin. The wear limit is 0.50 mm.

- The remaining installation is a reversal of the removal procedure, but special instructions are given for the installation of the bottom section of the crankcase in the case of the 628 engine in the ML 400 CDI. First fit all bolts as shown in Fig. 1.43 in accordance with the diameter AND their length. The tightening of the crankcase is carried out in two stages.

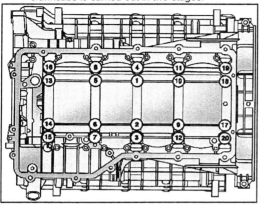

Fig. 1.51 – Initial sequence to tighten the bolts of the crankcase bottom section.

- Refer to Fig. 1.51 and tighten the M11 bolts 1 to 20 in the order shown to 2.0 kgm (14.5 ft.lb.), starting with bolt (1). The bolts are now tightened again in the same order to 5.0 kgm (36 ft.lb.). From the final position tighten the bolts a further 90° and then AGAIN a further 90°. The tightening sequence must be followed.

- The next operation is carried out by referring to Fig. 1.52, noting the different tightening sequence. Tighten the M11 bolts 1 to 20 in the order shown to 2.0 kgm (14.5 ft.lb.), starting with bolt (1). The bolts are now tightened again in the same order to 5.0 kgm (36 ft.lb.). From the final position tighten the bolts a further 90° and then AGAIN a further 90°. The tightening sequence must be followed.

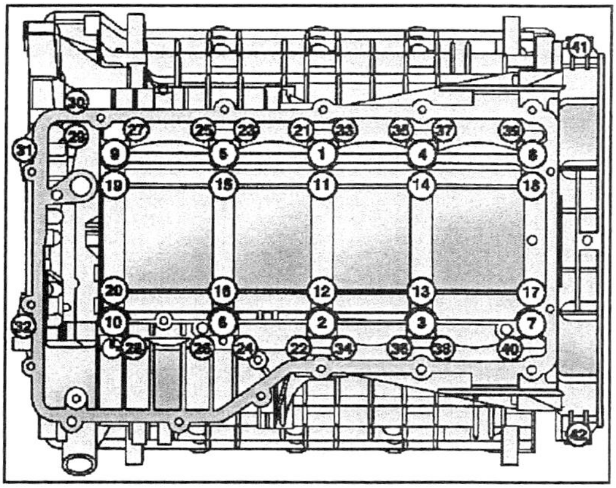

Fig. 1.52 – Second stage and sequence to tighten the bolts of the crankcase bottom section.

- Finally tighten the M6 and M8 bolts 21 to 42 in the given sequence. M6 bolts are tightened to 0.85 kgm, M8 bolts are tightened to 2.0 kgm (14.5 ft.lb.).

1.4.2. CYLINDER BLOCK

The cylinder block consists of the crankcase and the actual block with the cylinder bores. Special attention should be given to the cylinder block at each major overhaul of the engine, irrespective of whether the bores have been re-machined or not.

Thoroughly clean all cavities and passages and remove all traces of foreign matter from the joint faces. If any machining of the bores has taken place, it is essential that all swarf is removed before assembly of the engine takes place.

Measurement of the cylinder bores should be left to an engine shop, as they have the proper equipment to measure cylinder bores. It is, however, feasible to check the cylinder block face for distortion, in a similar manner as described for the cylinder head. The max. permissible distortion is 0.05 mm.

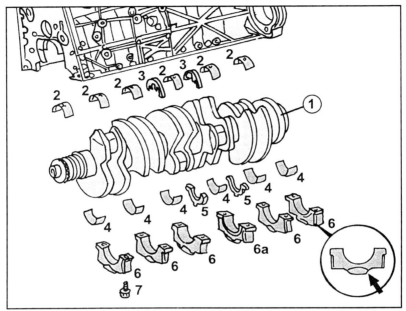

Fig. 1.53 – Crankshaft and bearings of a 612 engine. All bearing caps are numbered (arrow).
1 Crankshaft
2 Bearing shells, crankcase
3 Thrust washers, crankcase
4 Bearing shells in bearing caps
5 Thrust washers, cap
6 Main bearing caps
6a Fitted bearing cap
7 Bearing cap bolts

1.4.3. CRANKSHAFT AND BEARINGS
1.4.3.0. Technical Data

All dimensions in metric units. All data as available.

Max. run-out of main journals*:	
Journals Nos. 2 and 4 – 5-cyl:	0.07 mm
Journals Nos. 2 and 5 – 6-/8-cyl.	0.07 mm
Journal No. 3 – 5-cyl.:	0.10 mm
Journals Nos. 2, 4, 5 – 6-/8-cyl.:	0.10 mm
Max. out-of-round of journals:	0.005 mm
Max. taper of main journals	0.010 mm
Max. taper of crankpins:	0.015 mm
Max. run-out of main journals*:	
Journals Nos. II and IV	0.07 mm
Journal No. III:	0.10 mm

    * Crankshaft placed with Nos. I and V journals or I and IV journals in "V" blocks.

Main Bearing Journal Diameter – 612 engine:
  Nominal: .... 57.950 – 57.965 mm
  1st repair size: .... 57.700 – 57.715 mm
  2nd repair size: .... 57.450 – 57.465 mm
  3rd repair size: .... 57.200 – 57.215 mm
  4th repair size: .... 56.950 – 56.965 mm
Main Bearing Journal Diameter – Other engines:
  Nominal: .... 63.940 – 63.945 mm
Basic Bearing Bores (612 engine):
  For main bearings: .... 62.500 – 62.519 mm
  For big end bearings: .... 51.600 – 51.619 mm
Basic Bearing Bores (628 engine):
  For main bearings: .... 74.500 – 74.518 mm
  For big end bearings: .... 67.600 – 67.614 mm

Crankpin Diameter – 612 engine:
  Nominal dimension:.. .... 47.950 – 47.965 mm
  1st repair size .... 47.000 – 47.715 mm
  2nd repair size: .... 47.450 – 47.560 mm
  3rd repair size: .... 47.200 – 47.215 mm
  4th repair size: .... 46.950 – 46.965 mm
Width of Crankpins (612):
  Nominal Dimension... 27.960 – 28.044 mm
  Repair sizes: .... Up to 28.30 mm
Bearing Running Clearances:
  Main bearings – 612: .... 0.031 – 0.053 mm
  Main bearings – V6/V8: .... 0.026 – 0.050 mm
  Big end bearings – 612: .... 0.025 – 0.065 mm
  Big end bearings – V6/V8: .... 0.022 – 0.067 mm
  Wear limit (all engines): .... 0.080 mm
Bearing End Float:
  Main bearings (612): .... 0.10 – 0.25 mm
  Main bearings (remaining engines): .... 0.10 – 0.266 mm
  Big end bearings (all engines):................................... 0.12 – 0.25 mm
  Wear limit - Main bearings: .... 0.30 mm
  Wear limit - Big end bearings: .... 0.50 mm
Bearing shells: .... Depending on journal diameter (workshop)

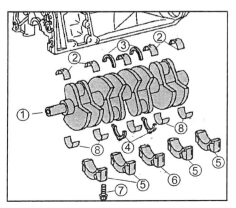

Fig. 1.54 – Crankshaft and bearing parts (V6 engine).
1 Crankshaft
2 Bearing shells in crankcase
3 Bearing shells in main bearing caps
4 Crankshaft bearing cap (end caps)
5 Fitted bearing cap
6 Thrust washers
7 Bearing cap bolt, M8 x 75 mm
8 Bearing cap bolt, M10 x 90 mm
9 Bearing cap side bolt, M8 x 40 mm
10 Crankshaft bearing cap

1.4.3.1. Crankshaft - Removal and Installation

The engine must be removed to take out the crankshaft. The operations are similar on all engines, but a different number of main bearings are fitted, depending on the engine. Fig. 1.53 shows the crankshaft of the 612 engine, Figs. 1.54 and 1.55 show the V6 engine. No bearing caps are used on the V8 engine (628). The instructions are given in general for all engines.

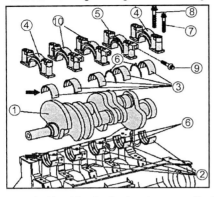

Fig. 1.55 – Crankshaft and bearing parts (V6 engine).
1 Crankshaft
2 Bearing shells in crankcase
3 Bearing shells in main bearing caps
4 Crankshaft bearing cap (end caps)
5 Fitted bearing cap
6 Thrust washers
7 Bearing cap bolt, M8 x 75 mm
8 Bearing cap bolt, M10 x 90 mm
9 Bearing cap side bolt, M8 x 40 mm
10 Crankshaft bearing caps

- Counterhold the flywheel in suitable manner and evenly slacken the clutch securing bolts. Use a centre punch and mark the clutch and flywheel at opposite points. Lift off the clutch plate and the driven plate. Immediately clean the inside of the flywheel and unscrew the flywheel.
- Remove the drive plate for a torque converter of an automatic transmission in the same manner.
- With the flywheel still locked, remove the crankshaft pulley bolt and remove the crankshaft pulley/damper as described later on.
- Remove the cylinder head together with the inlet manifold as described in Section 1.4.0.1.
- Remove the upper and lower timing cover.
- Remove the oil sump and oil pump.
- Remove the pistons and connecting rods as described in Section 1.4.1.1.

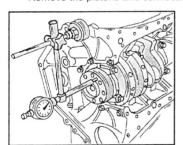

Fig. 1.56 – Checking the crankshaft end float with a dial gauge.

- The crankshaft end float should be checked before the crankshaft is removed. To do this, place a dial gauge with a suitable holder in front of the cylinder block and place the gauge stylus against the end flange of the crankshaft, as shown in Fig. 1.56. Use a screwdriver to push the crankshaft all the way to one end and set the gauge to "0" ' Push the shaft to the other side and note the dial gauge reading. The resulting value is the end float. If it exceeds 0.30 mm (0.012 in.) replace the thrust washers during assembly, but make sure to fit washers of the correct width. These are located left and right at the centre bearing. Note that only two washers of the same thickness must be fitted.
- Unscrew the oil seal flange from the rear of the cylinder block.

Five-cylinder Engine
- Unscrew the main bearing bolts (7) in Fig. 1.53 evenly across. The bearings caps are marked with the numbers 1 to 6. The numbers are stamped into the centre of the caps. No. 1 cap is located at the crankshaft pulley side.

- Remove the bearing shells (4) from the bearing journals (they could also stick to the caps) and immediately mark them on their back faces with the bearing number. Also remove the thrust washers (5).
- Lift the crankshaft (1) out of the cylinder block and remove the remaining thrust washers from the centre bearing location and the remaining bearings shells. keep the shells together with the lower shells and the bearing caps. These shells have an oil bore and a groove and must always be fitted into the crankcase when the crankshaft is installed.

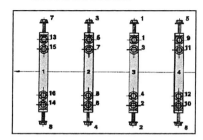

Fig. 1.57 – Tightening order for the crankshaft bearing cap bolts (V6). Note the different diameters and bolt length.

V6/8 Engines

The operations are similar on both types of engine. The instructions are given for the V6 engine, but Fig. 1.58 shows the respective parts for a V8 engine. Note that the lower section of the crankcase must be removed in the case of the 628 engine (ML 400 CDI) before access is gained to the crankshaft bearings. The operations are described in brief below.

- Unscrew the main bearing bolts in reverse order to the numbering in Fig. 1.57. Note that bolts of different diameter and length are used. Each bearing cap is secured with two bolts on either side from above and the side of each cap is additionally secured by a bolt inserted from the side. Mark each bearing cap and its position on the crankcase.
- Remove the crankshaft bearing caps (4), the bearing cap (10) and the fitted bearing cap (5). Cap (10) and (5) have a tight fit and must be levered out carefully. Remove the bearing shells (2) from the bearing journals (they could also stick to the caps) and immediately mark them on their back faces with the bearing number. The numbers refer to Fig. 1.54.
- Lift the crankshaft (1) out of the cylinder block and remove the remaining thrust washers (6) from the centre bearing location and the remaining bearings shells. Keep the shells together with the lower shells and the bearing caps. These shells have an oil bore and a groove and must always be fitted into the crankcase when the crankshaft is installed.

V8 Engine (ML 400 CDI, Model 163)

The following items must be removed to gain access to the crankshaft, engine removed and engine in an assembly stand: Again the work is more complicated when compared to other engines. Remove: Charge air cross pipe, high pressure pump, vacuum pump, front cover of cylinder head, Poly V-belt, charge air pipe on the left and on the right, cylinder head covers. The above operations are described in the section dealing with the cylinder head of the 628 engine, the Poly V-belt is covered in section „Cooling System".

Remove the driven plate, the crankshaft pulley, the engine end cover at the front, the alternator, the chain tensioner, the camshaft timing gears, the intermediate gear for the high pressure pump, the oil sump and the oil pump. The tensioner for the oil pump chain is pushed back to lift off the drive chain. The A/C compressor brackets with the compressor must be removed.

Remove the oil return flow lines at the turbo charger connection and the lower bolts on the side of the oil sump from the engine support on the lower crankcase section.

Rotate the engine until the crankcase is uppermost. The lower crankcase section is now removed as described in the section dealing with the removal of pistons and connecting rods for the 628 engine. Note the order of slackening of the bolts shown in Fig. 1.43. Lift off the lower section and remove the main bearing shells from the housing or the crankshaft journals. Mark their position by numbering them.

The pistons and connecting rods can be removed as described or left in the cylinder block (crankcase). In the latter case remove the big end bearing caps and take out the connecting rod bearing shells after marking their relative position.

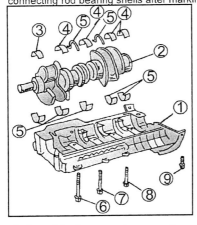

Fig. 1.58 – Removed crankshaft and bearing shells of a 628 V8 engine.
1   Lower crankcase section
2   Crankshaft
3   Upper bearing shells (oil hole)
4   Thrust washers
5   Lower bearing shells (no oil hole)
6   Bolt, M11 x 135 mm
7   Bolt, M11 x 113
8   M6 bolt
9   M8 bolt

Lift the crankshaft from the upper crankcase section and remove the upper bearing shells. Mark their position by numbering them. If the piston/connecting rod assemblies have been left in the cylinder block take out the upper big end bearing shells after marking them with their cylinder number in suitable manner. Fig. 1.58 shows the crankshaft together with the bearing shells and the lower crankcase section.

1.4.3.2. Inspection of Crankshaft and Bearings

Main and crankpin journals must be measured with precision instruments to find their diameters. All journals can be re-ground up to four times, depending on the engine, and the necessary bearing shells are available, i.e. repair size shells can be fitted. For this reason we strongly recommend to take the removed crankshaft to an engine shop to have the measurements carried out and, if required, the bearing shells replaced.

1.4.3.3. Crankshaft - Installation

Five-cylinder Engines (612)

Thoroughly clean the bearing bores in the crankcase and insert the shells with the drillings into the bearing bores, with the tabs engaging the notches. Fit the thrust washers to the centre bearing, with the oil grooves towards the outside.

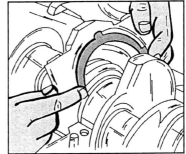

Fig. 1.59 – Fitting the main bearing cap together with the thrust washer.

Use the two forefingers as shown in Fig. 1.59 to hold the thrust washers against the bearing cap and fit the cap in position.

Lift the crankshaft in position and fit the bearing caps with the inserted shells (again shells well oiled and locating tabs in notches).

Fit the two thrust washers to the centre bearing cap, again with the oil groove towards the outside. Place this cap in position, guiding the two thrust washers in order not to dislodge them. Use the forefingers to hold the washers (Fig. 1.59).

Check the numbering of the bearing caps and fit them in position, with the shells inserted. Use a plastic mallet to tap them down. Caps can only be fitted in one position, but the bearing cap numbers must be observed.

Tighten the bolts from the centre towards the outside in several steps to a torque reading of to 5.5 kgm (39.5 ft.lb.) and from this position a further 90 – 100° (quarter of a turn).

Rotate the crankshaft a few times to check for binding.

Re-check the crankshaft end float as described during removal. Attach the dial gauge to the crankcase as shown in Fig. 1.56. The remaining operations are carried out in reverse order to the removal procedure. The various sections give detailed description of the relevant operations, i.e. piston and connecting rods, rear oil seal flange, timing mechanism, flywheel and clutch or drive plate, oil pump, oil sump and cylinder head.

V6/V8 Engines (642 and 628 engines)

The installation of the crankshaft of a **V8 (628) eng**ine is a reversal of the removal procedure. Refer to the section on pistons and connecting rods when refitting the connecting rods and pistons and refitting the lower crankcase section.

In the case of a **V6 (642) engine** thoroughly clean the bearing bores in the crankcase and lubricate the crankshaft bearing cap (4), bearing cap (10), fitted bearing (5) and the bearing shells in the crankcase (2) and the bearing cap (3) with engine oil. Insert the shells with the drillings into the bearing bores, with the tabs engaging the notches. Fit the thrust washers (6) to the bearing shown, with the oil grooves towards the outside. The numbers refer to Fig. 1.54.

Use the two forefingers as shown in Fig. 1.59 to hold the thrust washers against the bearing cap and fit the cap in position.

Lift the crankshaft in position and fit the bearing caps with the inserted shells (again shells well oiled and locating tabs in notches). Fit the two thrust washers to the centre bearing cap, again with the oil groove towards the outside. Place this cap in position, guiding the two thrust washers in order not to dislodge them. Use the forefingers to hold the washers (Fig. 1.59).

Check the numbering of the bearing caps and fit them in position, with the shells inserted. Use a plastic mallet to tap them down. Caps can only be fitted in one position, but the bearing cap numbers must be observed.

Tighten the bolts in the order shown in Fig. 1.57, but note the diameter and the length of the bolts:

- The M10 bolts securing the crankshaft bearing caps to the crankshaft bearing body (the centre bolts in Fig. 1.57) are tightened in three stages. First tighten the bolts to 3.5 kgm (25 ft.lb.) and from the final position a little more then a further quarter of a turn (95°) and then again by the same angle. When tightening the bolts follow the numbered sequence.
- The M8 bolts inserted into the side of the bearing caps Bolts 1 to 8 in Fig. 1.57) are tightened to 5.3 kgm (22 ft.lb.) and from the final position a further 95°. When tightening the bolts follow the numbered sequence.
- Rotate the crankshaft a few times to check for binding and re-check the crankshaft end float as described during the removal.
- The remaining operations are carried out in reverse order to the removal procedure. The various sections give detailed description of the relevant operations, i.e. piston and connecting rods, rear oil seal flange, timing mechanism, flywheel and clutch or drive plate, oil pump, oil sump and cylinder head.

1.4.3.4. Flywheel or Drive Plate (Automatic)

The flywheel or the drive plate for an automatic transmission model can be removed without removal of the crankshaft. The engine can also remain in the vehicle. Fig. 1.60 shows the attachment and the driven plate for reference. Note that two washers are used on the flywheel, one in front and one behind the flywheel in the case of a ML 270 CDI model, not as shown in the illustration. The drive plate, however, is only fitted with one washer on the outside of the drive plate (V6 and V8 models). Only the instructions for the flywheel apply to the 612 engine (ML 270 CD). The remaining models have a drive plate. Remove the part in question as follows:

Fig. 1.60 – View of flywheel and driven plate.
Refer to the information in the text above.
1 Securing bolt, always replace
2 Distance washer, drive plate or flywheel
3 Flywheel, manual transmission
4 Drive plate, automatic

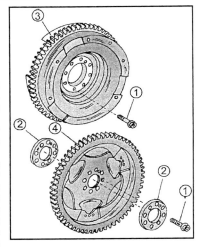

- Remove the transmission (Section 3.1.) or the automatic transmission. Remove the clutch in the case of a manual transmission.
- Remove the plastic cover at the rear end of the oil sump and remove the two bolts below.
- Counterhold the flywheel in suitable manner and remove the clutch after having marked its relationship to the flywheel. Remove the drive plate in a similar manner. 8 bolts are used to secure the flywheel. A dowel pin is fitted into the crankshaft flange to guide the flywheel or driven plate during installation.

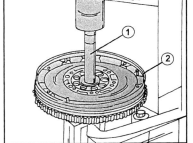

Fig. 1.61 – Pressing the guide bearing into the inside of the flywheel (2). A press mandrel (1) must be used.

- Remove the flywheel or the drive plate. Distance washers are used as explained above, which can also be removed. The securing bolts can be discarded, as they must be replaced. If a new flywheel or driven plate is to be fitted, quote the engine type and vehicle model.
- If the flywheel or the starter ring looks worn, take the wheel to your dealer to have the flywheel re-machined and/or the ring gear replaced.
- Fit the flywheel or drive plate as applicable. Always use new flywheel bolts if a dual-mass flywheel is fitted.

Engines for manual transmissions are fitted with a ball bearing inside the flywheel. The bearing must be pressed out of the flywheel, i.e. you will have to have access to a press. Place the flywheel onto a press table as shown in Fig.1.61, insert the bearing and press the bearing in position. Grease the bearing after installation.

Six-cylinder and eight cylinder engines (642 and 628 engines)

- Fit the drive plate with the dowel pin engaged. Fit a distance washer on top of the drive plate.
- Fit the bolts and tighten them evenly across to 4.5 kgm (32.5 ft.lb.). From this position tighten the bolts a further 90°. The angle is important to give the stretch bolts their correct tension. Fig. 1.62 demonstrates the angle-tightening in the case of a flywheel. The same applies to the driven plate.

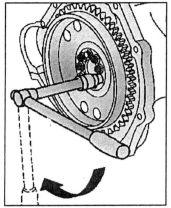

Fig. 1.62 – Apply the socket and extension as shown and tighten the bolts by 90° (quarter of a turn).

Five-cylinder engine (612 engine)

- The length of the bolts must be measured from the end of the thread to the underside of the bolt head before they are re-used. Either long bolts or short bolts are used. There is no need to measure the long bolts (approx. 2 in.). If the short bolts are longer then 22.5 mm, replace them.
- Fit the flywheel or the drive plate with the dowel pin engaged. Fit a distance washer underneath and on top of the drive plate (see Fig. 1.60 and explanation).
- Fit the bolts and tighten them evenly across to 4.5 kgm. From this position tighten the bolts a further 90° as shown in Fig. 1.62. Note that Torx-head bolts are used on some engines.

1.4.3.5. Crankshaft Pulley and Vibration Damper

Five-cylinder 612 Engine (ML 270 CDI)

The engine is fitted with a one piece crankshaft pulley/vibration damper assembly. The damper is located on the end of the crankshaft by means of a Woodruff key and secured by the central bolt in the end of the shaft. The tightening torque of the bolt is not the same on all models and depends on the marking of the bolt head (see below). Fig. 1.63 shows the attachment of the parts.

Fig. 1.63 – Details for the removal and installation of the crankshaft pulley/vibration damper assembly. Note the different tightening torque of the bolt (see below).
1 Crankshaft pulley/vibration damper
2 Central bolt
3 Washer

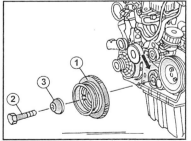

Remove the parts as follows, noting that a puller may be necessary to withdraw the hub:

- Remove the sound-proofing panel from underneath the engine compartment and release the tension of the drive belt, as described later on, and remove it.
- Engage a gear and apply the handbrake to lock the engine against rotation. In the case of a vehicle with automatic transmission remove the starter motor and

lock the starter motor ring gear in suitable manner. The same can be carried out when a manual transmission is fitted and the bolt cannot be removed by engaging a gear.
- Unscrew the crankshaft pulley/vibration damper bolt (2) in Fig. 1.63 and take off the washer (3). Note the fitted direction of the washer.
- Withdraw the assembly from the end of the crankshaft. A tight vibration damper can be removed with a suitable puller. You can also try two tyre levers, applied at opposite points of the damper.

The crankshaft pulley has a certain diameter. If replaced, quote the engine type and number.

The installation of the crankshaft pulley and the vibration damper is carried out as follows:
- Rotate the crankshaft until the Woodruff key is visible and slide the crankshaft pulley/vibration damper with the key way over the key and the shaft. Make sure that the Woodruff key has engaged and has not bee dislodged.
- Place the washer (3) the correct way round over the centre bolt (2), coat the bolt threads with engine oil and fit the bolt. If the bolt head is marked with "8.8" tighten the bolt to 20.0 kgm (144 ft.lb.) plus 90°. If the bolt head is marked with "10.9" tighten the bolt to 32.5 kgm (234 ft.lb.) plus 90°. The crankshaft must still be locked against rotation.
- Fit the drive belt as described later on.
- The remaining operations are carried out in reverse order.

V8 628 Engine (ML 400 CDI)
- Remove the sound-proofing panel from underneath the engine compartment. The electric fan and the charge air hose of the lower charge air pipe must be removed from the R.H., charge air cooler.
- Slacken the Poly V drive belt, as described later on, and remove it. Also remove the coolant hose from the water pump.
- To prevent the crankshaft from rotating a special counter holder is used in the workshop. You will have to remove the starter motor to lock the starter motor ring gear in suitable manner.
- Unscrew the crankshaft pulley/vibration damper bolt and withdraw the assembly from the end of the crankshaft. A tight vibration damper can be removed with a suitable puller. You can also try two tyre levers, applied at opposite points of the damper.

The installation of the crankshaft pulley and the vibration damper is carried out as follows:
- Rotate the crankshaft until the Woodruff key is visible and slide the crankshaft pulley/vibration damper with the key way over the key and the shaft. Make sure that the Woodruff key has engaged and has not bee dislodged.
- Coat the bolt threads with engine oil and fit the bolt. Tighten the bolt to 27.5 kgm (198 ft.lb.) and then a further 90°.
- Fit the drive belt as described later on.
- The remaining operations are carried out in reverse order.

V6 642 Engines (ML 280 CDI and ML 320 CDI)
The removal is similar as described for the V8 engine. The engine cover must be pulled upwards and removed. During installation tighten the crankshaft pulley bolt to 20.0 kgm (144 ft.lb.) and from the final position a further 90°. Then once more tighten the bolt a further 90°. The crankshaft must be prevented against rotation by locking the starter motor ring gear.

1.4.3.6. Rear Crankshaft Oil Seal and Oil Seal Carrier

Five-cylinder 612 Engine (ML 270 CDI)

The rear crankshaft oil seal is located inside a flange which is bolted to the rear of the crankcase. Flange and oil seal are made together and cannot be replaced separately. Two dowels locate the flange correctly in relation to the crankshaft centre. The flange is fitted with sealing compound ("Loctite"). Fig. 1.64 shows the attachment of the oil seal flange (cover) and the integral oil seal.

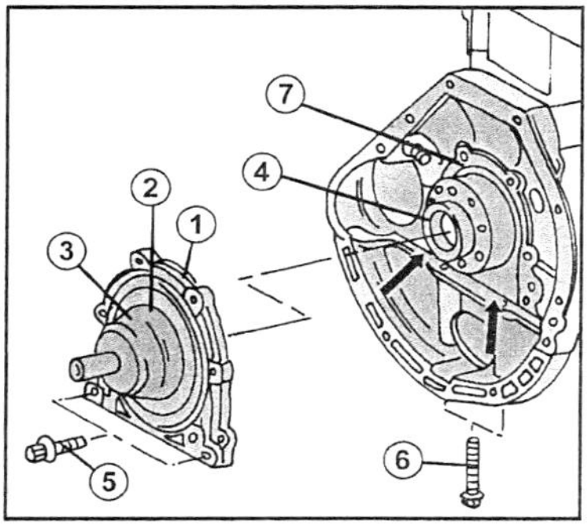

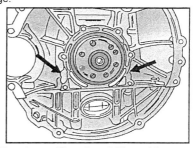

Fig. 1.64 – Removal and installation of the rear oil seal cover together with the oil seal. The faces marked with the arrows must be coated with "Loctite".
1 Cover with oil seal
2 Fitting sleeve (normally in repair kit)
3 Oil seal in cover
4 Crankshaft
5 Screws, inserted from front, 0.9 kgm
6 Screws, inserted from below, 0.9 kgm

Transmission and flywheel and/or drive plate must be removed to replace the cover/oil seal assembly. Also drain the engine oil.

- Place a jack underneath the engine (wooden block between jack head and engine) and lift the engine approx. 5 cm at the front axle in order to reach he bolts (6) in Fig. 1.64.
- Remove the bolts (5) from the front and the two bolts (6) from below.
- Insert two screwdrivers as shown in Fig. 1.65 and lever off the cover from the crankcase (7) without damaging the flange.

Fig. 1.65 – To remove the oil seal cover insert two screwdrivers carefully underneath two lugs shown by the arrows.

- Thoroughly clean the sealing faces and coat the cover face where it rests against the oil sump gasket. Push the cover against the crankcase. You should have a fitting sleeve (2) in Fig. 1.64 which will aid the fitting. Otherwise take care nct to damage the seal. After the cover is flush against the crankcase push it upwards until the upper face is against the crankcase and remove the fitting sleeve. The oil seal (3) must have a snug fit.
- Fit the two bolts (6) from below and then the remaining bolts from the front. First tighten the lower bolts and then the remaining bolts. All are tightened to 0.9 kgm (7 ft.lb.).
- All other operations are carried out in reverse order. Fill the engine with oil and check the oil level after the engine has been started. If necessary correct.

V8 628 Engine (ML 400 CDI)

The engine is fitted with a large rear cover and a separate rear oil seal. The automatic transmission and the drive plate must be removed to replace the seal. Prevent the crankshaft from rotating as described above to remove the drive plate bolts. Unscrew the rear engine cover and carefully remove the oil seal.

During installation fit the first fit the cover (1.0 kgm/7.2 ft.lb.) and then drive the oil seal carefully in position without damaging the sealing lip. Refit the drive plate as described earlier on. All other operations are carried out in reverse order. Check the oil level of the engine and if necessary correct.

V6 642 Engines (ML 280 CDI and ML 320 CDI)
The rear crankshaft oil seal is located inside a flange which is bolted to the rear of the crankcase. Flange and oil seal are made together and cannot be replaced separately. The automatic transmission and the drive plate must be removed to replace the seal. Prevent the crankshaft from rotating as described above to remove the drive plate bolts. Unscrew the rear engine cover and fir a new cover with the new seal. Tighten the bolts evenly around the outer edge to 0.8 kgm and then again to 1.0 kgm. Check the oil level of the engine and if necessary correct.

1.4.3.7. Front Crankshaft Oil Seal

The front crankshaft oil seal is located in the timing cover or in the case of the V8 engine in a separate front cover. Oil leaks at this position can also be caused by a leaking timing cover gasket. Check before replacing the oil seal.

Five-cylinder 612 and 642 Engine (ML 270 CD/280 CDI/320 CDI)
The crankshaft pulley/vibration damper as already described before the oil seal can be replaced. The seal can be carefully removed with a screwdriver (see Fig. 1.66). Screw a self-tapping screw into the outside of the seal and apply the screwdriver plate under the screw head. It is also possible to unscrew the oil seal cover to replace the seal.
Thoroughly clean the surrounding parts. Burrs on the timing cover bore can be removed with a scraper. Also clean the cylinder block face.
Fill the space between sealing lip and dust protection lip with grease and carefully drive a new oil seal into the timing cover and over the crankshaft until the ring outer face is flush. Fit the two bolts from below and then the remaining bolts. All bolts are tightened to 7.2 kgm (7.2 ft.lb.).

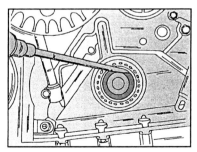

Fig. 1.66 – Removal of the front crankshaft oil seal if the seal is fitted to the timing cover.

Refit the vibration damper as described and carry out the remaining operations in reverse order.

V8 628 Engine (ML 400 CDI)
Remove the belt pulley/vibration damper as described in Section 1.4.3.5 for the V8 engine and unscrew the end cover around the crankshaft end. The oil seal is now removed carefully with a screwdriver.
Thoroughly clean the surrounding parts. Burrs on the timing cover bore can be removed with a scraper. No oil or grease must be smeared on the oil seal. Refit the cover (1.0 kgm) and then carefully drive a new oil seal in position into the cover and over the crankshaft until the ring outer face is flush.

The remaining installation operations are a reversal of the removal operations. Refit the vibration damper as described in Section 1.4.3.5.

1.4.3.8. Replacing Welsh Plugs in the Crankcase

Welsh plugs are fitted into the side of the cylinder block. These plugs will be "pushed" out if the coolant has been allowed to freeze and can be replaced with the engine fitted, provided the special tool 102 589 07 15 00 can be obtained.

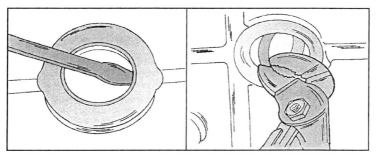

Fig. 1.67 – Removal of a welsh plug. Operation 1 on the left, operation 2 on the right.

Welsh plugs can be replaced as follows:

- Drain the cooling system and remove all parts obstructing the welsh plug in question, i.e. transmission, intermediate flange, injection pump, etc.
- The removal of a welsh plug is carried out in two stages. First place a small chisel or strong screwdriver blade below the lip of the welsh plug, as shown in Fig. 1.67 on the L.H. side and push the screwdriver in the direction of the arrow until it has swivelled by 90° Then grip the plug with a pair of pliers, as shown in Fig. 1.67 on the right and remove it.

Thoroughly clean the opening in the cylinder head from grease and coat the locating bore with "Loctite 241" (obtain from a dealer if possible). Fit the large new welsh plug with the special tool mentioned above or use a drift of suitable size and drive it in position until flush with the cylinder block face.

Refit all removed parts and allow the vehicle to stand for at least 45 minutes before the cooling system is filled and the engine is started. Then start the engine and check for coolant leaks.

1.4.3.9. Replacing the Pilot Bearing in the Crankshaft

Engines for manual transmissions are fitted with a ball bearing in the end of the crankshaft, sealed off with a sealing ring.

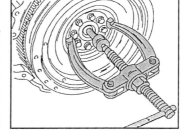

Fig. 1.68 – Removal of the pilot bearing with a two-arm puller.

The sealing ring must be removed to withdraw the ball bearing with a suitable puller, as shown in Fig. 1.68. The pilot bearing can be replaced with the engine fitted to the vehicle, but the transmission and the clutch must be removed. Then apply the extractor as shown in the illustration. The sealing ring will come away with the bearing. Coat the new bearing with heat-resistant grease and drive it into the end of the crankshaft, using a drift of suitable diameter as shown in Fig. 1.61. The ball bearing must be driven against its stop. Fit a new oil seal in a similar manner, taking care not to damage it.

1.4.4. TIMING MECHANISM – 612 Engine (ML 270 CDI)

The following description deals with the timing mechanism of the engine. The removal and installation of the two camshafts has already been described in conjunction with the cylinder head. The endless timing chain is engaged with the camshaft sprockets, the high pressure pump sprocket and the crankshaft sprocket. The chain is guided by slide rails. The tension of the chain is ensured by means of a hydraulic chain tensioner, which is located in the timing cover and pushes onto a tensioning rail. The camshaft sprockets are fitted by means of a bolt and located by a Woodruff key.

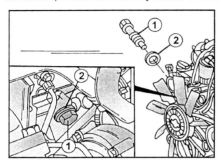

Fig. 1.69 – The chain tensioner (1) is fitted at the position shown and sealed off by means of sealing ring (2).

A second, smaller chain is used to drive the oil pump. The chain is fitted around a second sprocket on the crankshaft and around the pump drive sprocket and has its own chain tensioner.

1.4.4.0. Chain Tensioner – Removal and Installation

The chain tensioner is fitted into the R.H. side of the cylinder head as shown in Fig. 1.69. The tensioning force of the chain tensioner is a combination of the fitted compression spring and the pressure of the engine oil. The oil contained inside the tensioner also absorbs shock loads from the timing chain. A chain tensioner cannot be repaired, i.e. must be replaced if suspect.

The chain tensioner (1) can simply be unscrewed from the side of the engine. The sealing ring (2) must be replaced. Fit the chain tensioner with the new seal and tighten it to 8.0 kgm (58 ft.lb.). The pressure plunger of the tensioner will push against the tensioning rail.

1.4.4.1. Timing Case Cover – Removal and Installation

Fig. 1.70 shows most of the parts to be removed in order to take out the timing case cover. The illustration shows the similar four-cylinder engine. Any parts which can remain in the vehicle will be mentioned during the removal of the five-cylinder engine. The battery must be disconnected and the coolant and the engine oil drained after the bottom parts (1) and (2) of the noise encapsulation have been removed. Fig. 1.71 shows the remaining parts at the front of the engine.

- Remove the trim panels for the cylinder head cover (3) and (4) as described during the removal of the cylinder head.
- Disconnect the coolant hoses (9) and (10) from the thermostat housing. Check hoses and clamps before re-using them.
- Remove the air intake hose (5).
- Remove the charge air pipe (11) together with the charge air hose (6),
- Remove the electric fan (7) as described in section "Cooling System".
- Remove the injectors and the cylinder head cover as described during the removal of the cylinder head.

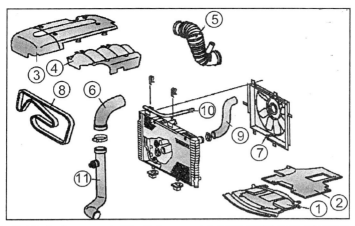

Fig. 1.70 – Details for the removal of the timing case cover. The numbers are referred to in the text. Also see Fig. 1.71.

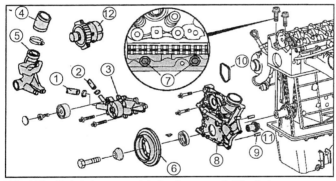

Fig. 1.71 – Parts to be removed during the removal of the timing case cover.
1 Coolant hose
2 Coolant hose
3 Coolant pump
4 Charge air hose
5 Charge air pipe
6 Belt pulley
7 M8 cylinder head bolts
8 Timing case cover
9 Dowel sleeve
10 Rubber seal
11 Return flow check valve
12 Alternator

- Set the piston of No. 1 cylinder to the top dead centre position by applying a socket to the crankshaft pulley bolt – not on the camshaft sprocket bolt – until the marks on camshaft and camshaft bearing cap are aligned as shown in Fig. 1.17. Do not rotate the crankshaft backwards.
- Remove the chain tensioner as described above.
- Remove the coolant thermostat and the front cover on the cylinder head (refer to the removal of the cylinder head for this engine).
- Remove the Poly V-belt (8) as described later on.
- Detach the connector plug from the A/C compressor and remove the compressor with the hoses/pipes attached and attach it in suitable manner at the bottom of the engine compartment.

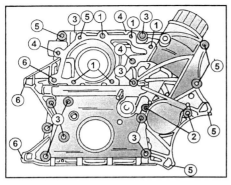

Fig. 1.72 - The location of the timing case cover bolts. Bolts (6) are not used on the 612 engine.
1   M6 x 28
2   M7 x 28
3   M8 x 60
4   M8 x 80
5   M8 x 90

- Detach the coolant hose to the oil-water heat exchanger at the crankcase connection.
- Detach all coolant hoses from the water pump (Fig. 1.71) and remove the pump ("Cooling System").
- Remove the charge air pipe and the alternator (Fig. 1.71).
- Remove the crankshaft pulley/vibration damper as already described.
- Unscrew the oil sump bolts in the area of the timing case cover. The remaining bolts must be slackened. M6 bolts are tightened to 0.9 kgm, M8 bolts to 2.0 kgm.
- Unscrew the M8 bolts (7) in Fig. 1.71 securing the timing case cover (8) to the cylinder head. The bolts are tightened to 2.0 kgm (14.5 ft.lb.).
- Remove the timing case cover (8).

The installation is a reversal of the removal procedure. Note that the length of the bolts is not the same. As you can see from Fig. 1.72 . Also note that M6, M7 and M8 bolts are used. Follow the tightening torques given above.

1.4.4.2. Removal and Installation of Timing Chain

The replacement of the timing chain is practically impossible without using the special tools available to Mercedes dealers. As the engine must be removed in any case you will be able to replace the chain in accordance with the instructions given during the removal of the cylinder head, camshafts, etc. and the instructions given below. The timing chain can then be removed in one piece and refitted. The workshop separates the chain and rivets are used to assemble it.

Removal and Installation of tensioning rail and slide rail in timing cover

The location of the tensioning rail and the slide rail in the timing cover is shown in Fig. 1.73. If it is necessary to replace the tensioning rail (1) you will also have to replace the slide rail (3) and the tensioning lever (5).

Fig. 1.73 – Removal and installation of the tensioning rail and the slide rail in the timing cover.
1 Tensioning rail
2 Bearing pin
3 Slide rail
4 Bearing pin
5 Tensioning lever
6 Bearing pin
7 Spring

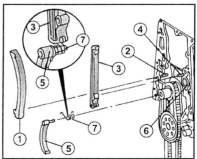

The engine must be removed to replace the parts shown in the illustration. Also remove the cylinder head and the timing cover as described earlier on. Proceed as follows:

- With the engine removed remove the cylinder head and the timing cover as described before.
- Pull the tensioning rail (1) off the bearing pin (2).
- Pull the slide rail (3) together with the tensioning lever (5) of the bearing pins (4) and (6) respectively.
- Release the spring (7) at the slide rail (3) and take it off the tensioning lever.

The installation is a reversal of the removal procedure. Ensure that the spring (7) is correctly installed to the tensioning lever.

Removal and Installation of slide rail in cylinder head

The location if the slide rail, located in the cylinder head, is shown in Fig. 1.74. The front cover of the cylinder head must be removed in order to gain access to the slide rail. Proceed as follows:
- Rotate the crankshaft in the direction of rotation until the piston of cylinder No. 1 is at top dead centre. The mark in the crankshaft pulley must be aligned.

Fig. 1.74 – Location of the slide rail (1) in the cylinder head. A 17 mm hexagon 3/8 in. square wrench is required to unscrew the driver (2) after removal of the cylinder head cover (3).

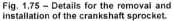

- Lock the camshafts to prevent them from rotating. This has already been explained during the removal of the camshafts. Otherwise make sure that the shafts cannot move.
- Remove the front cover from the cylinder head as described in connection with the cylinder head.
- Using the wrench mentioned above unscrew the driver (2) out of the inlet camshaft and take off the upper slide rail (1).

The installation is a reversal of the removal procedure. The driver is tightened to 5.0 kgm (36 ft.lb.). Refit the front cover to the cylinder head as described earlier on and refit the engine.

Fig. 1.75 – Details for the removal and installation of the crankshaft sprocket.
1 Crankshaft sprocket
2 Woodruff key
3 Oil pump drive chain
4 Tensioning lever
5 Timing chain
6 Puller

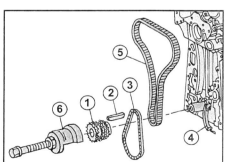

Removal and installation of crankshaft timing sprocket

Various parts must be removed to gain access for the removal of the sprocket. These are the oil sump and the high pressure pump drive gear. After the parts above have been removed you will be able to remove the sprocket in accordance with Fig. 1.75. Note that a puller is required to withdraw the sprocket, but the special tool shown in the illustration can be replaced by a two-arm puller

- Push the tensioning lever (4) down against the force of the spring and take off the drive chain for the oil pump (3).
- Lift the timing chain (5) off the crankshaft pulley. Immediately check the condition of the timing chain and replace it if necessary.
- Use the puller (6) shown in the illustration or one operating in a similar manner and withdraw the sprocket (1) from the end of the crankshaft. The tensioning lever (4) must again be pushed against the tension of the spring to facilitate the operation. Check the condition of the Woodruff key (3) and replace it if necessary. A side cutter can be used to remove the old key.

The installation is a reversal of the removal procedure. Use a hammer to tap in the Woodruff key. The flat face must be parallel with the crankshaft end. Use a piece of tube to drive the sprocket over the crankshaft end. A tight sprocket can be heated up if necessary (wear leather gloves in this case).

Rotate the crankshaft a few times, re-check the timing marks and assemble the engine.

Removal and installation of camshafts

The camshafts are not the same on all engines. A number stamped into the camshaft indicates to which engine the particular shaft is fitted.

The engine in question must also be fitted with the correct camshaft.

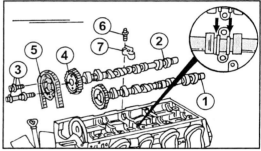

Fig. 1.76 – Camshaft installation shown in the case of the 611 four-cylinder engine. One more journal is fitted to the 612 engine. The arrows show where the alignment is checked at the camshaft bearing.
1 Inlet camshaft
2 Exhaust camshaft
3 Camshaft sprocket bolts (1.8 kgm)
4 Location of down pin
5 Camshaft sprocket
6 Bearing cap bolt (0.9 kgm)
7 Camshaft bearing cap

The camshafts are fitted to the upper end of the cylinder head and held in position by their bearing caps. The lower bearing bores are machined into the cylinder head. The camshafts are lifted out towards the top after removal of the camshaft bearing caps and the camshaft sprockets. The removal and installation has already been described in conjunction with the cylinder head. Fig. 1.76 shows the fitting of the camshafts in the case of a 611 four-cylinder engine.

1.4.5. TIMING MECHANISM – 642 Engine (ML 280/320 CDI)
1.4.5.1. Timing Case Cover – Removal and Installation

The vehicle must be resting on chassis stands as operations must be carried out from below. With the bonnet open proceed as follows, but note that the mixing chamber must be removed:

- Grip the engine trim panel and pull it upwards and towards the rear to free it from the pins. The trim panel is the panel covering the engine.
- Remove the Poly V-belt as described later and also the V-belt tensioning device. Looking at the front of the engine it is located on the R.H. side. On the opposite side remove the lower guide pulley.

- Remove the mixing chamber.
- Position the piston of No. 1 cylinder to the top dead centre position. Turn the crankshaft in the direction of rotation until the TDC marking on the crankshaft vibration damper is aligned with the bar on the timing case cover.
- From below the vehicle remove the bottom section of the sound-proofing capsule.
- Drain and collect the engine oil. The sealing ring for the drain plug should be replaced (tightened to 3.0 kgm /22 ft.lb.).
- Remove the lower part of the oil sump as described in section "Lubrication System". The bolts are tightened to 1.4 kgm (10 ft.lb.).
- Remove the crankshaft pulley/vibration damper as described earlier on. Before proceeding check once more the TDC position of the engine (timing cover can otherwise not be removed).
- Locate the timing cover securing bolts and remove them. Some are located around the pulley assembly, 5 in a row around the lower end. The timing cover can now be withdrawn. At the lower end you will find two guide sleeves which MUST BE REMOVED (only fitted during initial assembly) and not be refitted, as the sealing compound applied during installation would not seal properly. The oil seal in the cover can be replaced.

During installation in reverse order apply sealing compound "Loctite 5970" to the sealing face and fit the cover. The workshop uses a centering sleeve to fit the cover to protect the oil seal. Take care. First tighten the lower bolts and then all bolts to 0.9 kgm (7 ft.lb.). The tensioning device is tightened to 5.8 kgm (42 ft.lb.). Finally fill the engine with 8.5 litres of engine oil suitable for diesel engines.

1.4.5.2. Chain Tensioner – Removal and Installation

The chain tensioner is fitted into the R.H. side of the cylinder head as shown in Fig. 1.77. The tensioning force of the chain tensioner is a combination of the fitted compression spring and the pressure of the engine oil. The oil contained inside the tensioner also absorbs shock loads from the timing chain. A chain tensioner cannot be repaired, i.e. must be replaced if suspect.

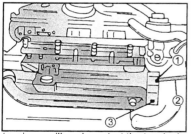

Fig. 1.77 – Details for the removal of the chain tensioner (642 engine. See Text.

The engine trim panel. The engine intake air duct on the R.H. side and the air filter housing on the R.H. side must be removed. Remove a cable strap (3) from the electrical cable (2) and unscrewed the tensioner (1) from the side of the engine. The sealing ring must be replaced. Fit the chain tensioner with the new seal and tighten it to 8.0 kgm (58 ft.lb.). The pressure plunger of the tensioner will push against the tensioning rail.

1.4.5.3. Removal and Installation of Timing Chain

The replacement of the timing chain is practically impossible without using the special tools available to Mercedes dealers. As the engine must be removed in any case you will be able to replace the chain in accordance with the instructions given during the removal of the cylinder head, camshafts, etc. and the instructions given below. The timing chain can then be removed in one piece and refitted. The workshop separates the chain and rivets are used to assemble it.

Briefly the following operations are necessary. Remove the engine trim panel (see above), unscrew the camshaft sprocket securing bolt (located opposite the locking pin of the R.H. camshaft, set the No. 1 piston to TDC as described above, but also check that the markings on the two camshaft sprockets are opposite each other, fully unscrew the camshaft sprocket, remove the chain tensioner as described above and remove the R.H. camshaft. The timing chain can now be lifted off.

Removal and Installation of tensioning rail and slide rails in timing case cover

The location of the tensioning rail and the three slide rails in the timing case is shown in Fig. 1.78. Any of the parts can be removed as follows if necessary: Again the operations are comprehensive. It is assumed that the rails are in the fitted engine. An impact hammer, together with a M6 threaded bolt of 100 mm in length is required to remove the slide rail bearing bolts. The 6 mm bolt is screwed into the end of the bearing bolt and the impact hammer (slide hammer) attached to the end of the bolt. Provided that these tools can be obtained, the rail can be removed as described below. Proceed as follows:

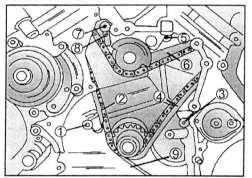

Fig. 1.78 – Details for the removal and installation of slide rails and tensioning rail. The numbers are referred to in the removal instructions.

- Remove the engine trim panel (see above), the mixing chamber and the L.H. cylinder head cover (see removal of cylinder head).
- Remove the oil filter and the high pressure pump and set the No. 1 piston to TDC.
- Remove the bottom section of the sound-proofing and drain the engine oil. Replace the sealing ring of the drain plug (3.0 kgm (22 ft.lb.).

Fig. 1.79 – Remove the two bearing bolts in the manner shown out of the cylinder block. This is a general view of the tool application.

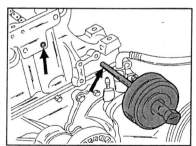

- Remove the crankshaft pulley/vibration damper as described earlier on.
- Remove the oil sump, the timing case cover and the chain tensioner.
- Withdraw the two bearing pins with the impact hammer and a threaded insert, as shown in Fig. 1.79 into the slide rail pins of the three slide rails (4), (6) and (8) to remove the slide rails. If no slide hammer is available, try the following: Slide a piece of tube over the bearing pin and place a washer over the tube. Screw in a 6 mm bolt and tighten it. With the washer pressing against the tube, the bearing pin will be dislodged as soon as the tube is under tension. All pins must be removed in the same manner (three in total).
- Remove the bolt (1) from the tensioning rail (2). The bolt is tightened to 1.2 kgm (9 ft.lb.) and pull out the tensioning rail downwards.

- Remove the exhaust camshaft. The timing chain and the sprocket must be marked at opposite points with paint, if possible. Lift off the timing chain, tie it up at the top and allow to hang down in the timing case.
- Remove the bolt (3) from the slide rail (4) – tighten to 1.2 kgm.
- Press the tensioning rail (9) acting against the oil pump chain upwards against the spring force and pull the slide rail (4) downwards. Then remove the bolt (5) of the slide rail (6) and again remove it downwards. The same operation is carried out with the slide rail (8) after removal of the bolt (7). Tighten the bolt to 1.2 kgm.

The installation is a reversal of the removal procedure. Follow the torques above. Finally fill the engine with oil.

Removal and installation of crankshaft timing sprocket

The removal and installation is carried out in a similar manner as described for the 612 engine earlier on.

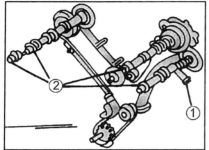

Fig. 1.80 – The camshaft drive of the 642 engine.
1   Chain tensioner
2   Camshafts

Removal and installation of cam-shaft sprockets

The camshafts are not the same for both sides of the cylinder head. A number stamped into the camshaft indicates to which cylinder head the particular shaft is fitted. Inlet valve L.H. cylinder head 642 10, R.H. cylinder head A 642 09, exhaust valve L.H. cylinder head A 642 12, R.H. cylinder head A 642 11. The engine in question must also be fitted with the correct camshaft.

The camshafts are fitted to cylinder head and secured by retainer brackets. The camshafts are lifted out towards the top after removal of parts described below. We must point out that a special hold-down device, the shape of which is shown in Fig. 1.81. The arrangement of the four camshafts is illustrated in Fig. 1.80. Removal and installation is not easy.

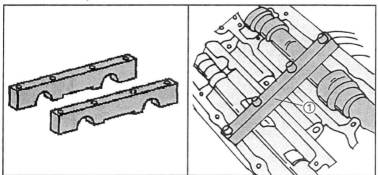

Fig. 1.81 – The L.H. view shows the shape of the hold-down device (1) for the camshafts (No. 642 589 00 31 00). The R.H. view shows where it is fitted in the centre of the cylinder head.

- Remove the engine trim panel and the cylinder head covers as described earlier on.
- Remove the camshaft sprockets in the following manner. Fit the hold-down device shown in Fig. 1.81 in the position shown on the R.H. side. The hold-down tool is fitted in the centre of the camshafts and acts as camshaft bearing to relieve the load on the camshaft retainer brackets at both ends.
- Set the piston of No. 1 cylinder to TDC as described above. Check the markings of the camshaft sprockets. On one side the marking on the sprocket must be opposite each other and the other sprocket the marking must be aligned with the cylinder head. Additionally the marking on the vibration damper must be opposite the rib on the timing case cover.
- Continue to rotate the crankshaft by one revolution exactly and remove the LOWER camshaft sprocket securing bolts from the camshaft sprockets. The bolts are tightened to 1.8 kgm (13 ft.lb.).
- Once more rotate the crankshaft by one revolution and re-set the No. 1 piston again to the TDC position as described above.
- Attach the timing chain with a strap (cable binder for example) to the camshaft sprocket and remove the UPPER sprocket securing bolts. The tightening torque is as given above.
- Withdraw the sprocket from the end of the camshaft.
- To remove the camshafts remove the hold-down device, remove the retaining brackets at either end and lift out the shaft(s). The hydraulic compensating elements can be removed.

During installation lubricate the compensating elements and the bearing journals with engine oil and insert the camshafts. Note the markings on camshaft sprockets as described above and align them accordingly. Fit the hold-down device and fit the retainer brackets. They are tightened to 0.8 kgm. Remove the hold-down device, refit the camshaft sprockets and the cylinder head covers. Place the engine cover in position.

Checking the Camshaft Timing position
As already mentioned: Camshafts and associated parts can only be removed when the camshafts are in their basic timing position. The cylinder head covers and the mixing chamber must be removed to carry out the check.
- Rotate the crankshaft until the markings on the inside of the camshaft sprockets are positioned opposite each other. Two other markings on the sprockets must be level with the cylinder head face on the L.H. side. Also check that the TDC marking on the vibration damper is aligned with the rib on the timing cover.
- A further check is necessary on the balance shaft. The balance shaft drive gear (this is the sprocket immediately above the crankshaft sprocket) has a mark which must be vertically at the upper end.

1.4.6. TIMING MECHANISM – 628 Engine (ML 400 CDI
1.4.6.0. Chain Tensioner – Removal and Installation

The chain tensioner is located immediately above the alternator, above the hose. To remove it unscrew it. The sealing ring underneath must be replaced. Tighten the tensioner plug to 8.0 kgm (58 ft.lb.). Check the oil level in the sump and correct if necessary. Check for oil leaks around the chain tensioner.

1.4.6.1. Timing Chain – Removal and Installation

As in the case of the other engines we cannot recommend the replacement of the timing chain as a DIY operation when the engine is fitted to the vehicle. If the engine is removed you can replace the chain in accordance with the instructions given, as the new chain is placed in position over the various sprockets. The remaining operations can be taken from the various operations described in this section.

1.4.6.2. Chain Tensioning Rail – Removal and Installation

The following instructions assume that the engine has been removed from the vehicle as described earlier on. Fig. 1.82 shows where the tensioning rail is located on the timing chain. To reach the tensioning rail in the inside of the timing chain housing, you will have to expose the front end of the engine. This requires the removal of the injectors, the cylinder head covers, the charge air cross pipe, the Poly V-belt, the crankshaft pulley/vibration damper, the vacuum pump. The high pressure pump and the alternator. Most of the operations have already been described and must be followed.

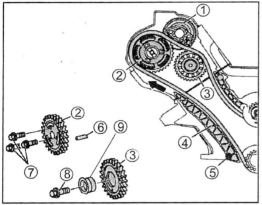

Fig. 1.82 – Details for the removal and installation of the chain tensioning rail.
1. Inlet camshaft sprocket
2. Camshaft drive gear
3. High pressure pump gear
4. Tensioning rail
5. Slide rail pin
6. Dowel pin
7. Bolt
8. Mounting bolt
9. Bush

The tensioning rail is fitted to the lower end by means of a bearing bolt, which must be extracted from the crankcase in the same manner as described during the removal of the cylinder head. In Fig. 1.79 you will see the arrangement of extractor bolt and impact hammer to remove such a bearing bolt. Proceed as follows:

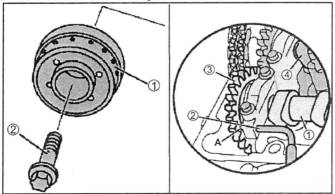

Fig. 1.83 – The L.H. view shows the centrifuge (1) in front of the balance shaft, secured with bolt (2) – L.H. thread. The R.H. view shows the locking of the camshaft sprocket. The numbers are referred to in the description.

75

- Set the No. 1 piston to the top centre position as described above.
- Remove the so-called centrifuge which has the shape shown in Fig. 1.83 in the L.H. view is fitted to the end of the balance shaft. The centrifuge (1) is located immediately above the crankshaft pulley and is secured by means of a bolt. To remove the part remove the bolts securing the cover in front of the centrifuge. The crankshaft pulley will have to be rotated slightly to reach the lower bolt. The cover sealing ring must be replaced. The bolt (2) in Fig. 1.83 can now be removed. As the thread is a left-hand thread, you will have to remove the bolt it as if you would tighten a bolt. The bolt is tightened to 2.2 kgm (as if you would slacken a bolt), the cover bolts to 0.8 kgm during installation. If you rotate the crankshaft pulley reset the TDC position.

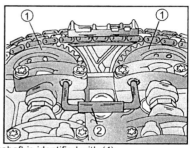

Fig. 1.84 – The two camshaft sprockets (1) are locked in position by inserting the timing pins (2) as shown from the rear of the camshaft caps as described (shown on a similar engine).

- Lock the L.H. and R.H. inlet camshafts. Fig. 1.83 on the R.H. side will help. Locking pins are used in the workshop of course, the shape of which can be seen in Fig. 1.84. The pin (2) is inserted through the first camshaft bearing cap for the inlet camshaft (1) into the hole (A) in the inlet camshaft sprocket (3) in Fig. 1.83. The exhaust camshaft is identified with (4).
- Mark the camshaft timing sprocket in relation to the timing chain (paint mark if possible) and remove the chain tensioner as described above. Then unscrew the camshaft timing sprocket (2) in Fig. 1.82 from the exhaust camshaft (4 in Fig. 1.83, right). The bolts (7) must be removed. A dowel pin (6) guides the sprocket. Always replace the bolts. Tightened to 1.8 kgm (13 ft.lb.).
- Remove the intermediate gear of the high pressure pump (10) by removing bolt (8) and take out the bush (9). Tighten the bolt to 4.0 kgm (29 ft.lb.).
- The impact extractor is now used as described above (see also Fig. 1.79) to remove the guide rail pins (5) in Fig. 1.82. The tensioning rail is now pulled upwards and then remove it.

The installation of the tensioning rail is a reversal of the removal procedure. The instructions to fit various parts and the tightening torques must be followed. Guide pins are fitted with sealing compound.

1.4.6.3. Camshafts – Removal and Installation

The following instructions will remove the camshafts with the engine fitted. Some of the operations have already been described earlier on. **As already mentioned:** Camshafts and associated parts can only be removed when the camshafts are in their basic timing position. The workshop uses a locating plate which is inserted into a groove in the camshaft, but by carefully turning the crankshaft this can be avoided. Camshafts of the L.H. and R.H. cylinder bank can be removed individually. If the engine is removed ignore the preliminary operations. Most of the operations are referred to during the removal of the cylinder head. Various illustrations must be followed to carry out the removal. We must point out that a special retainer is necessary to remove the camshafts, referred to in the text. Some mechanical knowledge is required.

- Detach the charge air distribution pipe.

- Unscrew the charge air intake pipe to cylinder head cover and press to one side (valid for both cylinder heads).
- Remove the covers for the injectors and remove the injectors (valid for both cylinder heads).
- Remove the cylinder head covers (valid for both cylinder heads) and in the case of the R.H. cylinder head remove the charge air cross pipe. Also remove the vacuum pump.
- . Set the piston of No. 1 cylinder to the top dead centre position. To make sure that the correct position is obtained refer to Fig. 1.85. The markings at the camshaft and the camshaft bearing caps must be aligned as shown. The markings can be found on the third bearing cap, counting from the side opposite to the camshaft sprockets.

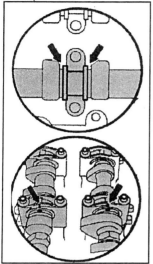

Fig. 1.85 – Camshaft and camshaft bearing cap markings must be aligned as shown to obtain the TDC position.

- Lock the inlet camshaft as described above, using the timing pins shown in Fig. 1.84.
- Remove the camshaft timing drive gear from the exhaust camshaft. Fig. 1.86 shows a front view of the drive with the location of the sprockets. Then remove the camshaft timing gear (2) in Fig. 1.86 from the exhaust camshaft. Do not rotate the engine during this operation.
- Slide the retainer (628 589 00 61 00) shown in Fig. 1.87 through the opening of the front cover onto the camshaft timing gear (2) in Fig. 1.86 in the case of the camshafts of the R.H. cylinder head. In the case of the L.H. cylinder head fit the retainer onto the head, push it onto the camshaft drive gear (2) and attach with the bolts removed from the cylinder head cover.

Fig. 1.86 – Details for the removal of the camshaft sprockets. The markings are positioned at (A).
1 Inlet camshaft sprocket
2 Camshaft drive gear
3 Exhaust camshaft sprocket

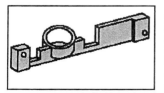

Fig. 1.87 – The special retainer required for the removal of the camshafts.

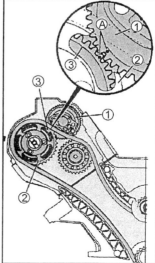

- Remove the camshaft bearing caps, each held by two bolts. Each bearing cap has a number, located at the positions shown by the arrows in Fig. 1.88. Both camshafts have the same identification. Refer to the L.H. view and remove the bearing caps marked E1, E3, E5, A1, A3 and A5 and then cap E2 and E4 at the inlet camshaft and A2 and A4 at the exhaust camshaft, shown with the arrows in the R.H. view. Note that the identification is only given for the removal and installation. The actual bearing identification is shown in Fig. 1.89. All bolts must be slackened in several stages when the bolts in the R.H. view are removed. Remove the bearing caps. The camshafts can now be removed. The camshaft timing gear remains on the retainer.

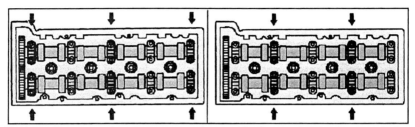

Fig. 1.88 – The arrows show the sequence of removal for the camshaft bearing caps. Both cylinder heads are identical.

Install the camshafts as follows:
- Lubricate the compensation elements and the camshaft journals with engine oil and insert the two camshafts into the bearing bores. If new camshafts are fitted make sure you fit the correct one.
- Align the camshaft sprockets of the two camshafts. Note the difference. In the case of the R.H. cylinder head the markings (A) in Fig. 1.86 must be positioned exactly opposite each other. In the case of the L.H. cylinder the markings (A) can be slightly offset. Align both camshafts at the thrust bearing as shown in Fig. 1.85.

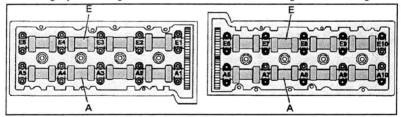

Fig. 1.89 – The identification of the camshaft bearing caps. Inlet camshafts are identified by (E), exhaust camshafts by (A). The L.H. view shows the R.H. cylinder head, the R.H. view shows the L.H. head.

- Fit the camshaft bearing caps in accordance with their numbering in Fig. 1.89. The marking on the camshaft and the marking on the bearing cap must be aligned as shown in Fig. 1.88. Tighten the bolts in several stages to 0.9 kgm (7 ft.lb.) in the order shown in Fig. 1.88.
- Lock the inlet camshaft by inserting the timing pin through the 1st camshaft bearing cap into the hole in the inlet camshaft sprocket. Then fit the camshaft timing gear (2) in Fig. 1.86 onto the camshaft. The timing gear must engage with the dowel pin. Fit the bolt and tighten it to 1.8 kgm (14 ft.lb.). Check the basic position of the camshafts before proceeding.
- The remaining operations are carried out in reverse order, depending to which extend the engine has been dismantled.

1.4.6.4. Balance Shaft

The transmission together with the torque converter must be removed to take out the balance shaft. Apart from this we consider the removal and installation of the balance shaft a very complicated operation and we do not recommend to attempt it. You may find no problems with the shaft or its drive. If so, we are sorry to refer you to your dealer.

1.5. Tightening Torque Values

The tightening torques for the various engines are given in the instructions to remove and install the various parts. We have tried to list every possible item you may have to tighten during the installation.

1.6. Lubrication System

The lubrication system is a pressure-feed system. A gear-type oil pump is driven via the crankshaft timing sprocket by means of a separate single roller chain and is kept under tension with its own chain tensioner with torsion spring.
The oil filter is fitted in vertical position on the side of the cylinder block. The filter element is held in the filter housing by means of a screw cap, fitted to the top of the filter housing. The workshop uses a special wrench to undo this cap. The filter consist of the lower part and a throw-away oil filter. An oil pressure switch is fitted to the side of the filter lower housing.
The engine is fitted with a light-metal oil sump, containing an oil level sensor. The oil sump can be removed with the engine fitted to the vehicle. Note that the oil sump can consist of one parts or two parts, depending on the engine.

1.6.0. TECHNICAL DATA

Oil Capacities:... See Page 8
Oil pressure at idle speed: .... Workshop operation
Oil pressure at 3000 rpm:... Workshop operation

1.6.1. OIL SUMP – REMOVAL AND INSTALLATION

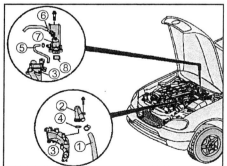

Fig. 1.90 – Details for the removal of the oil sump, showing parts to be disconnected or removed (see text).

612 Engine (ML 270 CDI - 163)

The oil sump can be removed with the engine fitted. A one-piece sump is fitted. Various parts must be disconnected and can be found at the positions shown with the numbers in Fig. 1.90. The instructions will refer to the individual items. With the battery disconnected, proceed as follows:

- Remove the bottom section of the sound-proofing panel. Three panels must be removed. Drain the engine oil and the coolant.
- Remove the trim panels for the cylinder head (see removal of cylinder head) and then refer to Fig. 1.90.

- Disconnect the coolant hose (1) from the coolant connecting pipe (2) and then remove the pipe from the exhaust gas re-circulation part (3). The seal (4) must be replaced.
- Use a suitable hose clamp and pinch off the fuel hose (5) as close as possible to the pre-heater for fuel system (7) and disconnect the pipe. Some fuel may run out. Then disconnect the fuel outlet line (6) from the pre-heater on the exhaust gas re-circulation unit (3). Replace the gasket (8).
- The next operations are more complicated as you have to locate the various items. First remove the coolant expansion tank, followed by the intake air scoop, the charge air pipe and the charge air hose. Some items are covered during the removal of the cylinder head.
- Remove the electric fan and remove a coolant hose from the radiator.

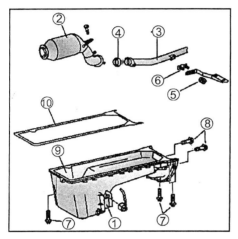

Fig. 1.91 – Final removal of the oil sump. The numbers are referred to in the instructions.

- The next operations are carried out with the help of Fig. 1.91. At the side of the oil sump disconnect the connector plug from the oil level sensor (1). Slacken the mounting clamp securing the pre-catalytic converter (2) and the catalytic converter (3). A new sealing insert (4) must be used.
- Unscrew the self-locking nuts (5) on the threaded plate (6) of the converter (2). The nuts must be replaced (2.0 kgm/14.5 ft.lb.).
- Detach the stabiliser bar as described in the section in question.
- Unscrew the nuts securing the front engine mountings and lift the engine in suitable manner (hand crane or lifting tackle) out of the mountings to create space for the removal of the oil sump. Take care not to damage any parts when the engine is lifted.

Fig. 1.92 – Location of the various oil sump bolts.
1 Bolt, M6 x 30
2 Bolt, M6 x 35
3 Bolt, M6 x 85
4 Bolt, M8 x 40

- Remove the bolts (7) and (8) securing the oil sump (9) and lower the oil sump. Take off the oil sump gasket (10). Note the different bolt length, shown in Fig. 1.92.

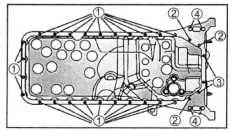

The installation of the oil sump is a reversal of the removal procedure. Refer to Fig. 1.92 to insert and tighten the bolts. All M6 bolts are tightened to 0.9 kgm (7 ft.lb.), M8 bolts to 2.0 kgm (14.5 ft.lb.), transmission to oil sump bolt to 4.0 kgm (29 ft.lb.). Tighten the oil drain plug to 3.0 kgm (22 ft.lb.). If the oil pump has been removed tighten the bolt to 1.8 kgm (13 ft.lb.). After installation fill the engine with 7.5 litres of oil, suitable for diesel engines.

628 Engine (ML 400 CDI - 163)
The oil sump of this engine consists of an upper and lower section. The removal of the lower oil sump section is fairly easy.
- Detach the intake air distribution pipe (page 39). From underneath the vehicle remove the noise encapsulation panels, unscrew the engine drain plug and drain the engine oil. Remember 10 litres must be collected. Refit the drain plug and tighten to 3.2 kgm (23 ft.lb.).
- Attach a handcrane or suitable lifting device to the engine hangers and lift the engine is far as possible, taking care not to damage any parts of the engine as the engine is lifted. The engine mountings must be unscrewed (5.3 kgm).
- On the front axle carrier locate two hydraulic lines and remove the line retainers.
- On the R.H. side of the oil sump bottom section unscrew the bracket securing the lower charge air pipe. The lower part of the oil sump can now be removed. All bolts are M6 bolts (20 mm long) and are tightened to 0.9 kgm. If necessary use a plastic/rubber mallet to free the sump part. No gasket is used.
- If necessary unscrew the upper sump section. Again all bolts are M6 bolts and have the same length (40 mm) and are tightened to the torque given above. Note that sleeves are fitted to some bolt. The oil sump parts is removed towards the front, direction of travel.

The installation is a reversal of the removal procedure. Tighten all bolts evenly around the sump faces. Coat all sealing faces with "Loctite 5970" sealing compound. Fit the oil sump part(s) within 10 minutes of applying the sealant. Fill the engine with 10 litres of oil suitable for diesel engines.

642 Engine (ML 280/320 CDI - 164)
The oil sump of this engine consists of an upper and lower section. We do not recommend the removal of the upper section. The lower parts can be removed as follows:
- Remove the oil dipstick guide tube and place the front end of the vehicle on chassis stands.
- From underneath the vehicle remove the noise encapsulation panels, unscrew the engine drain plug and drain the engine oil. Remember 8.5 litres must be collected. Refit the drain plug and tighten to 3.0 kgm (22 ft.lb.).
- Attach a handcrane or suitable lifting device to the engine hangers and lift the engine is far as possible, taking care not to damage any parts of the engine as the engine is lifted. The engine mounting bolts must be removed (5.3 kgm).
- Locate the oil temperature sensor on the oil sump and disconnect the cable plug.
- Remove the M6 bolts around the outside of the oil sump section and remove the sump. We would like to add that the workshop uses a hot air gun to facilitate the detachment of the sealing compound. You may be able to use a hair dryer (ask your for permission first) to heat up the sealant.

The installation is a reversal of the removal procedure. All bolts are tightened to 1.4 kgm (10 ft.lb.). Coat all sealing faces with "Loctite 5970" sealing compound. Fit the sump parts within 10 minutes of applying the sealant. Fill the engine with 8.5 litres of oil suitable for diesel engines.

1.6.2.   OIL PUMP - REMOVAL AND INSTALLATION
612 Engine (ML 270 CDI) and 628 Engine (ML 400 CDI) – 163)
As already described above the oil pump of the 612 engine or 628 is removed after removal of the oil sump. Removal and installation are similar. Remove the bolts and withdraw the pump towards the bottom. The chain tensioner must be pushed away

from the chain and the chain detached. A sealing ring is fitted to the inside of the pump (replace).
The installation is a reversal of the removal procedure, noting the following points:
- Clean the oil strainer before installation. Fill the oil pump with oil to assure initial lubrication.
- Refit the pump to the cylinder block and insert and tighten the bolts to 1.8 kgm (14 ft.lb.) – **612 engine** or 0.8 kgm (6 ft.lb.) – **628 engine.**
- Refit the oil sump as described for the 612 or 628 engine and fill the engine with oil. Start the engine and check all sealing faces for oil leaks.

642 Engine (ML 280/320 CDI) - 164
As the complete oil sump must be removed to gain access to the attachment of the oil pump and section 1.6.1 does not describe the removal of the upper section of the sump you will have to have the work carried out at a dealer when the engine is fitted. If the engine is removed it will be obvious which parts/items must be removed to reach the pump.

1.6.3. OIL PUMP - REPAIRS

Oil pumps should not be dismantled and/or repaired. If a new pump is fitted check the drive chain and the chain sprocket to prevent fitting a new pump together with new drive components.

1.6.4. OIL LEVEL SENDER UNIT – REMOVAL AND INSTALLATION

The oil level sender unit in the side of the oil sump can be replaced with the engine fitted. After draining the engine oil withdraw the cable connector plug from the sender unit (switch) and remove the two screws. Remove the oil seal below the sender unit (always replace).
Install in reverse order. Tighten the screws to 1.2 kgm (9 ft.lb.). Finally fill the engine with oil.

1.6.5. OIL PRESSURE SWITCH – REMOVAL AND INSTALLATION

The switch is located at the front end of the engine, L.H. side above one of the belt pulleys. The switch can be removed after withdrawing the cable connector. The switch is tightened to 2.0 kgm (14 ft.lb.).

1.6.6. OIL FILTER – REMOVAL AND INSTALLATION

The filter element is removed with a special filter wrench. The workshop uses a special tool, shown in Fig. 1.93, which is placed over the screw cap at the top of the filter and engages with the ribs.

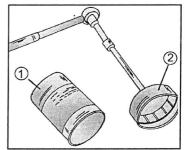

Fig. 1.93 – The screw cap on top of the oil filter (1) is removed with the special tool (2) as shown. Alternatively follow the description below.

A suitable socket, extension and ratchet complete the arrangement. Some engines have an oil cooler fitted, which reduced the oil temperature by about 15° C.
Fig. 1.94 shows where the oil filter is located. The following text describes the removal and installation of the filter and is valid for both

engine types. We would like to point out that a special filter wrench is used in the workshop. The hexagon fitted to the top of the oil filter cover on earlier and similar engines has now been removed. If you intend to carry out regular servicing of your vehicle we recommend to obtain such a filter wrench, available under Parts No. 103 589 02 09 00. Otherwise it may be possible to use a large pair of pliers or grips, but remember that access is limited. Remove the filter as follows:

Fig. 1.94 – Fitted oil filter (all engines).
1 Filter screw cap, 2.5 kgm
2 Filter insert (element)
3 Sealing ring

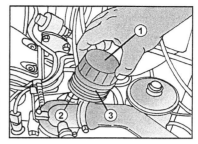

- In the case of a 642 engine (V6) remove the engine trim panel and the engine cover. In the case of other engines remove any parts obstructing the filter.
- Disconnect the battery. If the engine oil is to be changed (in most cases) remove the sound-proof panel underneath the engine.
- On all models use a filter chain wrench and unscrew the screw cap (1) in Fig. 1.93 (unless you have the special tool 103 589 02 09 00). Fully unscrew the screw cap and remove it. The filter element (2) will be attached to the cap (catch dripping oil) and can be carefully knocked off with a small drift, applied to the centre rod. Take off the sealing ring (3).
- Thoroughly clean the inside of the filter housing with a clean rag.
- Check the oil level in the engine and correct if only the oil filter element has been replaced. Otherwise fill the engine with the correct amount of oil.
- Start the engine and allow it to run for a while. Then switch off and check the filter surrounding for oil leaks.
- Fit the new filter element (2) to the screw cap, replace the sealing ring (3) and fit the cap to the filter housing. Tighten the cap to 2.5 kgm (18 ft.lb.). You will have to estimate the torque without the filter wrench.

1.6.7. ENGINE OIL COOLER

The oil cooler, also referred to as oil-water heat exchanger is difficult to see when the engine is installed, as it is located near the oil filter. The oil cooler is attached to the rear of the timing cover. Removal and installation is carried out by referring to Fig. 1.95, shown for the 612 engine in model ML 270 CDI.

Fig. 1.95 – Component parts of the removed oil cooler.
1 Oil cooler
2 Hose clamp
3 Coolant hose
4 Bolt, 2.5 kgm
5 Gasket

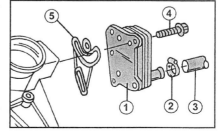

612 Engine (ML 270 CDI) – 163 model
This engine is fitted with a fuel cooler which must be removed during the removal of the engine oil cooler.

- Remove the trim panels of the cylinder head cover (see removal of cylinder head).
- Remove the bottom section of the sound-proofing capsule.

83

- Remove the oil filter screw cap from the top of the filter as described above. This will allow oil inside the filter housing to drain into the oil sump.
- Drain the cooling system as described later on.
- Remove the fuel filter as already described.
- The next step is the removal of the fuel cooler. Fig. 1.96 shows where the cooler (5) can be found. Disconnect the fuel hose (1). Protect the open hose end from entry of foreign matter. Do the same with the fuel outlet hose (2). Clamp off the coolant return flow hose (4) to the thermostat housing and disconnect the coolant feed hose (3) from the cooler. Remove the bolts (7) and lift the cooler upwards.

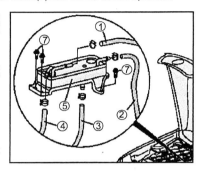

Fig. 1.96 – Details for the removal of the fuel cooler (612 engine). The numbers are referred to in the text.

- Remove the fuel distributor rail.
- Remove the charge air distribution pipe above the exhaust pipe (removal of cylinder head, page 27).
- Remove the coolant hose (3) in Fig. 1.95 after slackening the hose clamp (2) from the oil cooler (1).
- If an automatic transmission is fitted you will have to disconnect the disconnect the oil lines at the same side as the coolant hose.

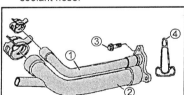

Fig. 1.97 – Removal of the coolant and vent line during the removal of the oil cooler (628 engine). The numbers are referred to in the text.

- Remove the bolts (4) from the timing case cover and withdraw the oil cooler (1). Remove the gasket (5) below it.

The installation is a reversal of the removal procedure. The gasket (5) must always be replaced. Tighten the bolts (4) to 1.5 kgm (11 ft.lb.). Finally check and correct the oil level.

628 Engine (ML 400 CDI) – 163 model

The engine oil cooler is attached to the oil filter housing in the case of this engine. Remove as follows:

- Pull the engine cover upwards and remove it from the engine.
- Remove the oil filter screw cap as described during the removal of the oil filter and take out the filter insert (element). This will allow oil inside the filter housing to drain into the oil sump. Tighten the cap to 2.5 kgm (18 ft.lb.) during installation.
- Jack up the front end of the vehicle and remove the L.H. wheel. Then remove the wing liner inside the L.H. wheel arch and the bottom section of the sound-proofing capsule.
- Drain the coolant.
- The coolant pipe (1) and the vent pipe (3) in Fig. 1.97 must now be removed from the oil filter housing. Remove the bolts at the flange. The gasket (4) must be replaced. Tighten the bolts to 1.1 kgm (8 ft.lb.).
- Unscrew the oil cooler from the oil filter housing. Remove the gasket.

The installation is a reversal of the removal procedure. The gaskets must be replaced, the oil cooler bolts are tightened to 1.5 kgm (11 ft.lb.). Finally check and correct the oil level.

642 Engine (ML 280/320 CDI) - 164
The oil cooler is located in the centre, at the bottom of the "V", to the cylinder block. The cooler can be removed after removal of the engine trim panel and the charge air distribution pipe. The cooling system must be drained. Unscrew the bolts and lift off the cooler. Two small gaskets seal off the cooler. Always replace them. The bolts are tightened to 1.2 kgm (9 ft.lb.) during installation.

1.6.8. ENGINE OIL CHANGE

The engine oil should be changed in accordance with the recommendations of the manufacturer. Remember that there are a few litres of engine oil to handle and the necessary container to catch the oil must be large enough to receive the oil. Dispose of the old oil in accordance with the local laws. You may be able to bring it to a petrol station. **Never discharge the engine oil into a drain.** Drain the oil as follows, when the engine is fairly warm:

- Jack up the front end of the vehicle and place the container underneath the oil sump. Unscrew the oil drain plug (ring spanner or socket). Take care, as the oil will "shoot" out immediately. Remove the oil filler cap to speed-up the draining.
- Check the plug sealing ring and replace if necessary. Clean the plug and fit and tighten to 3.0 kgm (22 ft.lb.) or in the case of the 628 engine to 3.2 kgm (23 ft.lb.).
- Fill the engine with the necessary amount of oil. Make sure that the oil is suitable for diesel engines.
- Refit the oil filler cap and drive the vehicle until the engine operating temperature is reached. Jack up the vehicle once more and check the drain plug area for oil leaks.

1.6.9. ENGINE OIL PRESSURE

The oil pressure can only be checked with an oil pressure gauge, which is fitted with a suitable adapter in place of the oil pressure switch. We recommend to leave the oil pressure check to a workshop. Low oil pressure can also be caused through a low oil level in the sump.

1.7. Cooling System

The cooling system operates with an expansion tank, at the R.H. side of the engine compartment. A coolant level indicator is fitted into the expansion tank. If the level drops below the "Min" mark for any reason, the switch contacts will close and light up a warning light in the instrument panel. A check of the coolant level is therefore redundant.

The water pump is fitted to the front at the bottom of the cylinder block, is sealed off by means of an "O" sealing ring and secured by means of four bolts. The pump cannot be repaired. The thermostat is mentioned later on.

1.7.0. TECHNICAL DATA

Type: .... Water pump-assisted thermo-siphon system with
impeller-type water pump

Filling Capacity:
- 612 engine: .... 8.5 litres

- 628 engine: .... 11.0 litres
- 642 engine: .... 10.0 litres
Anti-freeze amount: .... See Section 1.7.1.0

1.7.1 COOLANT - DRAINING AND REFILLING

Although there are differences within the model/engine range the following applies in general to all vehicles. We must, however, point out that models with 642 engine (280 and 320 CDI) are filled with the anti-freeze by means of a special vacuum-operated system filler in the workshop.

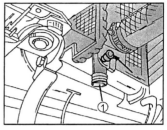

Fig. 1.98 – The arrow shows the small connection where the hose can be connected before the drain plug (1) is opened.

- If the engine is hot open the expansion tank cap to the first notch and allow the pressure to escape. The coolant must have a temperature of less than 90° C. but we recommend to wait until the temperature has dropped to 50° C. In all cases use a thick rag to cover the expansion tank cap to protect your hand.
- Remove the noise dampening panel from underneath the vehicle.
- Unscrew the coolant drain plug at the bottom of the radiator. You can push a hose over the nipple (1) in Fig. 1.98 (shown in general) and guide the hose into a container to drain and collect the coolant. If the anti-freeze solution is in good condition, your can re-use it. Poke a piece of wire into the bore of the drain hole to dislodge sludge, if the coolant flow is restricted.

To ensure that the cooling system is filled without air lock, proceed as follows when filling in the coolant. Refer to Section 1.7.1.0 for the correct anti-freeze amount to be added. Anti-freeze marketed by Mercedes-Benz should be used, as this has been specially developed for the engine.

- Set both heater switches to the max. heating capacity, by moving the controls. If an automatic climate control system is fitted, press the "DEF" button.
- Fill the pre-mixed anti-freeze solution into the expansion tank filler neck until it reaches the "Cold" mark. Do not fit the expansion tank cap at this stage.
- Start the engine and run it until the operating temperature has been reached, i.e. the thermostat must have opened. Fit the cap when the coolant has a temperature between 60 to 70° C. A thermometer can be inserted into the radiator filler neck to check the temperature.
- Check the coolant level after the engine has cooled down and correct if necessary.
- Refit the noise dampening panel underneath the vehicle.

1.7.1.0. Anti-freeze Solution

The cooling system is filled with anti-freeze when the vehicle leaves the factory and the solution should be left in the system throughout the year. When preparing the anti-freeze mixture, note the following ratio between water and anti-freeze solution. We recommend to use the anti-freeze supplied by Mercedes-Benz. It may cost you a little more, but your engine will thank you for it. The following ratios should be observed:
To –37° C:
– 612 engine – 4.5 litres of anti-freeze
– 628 engine – 5.0 litres of anti-freeze

- 642 engine – 5.0 litres of anti-freeze
To –45° C:
- 612 engine – 5.0 litres of anti-freeze
- 628 engine – 6.25 litres of anti-freeze
- 642 engine – 5.5 litres of anti-freeze

1.7.2. RADIATOR AND COOLING FAN
1.7.2.0. Checking Radiator Cap and Radiator

The cooling system operates under pressure. The expansion tank cap is fitted with a spring, which is selected to open the cap gasket when the pressure has risen to value engraved in the cap. If the cap is replaced, always fit one with the same marking, suitable for the models covered.

To check the radiator cap for correct opening, a radiator test pump is required. Fit the pump to the cap and operate the pump until the valve opens, which should take place near the given pressure (1.4 kg/sq.cm). If this is not the case, replace the cap. Fig. 1.99 shows the working principle of such a test pump.

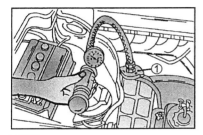

Fig. 1.99 – A radiator test pump (1) is used to check the cooling system for leaks and the expansion tank cap for correct opening. The pump is connected to the expansion tank.

The same pump can also be used to check the cooling system for leaks. Fit the pump to the expansion tank filler neck and operate the plunger until a pressure of 1.0 kg/sq.cm. is indicated. Allow the pressure in the system for at least 5 minutes. If the pressure drops, there is a leak in the system.

1.7.2.1. Radiator – Removal and Installation

Different radiators are fitted depending on the model. When the radiator is replaced make sure you obtain the correct one. Note the differences of the different engines, given below, depending if the model in question belongs to the 163 or 164 range of models.

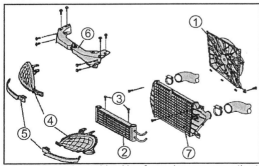

Fig. 1.100 – Removal of the radiator (612 engine). The numbers are referred to in the text.

612 Engine (270 CDI) – 163 model

The parts shown in Fig. 1.100 must be initially removed before access is possible to the radiator. The remaining parts are shown in Fig. 1.101.

- Disconnect the battery negative cable. Also from above remove the trim panel of the cylinder head cover (1.0 kgm/7.2 ft.lb.).

87

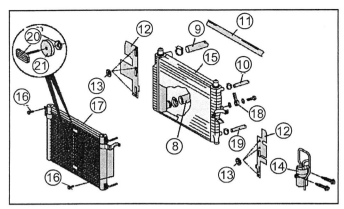

Fig. 1.101 – Removal of the radiator (612 engine). The numbers are referred to in the text.

- Remove the bottom part of the noise encapsulation at the front.
- Drain the cooling system as described in Section 1.7.1. On a model with automatic transmission, use clamps and clamp off the two hoses for the oil cooler. Disconnect the hoses from the R.H. side of the radiator. Some fluid will drip out. Immediately plug the hose ends and connections in suitable manner.
- Remove the electric fan (1) in Fig. 1.100 and the charge air cooler (7). The low temperature cooler (2) must be removed (unscrew bolts 3), the headlamp units (4) and the cover strips (5) must be removed before the radator crossmember at the upper end is unbolted.
- Remove the sealing strip (11) in Fig. 1.101.
- Empty the steering fluid reservoir, if possible with a hand pump, and disconnect the connection (18) in Fig. 1.101 (remove banjo bolt). New seals must be used during installation. Tighten the banjo bolt to 3.0 kgm (22 ft.lb.). Also disconnect the steering gear feed hose (19). This time remove the hose clamp.
- Disconnect all coolant hoses from the radiator (top and bottom), from the water pump and the coolant expansion tank.
- Detach the air guides (12), secured by mounting clips. The clips (13) should be replaced.
- Remove the bolts (16) securing the condenser (17) to the radiator. Do not disconnect the condenser lines and do not damage them when the condenser is taken out.
- Remove the attachment parts (20) and the rubber damper. During installation it is possible that the rubber damper drops down. Take care.
- Take off the fluid reservoir (14) for the A/C system at the radiator and place it to one side with the lines connected.
- The radiator can now be removed. Take care not to damage the radiator core. The workshop inserts a metal plate in front of the radiator to protect it.

The installation is a reversal of the removal procedure. After installation of the radiator check that the gap between the fan blades and the radiator air baffle is the same on all sides. If necessary remove the securing clips and centre the baffle.

Finally refill the cooling system as described in Section 1.7.1. Start the engine and check all cooling hose and drain points for leaks. The headlamp setting must be checked (workshop recommended).

628 Engine (400 CDI) – 163 model and 642 Engine – ML 280/320 CDI – 164 models
Apart from slight differences the specified models can be summarised. The operations can be carried out by referring to Fig. 1.5. Preliminary operations necessary are the draining of the steering fluid reservoir (hand pump), the removal of the two headlamp units and the removal of the front end crossmember, i.e. the upper radiator crossmember. The operations are described on page 29 (see also Fig. 1.4). Also remove the electric fan as described later on.

- Remove the bottom section of the sound-proofing capsule.
- Drain the cooling system as described later on – engine cold.
- For the next operations you can refer to Fig. 1.5. Disconnect the charge air hose (12) of the R.H. charge air cooler (11) and remove the charge air cooler.
- Disconnect the coolant vent hose (5) and the coolant feed hose (6) from the radiator. Also in Fig. 1.5 disconnect the oil cooling hoses for the transmission oil (2) and (3) from the radiator. Escaping oil must be collected. Use new sealing rings during installation. Tighten the union nut to 1.8 kgm (13 ft.lb.).
- Disconnect the fluid line for the steering oil cooling (7) and (8) in Fig. 1.5 at the radiator. Tighten the banjo bolt to 3.0 kgm (22 ft.lb.).
- Disconnect the coolant return hose (4), the coolant feed hose (6) and the coolant bleed hose (5) from the radiator (1).
- Similar as shown in Fig. 1.101 remove the attachment parts (20) and the rubber (21) damper. New clips (20) are required. During installation it is possible that the rubber damper drops down. Take care.
- Remove the bolts (16) securing the condenser (17) to the radiator (in Fig. 1.101). Do not disconnect the condenser lines and do not damage them when the condenser is taken out. The capacitor must be lifted and attached with wire slings.
- Pull the radiator (1) out of the rubber mounts (21) in Fig. 1.101. During installation make sure that the rubber mounts are correctly fitted.

The installation is a reversal of the removal procedure. Finally refill the cooling system as described in Section 1.7.1. Start the engine and check all cooling hose and drain points for leaks. The headlamp setting must be checked (workshop recommended).

1.7.3. WATER (COOLANT) PUMP

612 Engine (270 CDI) – 163 model
The water pump is fastened to a light-alloy housing which is bolted to the lower front of the crankcase. The removal and installation can be carried out by referring to Fig. 1.103.

Fig. 1.103 – Parts to be removed during the removal of the water pump. The numbers are referred to in the text.

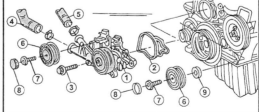

To remove the water pump proceed as follows:

- The front of the engine must be exposed to remove the pump. This means you will have to remove cylinder head cover panel and the charge air distribution pipe panel (described during the removal of the cylinder head), the electric fan (see below) and the poly V-belt
- Drain the cooling system. It is enough to open the drain tap in the radiator. Never open the expansion tank if the coolant temperature exceeds 90° C.

89

- Remove the two fuel lines (2) and (3) in Fig. 1.104 from the brackets (1) above the coolant pump.

Fig. 1.104 – Attachment of the fuel lines (2) and (3). These are attached to the brackets (1) at the top of the water pump.

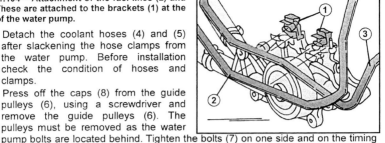

- Detach the coolant hoses (4) and (5) after slackening the hose clamps from the water pump. Before installation check the condition of hoses and clamps.
- Press off the caps (8) from the guide pulleys (6), using a screwdriver and remove the guide pulleys (6). The pulleys must be removed as the water pump bolts are located behind. Tighten the bolts (7) on one side and on the timing cover on the other side to 3.5 kgm (25 ft.lb.).
- Remove the M6 and M8 bolts securing the water pump and remove the pump (1). The gasket (2) must be removed during installation.
- If a new pump is to be fitted remove the drive pulley from the old pump and fit it to the new pump. Tighten the bolt to 0.8 kgm (6.5 ft.lb.).

The installation of the water pump is a reversal of the removal procedure. Tighten the M6 bolts to 1.4 kgm (10 ft.lb.) and M8 bolts to 2.0 kgm (14.5 ft.lb.). Finally refit all removed parts and fill the cooling system.
Start the engine and check all connections of the cooling system for leaks.

628 Engine (400 CDI) – 163 model

Details of the removal are shown in Fig. 1.105. The electric fan, the charge air cross pipe (see section "Diesel Engines) and the Poly V-belt must be removed. Remove the cover (1) in front of the guide pulley (4) with a screwdriver and remove the bolt (2) securing the pulley. Take off the washer (3). The bolt is tightened to 2.5 kgm (18 ft.lb.).

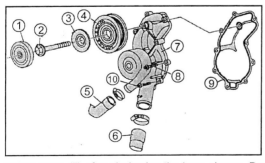

Fig. 1.105 – Details for the removal of the water pump (628 engine).
1   Cover
2   Securing bolt, 2.5 kgm
3   Washer
4   Guide pulley
5   Coolant hose
6   Coolant hose
7   Water pump
8   Pump securing bolt
9   Water pump gasket
10 Pump securing bolt

Disconnect the coolant hoses (5) and (6) from the coolant pump (7) after slackening the hose clamps. Replace clamps/hoses of not in good condition. The coolant pump can now be removed after unscrewing bolts (8) and (10). Note the different length of the bolts (25 or 45 mm). Make a note where they are fitted. The crankshaft must be rotated until all bolts can be reached. Take off the gasket (9). Must be replaced.

The installation is a reversal of the removal procedure. All bolts are tightened to 0.9 kgm (7 ft.lb.) – except the one securing the tensioning pulley bolt at the upper end.

642 Engine – ML 280/320 CDI – 164 models

Removal and installation is similar as described above. The engine trim panel and the mixing chamber must be removed in addition to the Poly V-belt. The pump is fitted with a sealing ring which must be replaced. All 5 bolts have the same length and are tightened to 0.9 kgm (7 ft.lb.). Clean the sealing faces of pump and engine front before installation.

1.7.4. DRIVE BELTS AND DRIVE BELT TENSION

A single drive belt, also known as poly V-belt, is fitted to the front of the engine, but the layout of the belt is not the same on all engines and depends on a fitted of an air conditioning system or a vehicle without A/C system. If a compressor is fitted it will also be driven by the same belt. The same belt drive system is, however, fitted to all engines and is held in its correct tension by means of an automatic tensioning device.
Different is also the length of the belt in the case of engines without A/C system or in the case of a fitted A/C system. If a new belt is fitted make sure your obtain the correct one.
The removal of the belt requires a drift or pin of 4 mm diameter or a 4 mm drill, the use of which is described in the following instructions. After the front of the engine has laid bare of all obstructing parts remove the belt as follows. Fig. 1.106 shows details for the removal and installation in the case of a **engine type 612 (270 CDI)**.

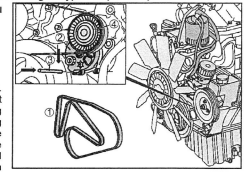

Fig. 1.106 – Details for the removal and installation of the poly V-belt.
1 Poly V-belt
2 Tensioning device
3 4 mm pin
4 Tensioning pulley

- Disconnect the battery.
- Refer to the L.H. view of Fig. 1.107 and turn the front part (1) of the pulley tensioning device against the spring force, i.e. turn it in the direction of the arrow. The refer to the R.H. view and insert the pin (2) of 4 mm diameter (or drift, or drill shank) into the holes, positioned in line in the front part and in the housing (3) in order to lock the tensioning pulley (4) in this position. The V-belt can now be removed from the various pulleys.

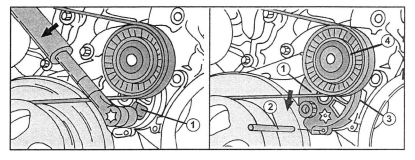

Fig. 1.107 – Removal of the poly V-belt. The numbers are referred to on the text.

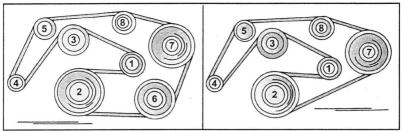

Fig. 1.108 – The poly V-belt is fitted over the various pulleys as shown. On the L.H. side for vehicles with A/C system, on the R.H. side for vehicles without one. Legend next page.
1 Tensioning pulley
2 Crankshaft pulley
3 Water pump pulley
4 Generator pulley
5 Belt guide roller
6 Compressor pulley (A/C)
7 Steering pump pulley
8 Belt guide roller

Check the removed V-belt for damage and traces of wear before installation. Replace the belt if necessary, fitting the correct belt.

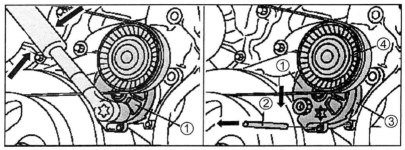

Fig. 1.109 – Details for the installation of the poly V-belt. The numbers refer to the description below.

The installation is carried out as follows:
- Fit the V-belt over the various pulleys, in all cases first over the tensioning pulley (4) in Fig. 1.106. Then depending on the version fit it over the remaining pulleys shown in Fig. 1.108. Make sure the belt engages with the grooves in the pulleys.
- Refer to Fig. 1.109 and turn the front part (1) of the tensioning device sufficiently against the force of the spring (direction of the arrow, R.H. view) until it is possible to withdraw the inserted pin (2) or drift/drill bit, depending what has been used out of the holes in the front part (1) and the housing (3) of the tensioning device (3).
- Pull out the pin (2).
- Slowly turn the front part (1) of the tensioning device in the L.H. view in the direction of the arrow until the V-belt is automatically tensioned by the force of the spring. The belt is now tensioned and no further operations are necessary. Rotate the crankshaft a few times before and re-check the belt drive before the removed parts are refitted.

628 Engine (400 CDI) – 163 model

Fig. 1.110 shows how the belt is fitted over the pulleys. The removal and installation requires that the vehicle is placed on chassis stands, as bottom section of the sound-proofing panel and the charge air hose from the lower charge air pipe must be removed to gain access. To remove the belt, turn the tensioning device above one of the pulley in a clockwise direction and lift off the belt (socket and extension required). The installation is a reversal of the removal procedure. Place the belt over the pulleys as shown in Fig. 1.110.

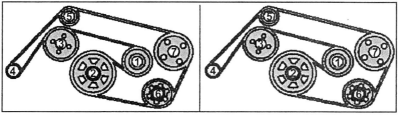

Fig. 1.110 – The layout of the drive belt of a V8 engine (model series 163). On the left for vehicles without A/C system, on the right with A/C system (valid for this model). Note that two guide pulleys are fitted to models without A/C.

On the left::
1 Tensioning roller
2 Crankshaft pulley
3 Water pump pulley
4 Alternator pulley
5 Guide pulley
6 Guide pulley
7 Power steering pump pulley

On the right:
1 Tensioning roller
2 Crankshaft pulley
3 Water pump pulley
4 Alternator pulley
5 Guide pulley
6 A/C compressor pulley
7 Power steering pump pulley

642 Engine – ML 280/320 CDI – 164 models

The removal is fairly straight-forward. Pull out the front engine cover upwards and out of the mountings. Study the layout of the pulleys. Seen from the front you will see two larger pulleys. The bottom one belongs to the A/C compressor, the one immediately above to the power steering pump. Fig. 1.111 shows a view of the pulleys. The smaller pulley in the centre is the tensioning pulley (2). This pulley must be rotated in an anti-clockwise direction by applying a socket to the hexagon located under the pulley. Remove the Poly V-belt as soon as it is slack, but remember the routing.

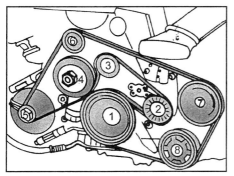

Fig. 1.111 – The layout of the drive belt of a 642 engine.
1 Crankshaft pulley
2 Tensioning pulley
3 Guide pulley
4 Water pump pulley
5 Alternator pulley
6 Guide pulley
7 Steering pump pulley
8 Compressor pulley (A/C)

The tensioning device must now be locked. To do this, apply a socket to the hexagon and turn it anti-clockwise until a drift can be inserted into the visible bore to keep the tensioning device in position.

The installation is a reversal of the removal procedure. The bolt securing the tensioning device is tightened to 3.5 kgm (25 ft.lb.).

1.7.5. THERMOSTAT

The thermostat of all engines is fitted into a cover, where the large cooling hose is connected, as can be seen in Fig. 1.112 in the case of the 612 engine (270 CD) and Fig. 1.113 for the 628 engine (400 CDI). It should be noted that the thermostat cannot be removed from its cover, i.e. a new thermostat means that a complete cover must be fitted. The removal is carried out as follows:

Fig. 1.112 – Thermostat removal – 612 engine. Refer to text.

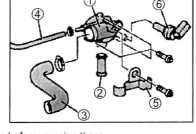

612 Engine (270 CDI) – 163 model

Refer to Fig. 1.112 where necessary. The cooling system must be drained.

- Remove the trim panels for the cylinder head cover as described during the removal of the cylinder head.
- Disconnect the connector plug from the coolant temperature sensor (6).
- Disconnect the coolant hose (3) and the vent/bleed hose (4) from the thermostat housing (1). Check the hoses and clamps before re-using them.
- Remove the thermostat housing (1) after unscrewing the securing bolts. The bolts are tightened to 0.9 kgm (7 ft.lb.).

Fig. 1.113 – Thermostat removal – 628 engine. Refer to text.

The installation is a reversal of the removal procedure. The gasket must be replaced. Ensure the correct installation of the connection fitting (2) to avoid overflow of coolant. Fill the cooling system, start the engine and check for coolant leaks.

628 Engine (400 CDI) – 163 model and 642 Engine (280/320 CDI) – 164 model

The operations are similar. Refer to Fig. 1.113 where necessary. The cooling system must be drained.

- Remove the charge air cross pipe (see removal of cylinder head).
- Disconnect the coolant hose (3) from the thermostat housing (2). Check the hose and clamps (4) before re-using them. **In the case of the 642 engine** the leak oil line must be removed from a bracket on the thermostat housing.
- Remove the thermostat housing together with the thermostat. The "O" sealing ring (1) must be replaced. The housing bolts are tightened to 0.9 kgm (7 ft.lb.).

The installation is a reversal of the removal procedure. The thermostat cannot be repaired and must be replaced as specified above.

1.7.6. ELECTRIC FAN – REMOVAL AND INSTALLATION

ML 270 CDI – 163 Models

The battery must be disconnected. The front end of the vehicle must be placed on chassis stands. Remove to Fig. 1.114 to remove the fan:

- At the upper end of the electric fan assembly (4) locate the connector at the control unit and disconnect the electrical cable (located top left, when looking at the fan assembly). Unclip the wiring harness from the bracket.
- Remove the front part of the noise encapsulation.

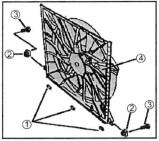

Fig. 1.114 – Removal of electric fan (612 engine, ML 270 CDI). See text.

• Detach the clamps/clips (1) from the bottom of the electric fan, remove the bolts (3) and take off the captive nuts (2).

• Unhinge the electric fan together with the integrated control unit at the upper end of the radiator and take it out towards the bottom.

Installation is a reversal of the removal procedure.

ML 400 CDI – 163 Models

The battery must be disconnected. The front end of the vehicle must be placed on chassis stands. Remove to Fig. 1.115 to remove the fan:

Fig. 1.115 – Removal of electric fan (628 engine, ML 400 CDI). See text.

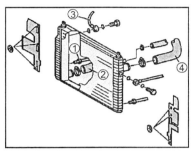

• Remove the front part of the noise encapsulation and drain the coolant. We suggest to disconnect the bottom coolant hose (2). Collect the anti-freeze.
• Disconnect the bottom oil pipe (1) for the oil cooling of the transmission. Some fluid will run out – collect it. Use new sealing rings during installation.
• Detach the clamps at the lower end of the fan assembly.
• Unscrew the bolts securing the electric fan with the integrated control unit (in the centre) at the bottom left and right.
• At the upper end of the electric fan assembly locate the connector at the control unit and disconnect the electrical cable (located top left, when looking at the fan assembly). Unclip the wiring harness from the bracket.
• Disconnect the upper coolant hose (4) and the upper oil pipe (3) from the radiator. Some fluid will run out – collect it. Use new sealing rings where necessary.
• Remove the electric fan together with the integrated control unit at the upper end of the radiator and take it out towards the top.

Installation is a reversal of the removal procedure.

ML 280/320 CDI – 164 Models

The operations are more complicated. The battery must be disconnected, the R.H. intake air duct must be removed.

• Unclip a coolant pipe at the fan shroud of the electric fan, locate and disconnect a connector plug at the fan shroud of the electric fan.
• Looking at the fan, on the R.H. side lift out the transmission oil line from the oil line mounts at the radiator and turn it towards the outside.
• Locate the securing screws, remove them and lift out the electric fan from the mountings together with the fan shroud towards the top.

Installation is carried out in reverse order.

1.8. Diesel Fuel Injection System
1.8.0. INTRODUCTION

Absolute cleanliness is essential during any repairs or work on the diesel fuel injection system, irrespective of the nature of the work in question. Thoroughly clean union nuts before unscrewing any of the injection pipes.

The high pressure injection pump, the injectors and the injection pipes are the main components of the fuel injection system. The injection system is different for the different engine capacities, but there are some systems which are the same on all engines.

The operations described on the following pages either apply to 612 engine or, when possible to the remaining engines, and are headed accordingly. In all cases we recommend to read the instructions in full before you commence with any removal work. In general there are no special tools required, but you will need some experience working on the engine. Many of the removal operations are only mentioned and you will have to refer to the relevant chapter or section for a full description.

1.8.0. PRECAUTIONS WHEN WORKING ON DIESEL INJECTION SYSTEMS

Whenever repairs are carried out on a diesel fuel injection system, whatever the extent, observe the greatest cleanliness, apart from the following points:

- Only carry out work on diesel injection systems under the cleanest of conditions. Work in the open air should only be carried out when there is no wind, to prevent dust entering open connections.
- Before removal of any union nut clean all around it with a clean cloth.
- Removed parts must only be deposited on a clean bench or table and must be covered with a sheet of plastic or paper. Never use fluffy shop rags to clean parts.
- All open or partially dismantled parts of the injection system must be fully covered or kept in a cardboard box, if the repair is not carried out immediately.
- Check the parts for cleanliness before Installation.
- Never use an air line to clean the exterior of the engine when connections of the injection system are open. With the availability of air compressors which can be plugged into a cigar lighter socket, you may be tempted to use air for cleaning.
- Take care not to allow diesel fuel in contact with rubber hoses or other rubber parts. Immediately clean such a hose if it should happen accidentally.
- Do not use naked lights anywhere near the engine. Although diesel fuel is less inflammable, there is always the risk of fire.

1.8.1. HIGH PRESSURE INJECTION PUMP – REMOVAL AND INSTALLATION

612 Engine – ML 270 CDI – 163 Model

The precautions given above must be observed at all times.

Fig. 1.116 shows the parts to be disconnected or removed during the removal of the pump.

- Disconnect the battery earth cable.
- Remove the trim panels of the cylinder head covers as described during the removal of the cylinder head and the Poly V-belt (Cooling System).

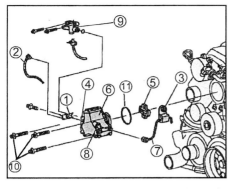

Fig. 1.116 – Details for the removal and installation of the high pressure pump. The **numbers** are referred to below (612 engine).

- Disconnect the high pressure line (7) from the high pressure pump (6). Never slacken the threaded connection (8). Use an open-ended spanner to counterhold at the threaded connection when slackening or tightening the union nut. When tightening the union nut do not exceed a torque of 2.3 kgm (16.5 ft.lb.) as it is possible that the threaded connection will be slackened the next time the union nut is removed. Take care not to bend the pipe during removal. The bracket (3) securing the pipe must be detached.
- Detach the bracket (1) at the high pressure pump. The bolts are tightened to 0.9 kgm (7 ft.lb.).
- Detach the fuel return line (2) at the high pressure pump. Some fuel may run out. The sealing ring must always be replaced.
- Remove the electric shut off valve (9) as described later on in this section.

Fig. 1.117 – The driver must engage correctly into the intermediate drive gear of the high pressure pump at the position shown by the arrow.

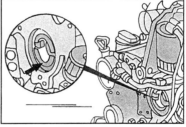

- Remove the high pressure pump (6) from the cylinder head after unscrewing the securing screws (10). We would like to point out that it is not easy to reach the lower bolt of the three shown in the illustration. **Warning:** The high pressure pump must not be opened. The driver (5) can be taken off. The sealing ring (11) must be replaced during installation. If the driver must be replaced it is also required to remove the intermediate drive gear.
- Detach the intermediate piece (adapter piece) (4) from the high pressure pump if a new pump is to be fitted. In this case replace the "O" seal underneath.

During installation of the driver pay attention to the relative position of the driver to the intermediate gear. This can be checked at the position shown by the arrow in Fig. 1.117. If the driver (5) looks worn, also replace the intermediate drive gear.

The installation is a reversal of the removal procedure. In addition to the tightening torques already given above tighten the pump securing screws to the cylinder head to 1.4 kgm (10 ft.lb.).

628 Engine – ML 400 CDI – 163 Model

In general the operations are carried out as described for the 612 engine. The charge air cross pipe must be removed. The pressure line is removed as described and must be removed at both ends (tighten to 2.2 kgm/16.5 ft.lb.). The same applies to the fuel return line next to the pressure line. The pump is fitted with a quantity control valve on one side. Remove the connector plug. Remove the pump securing bolts (1.4 kgm/10 ft.lb.). The notes regarding the driver also apply to this engine.

642 Engine – ML 280/320 CDI – 164 Model

In general the operations are carried out as described for the 612 engine, but you will have to located the various pipes, i.e. high pressure pipe and fuel hose. The pump also has a temperature sensor. Remove the connector plug for the cable. The pump securing bolts are tightened to 1.4 kgm (10 ft.lb.), BUT NEW BOLTS must be used. The high pressure pipe union nuts are tightened to 3.3 kgm (24 ft.lb.). *One important point, not applicable to the other engines*: The ignition must be switched off at least 15 seconds, before the engine is started. Otherwise the pump could be damaged.

Injection Pipes – Removal and Installation – 612 Engine – 163 model

- In the case of a 612 engine remove cylinder head cover trim panels as described in section "Engine" in connection with the cylinder head.

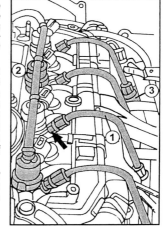

Fig. 1.118 – Counterhold the threaded fitting of the injectors (arrow) with an open-ended spanner at the injectors (2) and the injection rail (3) when removing the injection pipes (1). The illustration shows a four-cylinder engine   The 612 engine has one more injection pipe.

- Remove the union nuts securing the injection pipes (1) to the injectors (2) and to the injection rail (3) in Fig. 1.118. Counterhold the threaded fitting of the injectors (arrow) when slackening the union nut(s). Do not exceed the tightening torque of 2.3 kgm (16 ft.lb.) during installation. Otherwise the threaded fitting may unscrew during the next removal of the injector.
- Remove the injection pipes without bending or kinking them. Lay them out in the order shown in Fig. 1.119. Close the open ends of the pipes.

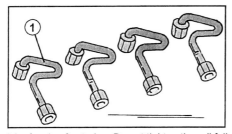

Fig. 1.119 – The injection pipes of a four-cylinder engine. The 612 engine will have one more pipe (1).

The installation is a reversal of the removal procedure, noting the tightening torque already given above. Ensure the exact seating the pipes. To install the pipes free of stress or tension, slacken the injection rail in order to avoid any risk of a pipe fracturing. Do not tighten the rail fully until all pipes have been secured.

Injection Pipes – Removal and Installation – 628 Engine – 163 model

Removal and installation is generally as described for the 612 engine, but more complicated. The intake air distribution pipe, the charge air intake pipe on the R.H. side must be removed and pressed to one side or the pipe on the L.H. side must be removed. To gain access, remove the wing panel inside the L.H. front wing and remove the charge air distribution pipe from the cylinder head cover and the turbo charger. Then press the pipe to one side. The pipes are removed from the injectors and the rail as described, noting the cautions given above. The same applies when installing the pipes.

Injection Pipes – Removal and Installation – 642 Engine – 164 model

Removal and installation is generally as described for the 612 engine, but more complicated. The engine cover must be removed. Then remove the air cleaner and the engine suction air duct after the air filter.

The engine has a leak oil line which is secured to the injectors and secured with catches. Pull the catches upwards to remove the line.

Looking at the injection lines/fuel rail, remove a bolt on the R.H. side and unscrew a bracket from the engine harness.

Remove the injection pipes as described for the 612 engine, noting the same precautions. In addition slacken the injection rail securing bolts to assure a stress-free installation of the pipes. The following tightening torques must be noted: Pressure line to high pressure pump and injection pipe union nut to injector = 3.3 kgm (24 ft.lb.), injection pipe to of high pressure pump to rail and injection pipe union nut to rail = 2.7 kgm (20 ft.lb.).

1.8.2. INJECTORS – REMOVAL AND INSTALLATION

The injectors have a tight fit in the cylinder head. The workshop has a puller to remove a very tight injector. Fig. 1.120 shows the parts of an injector for a 612 engine. An injector can be removed as follows, with the necessary preliminary operations as described during the removal of the injections pipes (all engines):

- In the case of a 612 engine remove the coolant reservoir and place it to one side (lines connected). Remove the cylinder head cover trim panels and remove the injection pipes (8) in Fig. 1.120 as described above.

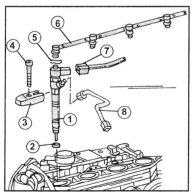

Fig. 1.120 – Details for the removal and installation of the injectors. The numbers are referred to in the text.

- Remove the connector plug (7) from the injector (1).
- Remove the securing clips (5) from the connection of the leak-off pipe (6) and push the pipe to one side.
- Remove the stretch bolts (4) and the tensioning clamp (3). The bolts must always be replaced. Tighten the bolts (4) to 0.7 kgm and from the final position a further 90°.

The injector can now be removed. As already mentioned a tight injector is removed in the workshop with a special puller (611 589 00 33 00) which is applied in place of the tensioning clamp. If a new injector is to be fitted quote the engine type and model year as injectors are sometimes changed to improve their performance.

The installation is a reversal of the removal procedure. Note the comment already given for the tightening of the injection pipes. The sealing ring (2) must always be replaced. The tensioning clamp bolts are tightened to 0.7 kgm and a further quarter of a turn.

1.8.3. MIXING CHAMBER – REMOVAL AND INSTALLATION

612 Engine

The mixing chamber is identified with (1) in Fig. 1.121 and is fitted to the charge air distribution tube (the plastic part). Removal and installation is carried out as follows on this engine:

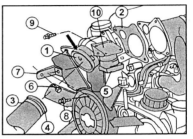

Fig. 1.121 – Details for the removal and installation of the mixing chamber in the case of the 612 engine. The numbers are given in the text.

- Disconnect the battery earth cable.
- Detach the charge air hose (3) at the mixing chamber (1). To disconnect, pull the spring marked by the arrow in an upwards direction. The sealing ring (4) must be replaced during installation.
- Disconnect the cable connector plug (5) at the exhaust gas re-circulation positioner (10).
- Remove the bracket (7) after unscrewing the screw (6).
- Unscrew the mixing chamber (1) from the charge air distribution tube. During installation replace the gasket (2). The bolts securing the mixing chamber to the charge air distribution tube are tightened to 1.4 kgm (10 ft.lb.).

642 Engine

The removal is fairly complicated as many parts must be removed to gain access and many parts must be located before they can be removed. Difficult is also the interpretation of the individual item identification. The mixing chamber is attached to the charge air distribution pipe. Proceed as follows, only when absolutely necessary:

- Remove the engine trim panel.
- Remove the R.H. intake air duct upstream of the air cleaner and the charge air hose downstream of the charge air cooler. The charge air channel on the turbo charger must also be removed.
- Locate and remove the bolts on the muffler downstream of the charge air cooler and the bolts on the bracket from the throttle valve actuator. Bolts are tightened to 0.9 kgm (7 ft.lb.)This item is located at the front of the engine, above two of the pulleys. Also disconnect the connector plug.
- Disconnect the plug connectors from the glow plug output stage and the plug from the charge air pressure sensor.
- Unclip the coolant line and unscrew the bolt on the glow plug output stage.
- Remove the bolts securing the mixing chamber to the charge air distribution pipe. The bolts are tightened to 0.9 kgm (7 ft.lb.).
- Push the removed hose bracket and the tubing bracket upwards and remove the mixing chamber towards the top.

The installation is a reversal of the removal procedure. Follow the tightening torques given above.

1.8.4. FUEL FILTER – REMOVAL AND INSTALLATION

The high pressure injection pump, the injectors and the associated injection pipes are sensitive to contamination. A fuel filter is responsible to remove any foreign matter. The filter element should be replaced approx. every 40.000 miles. Looking into the engine compartment you will find the fuel filter at the position shown in Fig. 1.122, when a 612 engine is dealt with. The other engines look similar.

Fig. 1.122 – View of the fuel filter as fitted to the 612 engine.

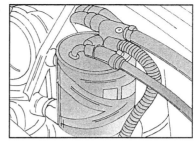

Fig. 1.123 shows the attachment of the filter. Although the fitting of the filter is not the same on all engine types, the removal and installation of the filter is practically the same. The 612 engine is, of course, fitted with the fuel cooler, which must be removed. All precautions given previously must be observed.

612 Engine – ML 270 CDI – 163 model

The fuel feed line (1) and the return flow line (2) are connected by means of locking arms. Some precautions must be taken during the disconnection of the fuel lines in order not to damage the locking arm (see description below).

Fig. 1.123 – Details for the removal and installation of the fuel filter. The numbers are referred to in the text.

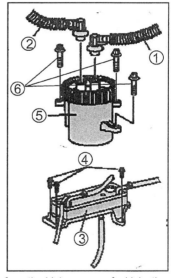

- In the case of the 612 engine remove the trim panel of the charge air distribution pipe
- Disconnect the fuel lines (1) and (2) in Fig. 1.123 from the full flow filter (5). Collect the escaping fuel.
- Take off the fuel cooler (3) after removal of the securing screws (4) and raise the fuel cooler slightly.
- Remove the fuel filter (5), attached with bolts (6). If the filter housing has been emptied during removal it must be filled with diesel fuel to ensure immediate distribution of the fuel.

The installation is a reversal of the removal procedure. Th filter securing bolts are tightened to 0.9 kgm (7 ft.lb.).

Disconnecting and Connecting low pressure fuel lines

These are the pipes which are not under pressure from the high pressure fuel injection system, leading to the fuel distributor rail and the fuel return lines. The pipes are fitted with a locking arm in place of a screw connection and are sealed off with a sealing ring. Fig. 1.124 shows details to disconnect and connect any of theses pipes in a schematic drawing. The disconnection and re-connection is difficult to describe if you have no experience.

Fig. 1.124 – Details for the disconnecting (L.H. view "A") and connecting (R.H. view "B") low pressure fuel pipes.
1   Locking arm
2   Sealing ring

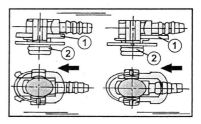

Disconnection

- Move the locking arm to its stop into the released position as shown by the arrow in view "A".
- Remove the connection from the low pressure line.
- Move the locking (1) back to the locked position as shown in view "A". The locking arm must not remain in the released position over an extended period as this could lead to leaks in the fuel line. *After disconnecting the fuel line make absolutely sure that the locking arm is back to the locked position, otherwise you will have to replace the fuel line.*

Connecting the Fuel Line

- Check that the locking lever (1) is in the fitting position as shown in view "B".
- Insert the fuel line connector. Check that the connection is free of fuel leaks after installation.

628 Engine – ML 400 CDI – 163 model

The fuel hoses are connected by means of hose clamps. Check them before re-use. May have to be replaced. The filter can be seen in the centre of the engine after the engine cover has been pulled upwards.

- Disconnect the fuel inlet hose (on the R.H. side of the filter) and the outlet hose (on the L.H. side) after slackening the hose clamps.
- From the top of the filter remove three bolts (two on one side, one on the opposite side) and remove the filter upwards. Tighten the bolts to 0.9 kgm (7 ft.lb.).
- Mark the edge of the filter relative to the filter clamp to assure installation in the same position, remove the clamp bolt and remove the clamp. The filter can now be taken out. Tighten the bolt to 0.9 kgm (7 ft.lb.).

Install in reverse order. If the filter housing has been emptied during removal it must be filled with diesel fuel to ensure immediate distribution of the fuel.

642 Engine – ML 280/320 CDI – 164 model

The removal and installation is similar as described for the 628 engine. After removal of the engine covering panel you will find the filter in the centre of the engine. The engine intake air duct downstream of the air cleaner must be removed for access. Two fuel hoses are secured with hose clamps. One bolt (0.5 kgm) secures the filter. The filter is removed in an upwards direction.

1.8.5. ELECTRIC SHUT-OFF VALVE – REMOVAL AND INSTALLATION

The valve is fitted at the position shown in Fig. 1.125. All precautions regarding fuel must be observed.

- Remove the heat shield above the turbocharger.
- Unplug the connector (2) at the electric shut-off valve (1) and detach the fuel line (3) from the valve. Fuel will run out and the poly V-belt must be protected with a thick rag to prevent contamination. The sealing ring between fuel line and valve must be replaced.

Fig. 1.125 – Details for the removal and installation of the electric fuel shut-off valve. The numbers are referred to in the text.

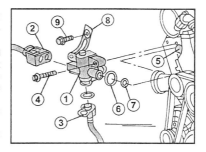

- Unscrew the bolts (4) and (9) and pull the valve (1) together with the bracket (8) off the intermediate piece (5) from the side and take it out. Replace the seals (6) and (7) during installation. The bracket (8) can be removed from the valve if a new valve is fitted.

Installation is a reversal of the removal procedure.

1.8.6. PRESSURE CONTROL VALVE – REMOVAL AND INSTALLATION

The location of the pressure control valve can be seen in Fig. 1.126 (612 and 628 engines), i.e. it is fitted at position (6) into the common rail, near the oil filter (7), Observe all precautions regards the fuel during removal.

Fig. 1.126 – Details for the removal and installation of the pressure control valve. The numbers are given in the text.

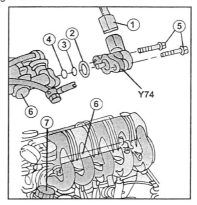

- Detach the charge air distribution pipe from the cylinder head and place it to one side with the engine wiring harness connected. Details of removal can be found in section "Engine", dealing with the cylinder head cover.
- Separate the cable connector plug (1) from the control valve (electrical identification Y74).
- Remove the pressure control valve after removal of the screws (5). Sealing rings (2) and (4) and the support ring (3) must be replaced during installation.

The installation is a reversal of the removal procedure. The sealing rings (2) and (4) are coated in the workshop with a special grease (No. 001 989 42 51 10). You may be able to obtain some. Take care not to damage the seals during installation of the valve as internal leaks may occur which are not visible from the outside. Fit the valve and secure with the screws (5) to 0.3 kgm and in a second stage to 0.5 kgm. Finally push the plug (1) over its connection. Refit the charge air distribution pipe to the cylinder head.
After installation start the engine and check for visible leaks around the valve.

1.8.8. COMMON RAIL – REMOVAL AND INSTALLATION

612 Engine (270 CDI) – 163 model
Fig. 1.127 shows the items to be disconnected or removed to take out or replace the common rail fuel distribution tube. Observe all precautions regards fuel when removing the rail.

- Remove the plastic charge air distribution pipe (14) as described in section "Engine" during the removal of the cylinder head cover and place it to one side with the engine wiring harness connected. Also remove the trim panel from the cylinder head cover.

Fig. 1.127 – Details for the removal and installation of the common rail as fitted to the 612 engine. Follow the numbers as given below.

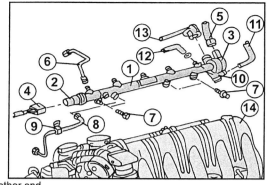

- Remove the injection pipes (6) as described earlier on in this section.
- Unplug the cable connector plug (4) from the rail pressure sensor (2) on one side of the rail and the plug (5) from the pressure control valve (3) at the other end.
- Detach the retaining clamp (9) securing the pressure pipe (8) to the high pressure pump-rail and disconnect the pipe from the rail and the high pressure pump, following the instructions already given during the removal of the injection pipes. Tighten the union nuts to 2.3 kgm16.5 ft.lb.
- Disconnect the fuel return flow line (13) from the rail (1). Pay attention to the locking arm (section 1.8.4, fuel filter, 612 engine). Replace the seal.
- Remove the screws (7) and take the fuel rail (1) off the cylinder head. If the fuel rail is replaced, fit it onto the existing angle piece (10). Replace the seals. The rail must be tightened to 1.4 kgm(10 ft.lb.) after the injection pipes have been fully connected.
- Disconnect the fuel return flow line (12) and the leak oil line (11) at the angled piece and remove the fuel rail towards the front.

The installation is a reversal of the removal procedure, noting the points already given above. The banjo bolt for the leak oil line must be tightened to 2.0 kgm (14 ft.lb.).

628 Engine (ML 400 CDI – 163 Model)

The removal and installation is not very difficult. Two common rails are fitted in the centre of the engine, one for each cylinder bank. The intake air distribution pipe must be removed. After disconnecting the fuel injection pipes and the pressure line from the rail, as described earlier on, remove the bolts securing the rail (in the centre and at the end) and lift off the rail.

Install in reverse order. First connect the injection pipe union nuts to the rail (2.3 kgm/16.5 ft.lb.) and then fit and tighten the rail securing bolts to the cylinder head (2.0 kgm/14.5 ft.lb.).

642 Engine (ML 280/320 CDI – 164 Model)

Two common rails are fitted in the centre of the engine, one for each cylinder bank. Removal can be carried out with the help of Fig. 1.128. The engine cover must be removed for access. After disconnecting the fuel injection pipes from the rail, as described earlier on, you will have to located and disconnect two connector plugs. Disconnect the plug (5) from the rail pressure sensor and the plug (6) from the pressure regulating valve.

Disconnect the fuel return pipe (2). Undo the union nuts connecting the pressure lines (near the fuel return pipe). The fittings must be counter held with an open-ended spanner.

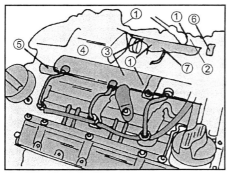

Fig. 1.128 – Removal and installation of common rails of a 642 engine- See text.

Refer to the illustration and unscrew the union nuts (3) on the connecting pipe (7) between the L.H. and R.H. rail. The end of the pipe must be sealed off to prevent entry of dirt. The connecting line has a tapered gasket and must be replaced if the gasket is not in perfect condition.

The bolts (1) can now be removed and the common rail or rails (4) taken out.

Install in reverse order. First fit and tighten the union nuts (3) of the connecting pipe (7) and of the pressure pipe finger-tight and then tighten the bolts (1) to prevent distortion of parts. Tighten as follows: Connecting pipe between the two rails and pressure pipe of high pressure pump to rail = 2.7 kgm (19.5 ft.lb.), pressure line to high pressure pump = 3.3 kgm (24 ft.lb.).

1.8.9. RAIL PRESSURE SENSOR – REMOVAL AND INSTALLATION

The pressure sensor is fitted to the common rail. Fig. 1.129 shows where it is located in the case of the 612 engine. Fig. 1.128 identifies the location of the 642 engine. Observe all precautions regards the fuel.

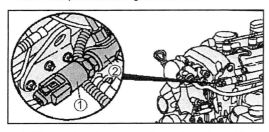

Fig. 1.129 – Details for the removal and installation of the rail pressure sensor in the case of the 612 engine.

612 Engine (ML 270 CDI – 163 Model)

Removal and installation is straight-forward. Withdraw the connector plug from the pressure sensor (1) and unscrew the sensor from the rail (2). The threaded connection in the rail must be counter-held with an open ended spanner. Fit in reverse order. Tighten the sensor to 2.2 kgm (16 ft.lb.).

628 Engine (ML 400 CDI – 163 Model)

First remove the intake air distribution pipe. The pressure sensor must now be located. We are trying to help. You will see a square box, secured by a black bracket and surrounded by various cables/hoses. One is a vacuum hose (the large one), secured by a bracket. Remove the bolt and place the hose to one side. Below the hose you will find the pressure sensor, screwed into the so-called valve block. Unplug the connector plug and unscrew the pressure sensor. Install in reverse order. Clean the sealing faces and use a new sealing ring. Tighten the sensor to 3.5 kgm (25 ft.lb.).

642 Engine (ML 280/320 CDI – 164 Model)

After removal of the engine trip panel you will have the view shown in Fig. 1.128 with the location of the pressure sensor (5). A few preliminary operations are necessary.
- Remove the engine intake air duct downstream of the air cleaner..
- Disconnect the connector plug from the sensor.

- Remove the engine suspension lugs (lifting lugs) and unscrew the pressure sensor from the injection rail (common rail). Prevent entry of foreign matter.

Install in reverse order. The pressure sensor is tightened to 1.4 kgm (10 ft.lb.). Make sure that the sealing faces are clean.

1.8.10. AIR CLEANER
1.8.10.1. Replacing the Air Cleaner Element

The air cleaner of the 612 engine consists of the parts shown in Fig. 130. The air cleaner is located, seen from the front of the vehicle, on the L.H. side of the engine compartment. The same applies to the 628 engine. As you will know, two air cleaners are fitted to the 642 engine, one to each side.

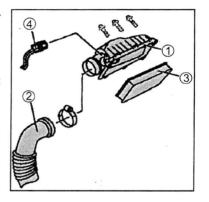

Fig. 1.130 – The component parts of the air cleaner element (612 engine).
1 Top part of air cleaner housing
2 Air intake hose
3 Air cleaner element
4 Hot film mass air flow sensor

Remove and install the air cleaner element as follows:

612 Engine (ML 270 CDI – 163 Model)
- Remove cylinder head cover trim panel as described during the removal of the cylinder head (bolts = 1.0 kgm).
- Slacken the hose clamp and remove the air intake hose (2).
- Disconnect the plug from the hot film mass air flow meter (4).
- Remove the top part of the air cleaner housing after removal of the bolt and lift it off. The air cleaner element (3) can now be withdrawn.
- Clean the inside of the air cleaner housing with a damp rag before fitting the new element. Make sure that the element is correctly seated at the sealing surfaces.
- Detach the air intake hose (1) at the upper part of the air cleaner housing (2) after slackening of the hose clamp. If fitted remove the hot film air flow sensor as described below.
- Unclip the top part of the air cleaner housing (2) at the lower part of the housing (4) and lift off the upper housing (cover). The filter element (3) can now be removed.

The installation is a reversal of the removal procedure. On one end of the air cleaner cover is a service indicator which must be reset by turning.

628 Engine (ML 400 CDI – 163 Model)
The upper part of the air cleaner housing must be removed to gain access to the element. The cover is secured by means of 6 clips around the outside. Locate the clips and remove them. The cover can be taken off and the element removed from the inside of the air cleaner housing. During installation ensure the correct sealing of the cover before fastening the clips.

642 Engine (ML 280/320 CDI – 164 Model)
First remove the engine cover in the centre of the engine. To gain access to the air cleaner element the air filter housing must be removed. Engine bonnet open.

The removal of the L.H. filter housing is more complicated. Before commencing read the instructions in full. Otherwise have the replacement of the element replaced in a workshop (recommended).
- Remove the seal on the edge of the engine compartment near the large air duct. Below locate and remove three bolts securing the partition above the air duct and remove the partition.
- Remove the clamp from the air duct, unscrew two bolts (0.9 kgm) and separate the connector from the sensor (for intake air temperature). The air cleaner housing can now be removed.

The removal of the R.H. filter housing is less complicated.
- Slacken the clamp securing the air inlet hose and locate and remove two securing bolts (0.9 kgm).
- Remove the air cleaner housing first towards the inside and then forward to remove it.

The filter element can now be removed from the housing. Remove four bolts on the outside (2 on each side) and remove the cover from the housing. Lift out the filter element. Install the removed parts in reverse order.

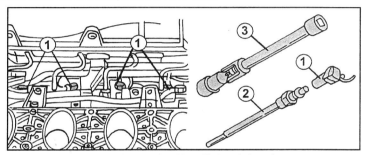

Fig. 1.131 – Removal and installation of glow plugs.

1.8.11. GLOW PLUGS

The glow plug system consists of the glow plugs, the glow time relay and the warning lamp in the instrument panel. In general:

When the ignition is switched on, the glow plug relay will receive current via terminal "15" ' The relay directs the current from the plus terminal "30" via a fuse to the glow plugs. The glow plugs receive a voltage of at least 11.5 volts and a current of 30 amps, which is however, reduced to 8 to 15 amps by means of a regulator, thereby preventing burning out of the plugs. The glow plugs heat up to 90° C within 10 seconds and can reach a temperature of 1180° C after 30 seconds.

The glow plug time relay determines the operating time of the glow plugs. This relay senses the outside temperature, i.e. at very low temperatures, for example – 30°) C, the plugs can glow as long as 25 seconds. During the summer months, however, glowing time may be as little as 2 seconds. If the engine is not started immediately after the warning light has gone "off", the current feed will be interrupted through a safety circuit. Subsequent starting of the engine will switch in the glow plug circuit via starter motor terminal "50".

Glow plugs must again be obtained by quoting the engine number and model year. The plugs are sometimes modified and only your MB parts supplier will be able to sell you the correct plugs.

The glow plugs are fairly hidden below as you can see in Fig. 1.131. A special socket with universal joint and extension are required to reach them. A ratchet is of advantage. Additionally you will have to remove various parts to gain access to the glow plugs.

Use a pair of pliers and unplug the cable connector plugs (1) from the glow plugs (2). Using the special wrench mentioned above and shown in Fig. 1.131 unscrew the plug(s) out of the cylinder head. If a plug is difficult to remove refit the connector plugs, start up the engine and allow it to reach operating temperature. Obviously this is more time consuming.

The installation of the glow plugs is a reversal of the removal procedure. Plugs are tightened to 2.0 kgm (14.5 ft.lb.). Do not over-tighten the cable securing nuts (0.4 kgm). Problems with glow plugs should always be investigated by a workshop dealing with diesel equipment as diagnosis is not a straight forward operation.

2 CLUTCH

2.0. Introduction

Only the ML270 CDI is fitted with a clutch and a manual transmission, but note that two different transmissions (type 716 and 717) can be fitted, each with a different clutch operating system. The clutch is operated by means of a hydraulic system. Pressure is generated by the depressing of the clutch pedal and transmitted via the clutch master cylinder to a so-called central clutch operator inside the clutch bell housing which takes the place of the clutch slave cylinder but incorporates the clutch release bearing, in the case of transmission type 716 or with a slave cylinder and a separate clutch release bearing in the case of type 717 (CDI models). We refer you to your MB parts department if the clutch must be replaced, quoting the engine type and engine number.

2.1. Technical Data

Type:	Single plate, dry clutch with diaphragm spring.
Clutch operation:	By hydraulic system (see below)
Pedal adjustment:	Automatic take-up
Clutch release bearing	Sealed ball-type bearing in constant contact with the clutch plate, incorporated in sealed clutch operator or as described above.

2.2 Clutch Unit

2.2.0. CHECKING THE CLUTCH OPERATION

The clutch can be checked for proper operation when fitted to the vehicle. To do this, proceed as follows:

- Start the engine and allow to idle. Depress the clutch pedal and wait approx. 3 secs. Engage the reverse gear. If grating noises can be heard from the transmission, it can be assumed the clutch or driven plate needs replacement, as the driven plate no longer connects the clutch pressure plate with the flywheel.
- To check the clutch for signs of slipping, drive the vehicle until the clutch and transmission have reached operating temperature. Stop the vehicle, firmly apply the handbrake and engage the 3rd gear. Keep the clutch pedal fully depressed and accelerate the engine to approx. 3000 - 4000 rpm. Release the clutch pedal suddenly. The clutch operates satisfactorily if the engine stalls immediately.

2.2.0. REMOVAL AND INSTALLATION

Important Note: Pressure plate and diaphragm spring cannot be dismantled and must be replaced together. Clutches and driven plates are sometimes modified to improve their operation. If a new clutch or driven plate is purchased always quote the model and the engine type and number.

The clutch cannot be removed without removing the transmission. Removal of the transmission is described in section "Manual Transmission". The operations are the same on all models. After the clutch has been removed you will have the parts shown in Fig. 2.1.

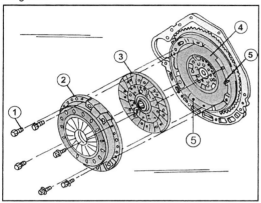

Fig. 2.1 – The component parts of the clutch. All clutches look similar
1 Clutch securing bolts
2 Clutch pressure plate
3 Clutch driven plate
4 Flywheel
5 Dowel pins

• Remove the engine and transmission or the transmission (Section 3.1).

• Mark the clutch in its fitted position on the flywheel if there is a possibility that the clutch unit is re-used. To remove the clutch, unscrew the six bolts (1) in Fig. 2.1, securing the pressure plate (2) to the flywheel (4) and lift off the clutch unit and then the driven plate (3), now free. Before removing the driven plate, note the position of the longer part of the driven plate hub, as the driven plate must be refitted in the same way. Note that the clutch plate is located in position by means of the dowel pins (5).

• Immediately check the friction face of the flywheel, as it is possible that the rivets of the driven plate have left their mark on the flywheel face if the linings have worn excessively.
• Check the separate clutch release bearing or the central clutch operator, depending which type is fitted and replace as necessary.

Fig. 2.2 – The clutch centring mandrel (1) is inserted into the driven plate and the flywheel before the clutch is fitted.

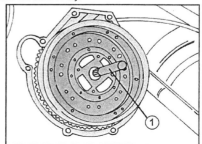

Install in the reverse sequence to removal, noting the following points:
• If the old clutch unit is fitted, align the marks made before removal. A new clutch can be fitted in any position.
• Coat the splines of the clutch drive shaft with a little Molykote BR2 grease.
• A centring mandrel is required to centre the clutch driven plate inside the flywheel. Tool hire companies normally have sets of mandrels for this purpose. An old transmission (clutch) shaft for the transmission in question, which you may be able to obtain from a Mercedes

workshop, can also be used. Experienced D.I.Y. mechanics will also be able to align the clutch plate without the help of a mandrel. Insert the mandrel as shown in Fig. 2.2. Fit the clutch pressure plate (2) over the dowel pins (5) in Fig. 2.1.

- Fit and tighten the six clutch to flywheel bolts (1) to a torque reading of 2.5 kgm (18 ft.lb.), in gradual steps. The flywheel must be locked against rotation when the clutch bolts are e tightened.
- Refit the engine and transmission or the transmission and operate the clutch pedal at least 5 times before the engine is started.

Fig. 2.3. – To check the driven plate for run-out, clamp it between the centres of a lathe and check with a dial gauge.

2.3. Servicing

The cover assembly – pressure plate and diaphragm spring – must not be dismantled. Replace, if necessary with a complete assembly from your dealer or distributor.

Inspect the driven plate and the linings, replacing the complete plate if the linings are worn down close to the rivets. A driven plate with the linings contaminated with grease or oil cannot be cleaned successfully and should also be replaced. All rivets should be tight and the torsion springs should be sound and unbroken.

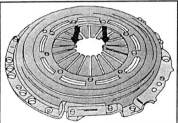

Fig. 2.4 – The "fingers" of the diaphragm spring can wear at the positions shown. All must be at the same height.

Check the condition of the driven plate splines. Clamp the driven plate between the centres of a lathe and apply a dial gauge to the outside of the plate as shown in Fig. 2.3, at a diameter of approx. 175.0 mm (6.4 in.). The max. run/out of the driven plate should be no more than 0.5 mm (0.02 in.).

Check the rivet fastening of the clutch pressure plate and replace the plate, if loose rivets can be detected.

Fig. 2.5 – Checking the clutch pressure plate for distortion. The gap should not be more than given below.

Check the inner ends of the clutch plate at the position shown in Fig. 2.4. If wear is detected (more than 0.3 mm) replace the clutch unit. The fingers of the diaphragm spring must all be at the same height. It may be possible to bend them slightly with a pair of pliers, but renewal is always the best remedy.

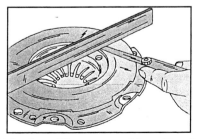

Place a straight edge (steel ruler) over the friction face of the pressure plate and insert feeler gauges between the ruler and the surface. If the gap at the innermost spot of the friction face is no more than 0.03 mm (0.012 in.), the plate can be re-used. Fig. 2.5 shows this check.

2.4. Clutch Release Mechanism

Engagement and disengagement of the clutch is by means of the central clutch operator inside the transmission housing with incorporated clutch release bearing if a transmission of type 716 is fitted. A separate clutch release bearing is fitted to the 717 transmission. The system is free of clearance and any wear of the driven plate is automatically compensated by the system.

2.4.0. HYDRAULIC CLUTCH OPERATOR – REMOVAL AND INSTALLATION – 6 speed transmission

Precautions when working with Brake Fluid

As the hydraulic system is filled with brake fluid read the notes below before any operations are carried out on the hydraulic clutch system.

Fig. 2.6 – Attachment of the central clutch operator inside the gearbox housing. The numbers are referred to during the removal instructions.

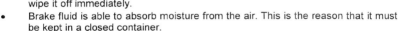

- Only store brake fluid in a closed container, tin, etc. which must be marked accordingly. Brake fluid can damage your health if swallowed.
- Protect your hand with gloves and if possible your eyes with goggles. If your hands come into contact with brake fluid immediately wash them with water and soap.
- Take care not to drip brake fluid onto painted areas of the vehicle. Brake fluid will damage the paint. If it happens, wipe it off immediately.
- Brake fluid is able to absorb moisture from the air. This is the reason that it must be kept in a closed container.
- Even the smallest quantity of oil in the brake fluid can damage the rubber parts of the hydraulic system.
- Brake fluid released from the system, as is the case during the bleeding operation, must not be re-used to top-up the fluid reservoir.

The transmission must be removed to gain access to the hydraulic clutch operator. Fig. 2.6 shows the attachment of the parts in question. With the transmission removed unscrew the four bolts (1) and take off the central clutch operator (2) from the gearbox (3).

Check the clutch release bearing for noises, rough operation, leakage or wear and replace the complete assembly if necessary.

The installation is carried out in reverse order. Use new micro-encapsulated bolts (1). Tighten the bolts to 1.0 kgm (7 ft.lb.). Mercedes-Benz recommends to use a suitable thread cutter to re-cut the bolt threads inside the gearbox housing before the clutch operator is fitted. After installation of the gearbox bleed the clutch system as described further on in the text.

2.4.1. CLUTCH RELEASE BEARING

Fitted to transmission type 717.

On this arrangement the engagement and disengagement of the clutch is by means of the slave cylinder push rod, acting on the clutch release lever and sliding the ball bearing-type release bearing along a guide tube on the clutch shaft of the transmission. The release system is free of play, as the wear of the clutch linings is compensated automatically.

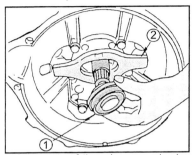

Fig. 2.7 – Removal of the clutch release bearing (1) from the release lever (2).

The transmission must be removed to replace the release bearing. Remove the bearing from the bearing sleeve on the front transmission housing cover, as shown in Fig. 2.7. To remove the release fork, refer to Fig. 2.8 and move it in direction of arrow (a) and then pull it from the ball pin in the clutch housing in direction of arrow (b).

Thoroughly grease the guide sleeve on the front transmission cover, the ball pin and all of the parts of the release mechanism in contact with the release bearing with long term grease. Push the release lever in reverse direction of arrow (b) over the ball pin until the spring clip of the release lever engages with the ball pin. Check for secure fitting. Then move the lever in reverse direction of arrow (a) until the slave cylinder push rod is engaged with the ball-shaped cut-out in the release lever.

Fig. 2.8 – Removal and installation of the clutch release lever (see text).
1 Ball pin   2 Release lever

Grease the release bearing on the inside and on both sides at the rear, where it rests against the release lever and slip the bearing over the guide sleeve. Rotate the bearing until it snaps in position into the release lever. Check that the bearing is properly fitted and refit the transmission.

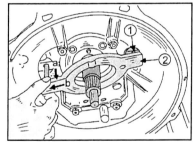

2.4.2.   CLUTCH SLAVE CYLINDER – 717 Transmission

The clutch slave cylinder is fitted to the side of the transmission. The cylinder can be removed as follows:

- Unscrew the fluid pipe from the slave cylinder, using an open-ended spanner. Close the end of the pipe in suitable manner to prevent fluid leakage (rubber cap for bleeder screw).
- Remove the two cylinder securing screws and take off the cylinder. Observe the fitted shim.
- When fitting, insert the shim with the grooved side against the clutch housing and hold in position. Fit the slave cylinder, engaging the push rod into the ball-shaped cut-out of the clutch release lever, and insert the two screws. Tighten the screws. Finally bleed the clutch system as described in the next section.

2.4.3.   CLUTCH MASTER CYLINDER

As the removal and installation of the clutch master cylinder is a complicated operation and the cylinder will have a long service lift, we suggest to have the cylinder replaced in a workshop.

2.5. Bleeding the Clutch System

A pressure bleeder is used by Mercedes workshops. The following description involves the brake system and is therefore to be treated with caution.

Fig. 2.9 – The bleeding screw (1) is located on the side of the gearbox if a central clutch operator is fitted. The attached bleeder hose (2) is inserted into a glass jar (3).

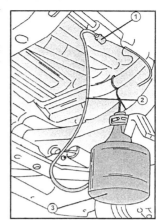

Make absolutely sure that the brakes have correct operating pressure after the clutch has been bled. A transparent hose of approx. 1 metre (3 ft.) in length is required. Proceed as follows, noting that the bleed hose is connected :

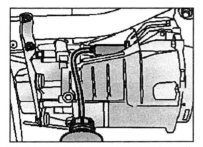

Fig. 2.10 – The bleeding screw is located at the end of the clutch slave cylinder, if one is fitted.

- Fill the brake/clutch fluid reservoir.
- Remove the dust cap of the bleeder screw in the side opening of the gearbox, shown in Fig. 2.9 or as shown in Fig. 2.10, if a slave cylinder is fitted, and push the hose over the bleeder screw and place the hose end into a glass container filled with some brake fluid. Open the bleeder screw.

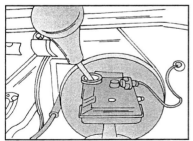

Fig. 2.11 – Brake fluid can be removed from the fluid reservoir in the manner shown.

- Ask a second person to operate the brake pedal until the hose is completely filled with brake fluid and no more air bubbles can be seen in the glass container. Place a finger over the hose end to prevent fluid from running out.
- Tighten the bleed screw and remove the hose from the end of the screw.
- Check the fluid level in the reservoir and, If necessary, top it up to the "Max." mark. Do not overfill. If necessary extract some fluid in the manner shown in Fig. 2.11. Start the engine, depress the clutch pedal and engage reverse. No grating noises should be heard.

2.6. Clutch Faults

Below we list some faults which may occur in connection with the clutch. The faults are not directed specifically to the models covered in this manual.

A Slipping Clutch
1 Clutch plate slipping — Replace driven plate
2 Clutch pressure to low — Replace clutch unit
3 Clutch plate linings full of oil — Replace driven plate, find oil leak
4 Clutch overheated — Replace driven plate, maybe clutch plate
5 Hydraulic operator leaking — Replace central clutch operator

B Clutch will not release
1 Air in the system — Bleed clutch system
2 Master cylinder or operator leaks — Replace cylinder in question
3 Distorted clutch driven plate — Replace driven plate
4 Driven plate linings broken — Replace driven plate
5 Driven plate jammed on shaft — Investigate and rectify
6 Clutch plate lining sticking on flywheel (after long lay off) — Engage 1st gear and depress clutch pedal. Have the vehicle towed a short distance, with ignition switched off

C Clutch jerky
1 Refer to point A3
2 Wrong driven plate (after repair) — Check and rectify
3 Release bearing defect — Replace central clutch operator
4 Pressure plate has uneven pressure — Replace pressure plate
5 Engine/gearbox mountings defect — Check and if necessary replace

D Clutch does not release and slips
1 Clutch pressure plate damaged — Replace pressure plate

3 Manual Transmission

The models covered in this manual are either fitted with a six-speed transmission, with the technical designation type "716", with different end numbers, depending on the fitted engine or an automatic transmission. Again a different transmission is fitted, allocated to the different engines. The type is important when it is intended to fit a second-hand transmission during the life-span of your vehicle. The transmission is also identified by different letters/numbers which can be identified details available from supplier. There are too many to list them all. Fig. 3.1 shows the layout of the gearchange mechanism.

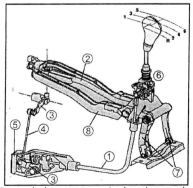

Fig. 3.1 – The component parts of the gearchange mechanism of the six-speed transmission "716".
1   Selector cable
2   Shift rod
3   Transfer lever
4   Selector rod
5   Bracket
6   Floor shaft
7   Swivel lever
8   Coupling arm

The overhaul of the transmission is not described in this manual. The description in the overhaul section is limited to some minor repair operations, not involving the gear train or the gear shafts. If the transmission appears to be damaged or faulty, try to obtain an exchange unit.

114

Transmission overhaul is now limited to specialised workshops which are equipped with the necessary special tools.

3.0. Technical Data

Fitted transmission – all diesel models: .... 716- different end numbers
Fitted transmission – early petrol models: .... 717- different end numbers

Transmission Ratios: **ML 270 CDI (163)**
- First gear: 5.100 : 1
- Second speed: 2.830 : 1
- Third speed: 1.790 : 1
- Fourth speed: 1.260 : 1
- Fifth speed: 1.000 : 1
- Sixth speed: 0.830 : 1
- Reverse speed: 4.570 : 1

Oil capacity: .... 1.5 litres
Lubrication oil: As in automatic transmissions

3.1. Removal and Installation

The following text describes the general removal and installation operations. The transmission is heavy and the necessary precautions must be taken when it is lifted out. We must point out that the transfer case must be removed before the actual transmission can be removed, irrespective of the type of transmission (five-speed, six speed or automatic). The battery must be disconnected.

Refer to Fig. 3.2 to remove the transfer case as follows:

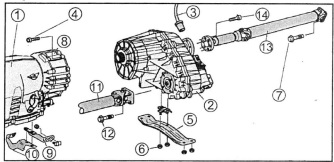

Fig. 3.2 – Details for the removal and installation of the transfer case (all transmissions). See text.

- Place the front end of the vehicle on chassis stands and remove the rear section of the sound-proofing panel underneath the vehicle.
- Unscrew the exhaust bracket (9) and the bracket (10) from the exhaust.
- Remove the bolts (14) and separate the propeller shaft (13) from the flange on the transfer case (2). The shaft can be removed after removal of bolts (7). Tighten the bolts to 4.0 kgm (29 ft.lb.) during installation when connecting to the case and rear axle. Then remove the bolts (12) and remove the propeller shaft (11) from the transfer case. Use a wire sling, push the shafts to one side and tie them up to the underbody. Take care not to damage the shaft universal joint and in the case of shaft (13) the joint and the centre bearing. Note that these bolts are tightened to

5.0 kgm (25 ft.lb.) when connecting to the front axle. In both cases new bolts must be fitted. Also remove the starter motor.
- Detach the plug connector (3) from the actuator motor (if fitted).
- Place a mobile jack or other lifting device underneath the transmission and remove the rear engine crossmember (5) with the engine mounting. The nuts (6) securing the rear crossmember to the body are tightened to 4.0 kgm (29 ft.lb.). The same torque applies when the engine mounting is fitted.
- Slightly lower the transmission unit and now support and lift the transfer case (2) on the jack. The workshop uses a plate to lift the case. Remove the bolts (4) and withdraw case the from the adapter housing (8) towards the rear (carefully).

The installation of the transfer case is carried out in reverse order. Tighten the bolts (4) to 2.0 kgm (14.5 ft.lb.), irrespective of the fitted transmission. Before installation check the oil level in the transfer case. The oil must be to the bottom edge of the filler plug opening. The plug is tightened to 3.0 kgm (22 ft.lb.).

Continue with the removal of the transmission as follows:
- Disconnect the connector plug from the reversing light switch and other plugs at the rear end of the transmission.
- On one side of the transmission separate the hydraulic pipe from the clutch housing after removal of a retainer. Plug the open pipe connection.
- Unhook and pull out a so-called "safety bolt" and unhook the shift rod from shift (gearchange) mechanism on the transmission.
- Disconnect the electrical leads from the starter motor, remove the starter motor mounting bolts and withdraw the starter motor from the engine and transmission.
- Place the jack underneath the transmission and lift it up slightly.
- Remove the transmission-to-crankcase bolts. The two upper bolts are removed last.
- Rotate the transmission towards the left and remove it horizontally towards the rear and away from the clutch housing before it is lowered. Make absolutely sure that the clutch shaft has disengaged from the clutch driven plate before the gearbox is lowered. Failing to observe this can lead to distortion of the clutch shaft or damage to the driven plate.

The installation of the gearbox is carried out as follows:
- Coat the dowel pin and the clutch shaft splines with long-term grease and lift the gearbox until it can be pushed in horizontal position against the engine.
- Engage a gear, slightly rotate the gearbox towards the left and rotate the drive flange at the end of the transmission to and fro until the splines of the clutch shaft have engaged with the splines of the clutch driven plate. Now push the gearbox fully against the engine until the gap is closed.
- Bolt the gearbox to the engine (4.0 kgm/29 ft.lb.).
- Fit the starter motor and re-connect the cable connections.
- Fit the gearchange linkages to the gearchange levers and secure them with the retaining clips.
- The remaining operations are carried out in reverse order. The clutch hydraulic system must be led of air as described in section "Clutch". Finally check and if necessary correct the oil level. Tighten the oil filler plug to 3.5 kgm (25 ft.lb.). If the transmission oil has been drained tighten the oil drain plug to 5.0 kgm (36 ft.lb.).

3.2 Transmission Repairs

Complete dismantling of the transmission requires special tools. A damaged transmission should be replaced by an exchange unit. We recommend to contact a

Mercedes-Benz dealer to enquire about the availability of exchange gearboxes. Make sure that the correct transmission for the model in question is obtained.

Fig. 3.3 – Location of the gearbox oil filler plug (1) and drain plug (2).

3.2.2. GEARBOX OIL LEVEL

The gearbox oil is only changed after the first 6000 miles and is then filled for life. To check the oil level remove the plug (1) in Fig. 3.3 (Allen key) and insert the tip of the forefinger to reach for the oil. If necessary top-up with the recommended oil. You may have to clean an oil can of old oil to use for the topping-up operation.

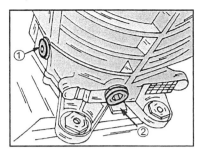

4 Propeller Shafts

All vehicles are fitted two propeller shafts, one between the transfer case and the front axle, the other one between the transfer case and the rear axle. This is shaft (13) in Fig. 3.2. The attachment of the front shaft on model series 163 is shown in Fig. 4.1. The arrangement on models series 164 is more or less identical but different tightening torques apply to the propeller shaft bolts. Bolts and nuts and the lock plates (shims) must always be replace if removed.

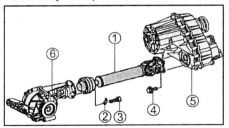

Fig. 4.1 – Propeller shaft between front axle drive and transfer case, shown in the case of a 163 model. See text.

4.1. Propeller Shafts – Removal and Installation

ML 270/400 CDI

The propeller shaft between the transfer case and the rear axle is removed as described during the removal of the transfer case in Section 3.2. Remove the front shaft, shown in Fig. 4.1 as follows:

- Place the vehicle on secure chassis stands.
- Remove the bolts (4) securing the shaft flange to the transfer case (5) and then remove the bolts (3) securing the shaft flange to the front axle drive. Take off the lock plates (shims).
- Remove the propeller shaft downwards.

During installation make sure that the flange faces are clean. If the universal joint or the double universal joint are worn replace the complete propeller shaft. The shaft flange is tightened to 5.0 kgm (36 ft.lb.) to the transfer case or 4.0 kgm (29 ft.lb.) to the front axle.

ML 280/320 CDI: All self-locking nuts and bolts must be replaced during installation. Removal and installation is carried out in a similar manner as described above, with the following differences:

- The exhaust heat protection plate must be removed from the propeller shaft intermediate bearing (remove the bolts) and from the propeller shaft (remove the bolts).
- Mark the propeller shaft flange and the rear axle drive flange at opposite points, using paint and the propeller shaft flange and the flexible coupling in the same manner.
- Remove the bolts securing the propeller shaft flanges at both ends and unscrew the propeller shaft intermediate bearing and remove the shaft. The flexible coupling remains on the shaft. The shaft must be supported by a helper before the last bolts are removed as it will drop down.

The installation is a reversal of the removal procedure. Make sure that the paint marks on the flanges are in line. The following tightening torques must be observed: Front propeller shaft on transfer case (rear axle end) = 5.4 kgm (37 ft.lb.), rear propeller shaft to rear axle centre = 6.4 kgm (46 ft.lb.), propeller shaft intermediate bearing bolts to frame floor = 4.0 kgm (29 ft.lb.).

5 Front Axle and Front Suspension

Different front suspensions are fitted to the models introduced during the beginning of January 2005, i.e. the model series 164. Model series 163 where fitted with upper and lower suspension arms and torsion bars. The later models retain the upper and lower suspension arms, but the torsion bars have been replaced by coil springs.

5.1. Front Axle Half – Removal and Installation – 163 Models

Fig. 5.1 shows details for the removal and installation of the front axle half. The complete front axle half can be removed as follows:

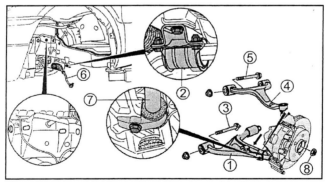

Fig. 5.1 – View of the assembled front suspension on one side. The numbers are referred to in the text.

- Jack up the front end of the vehicle and place chassis stands in position. Remove the front wheels. Make sure that the vehicle is adequately supported.
- Remove the collar nut (8) from the end of the drive shaft. The nut is tightened to a very high torque (49.0 kgm/353 ft.lb.).
- Remove the L.H. or R.H. front spring as described later on.
- Remove the panel inside the wing and remove the shock absorber as described later on.

- Locate the wheel speed sensor on the front suspension (follow the cable) and unplug the connector plug.
- Disconnect the brake hose from the brake pipe and remove the hose/pipe connection from the attachment. Close the open ends of hose and pipe in suitable manner to prevent entry of dirt. **Note the following during installation.** The union nut is tightened to 1.8 kgm (13 ft.lb.) without allowing the brake hose to twist. After installation have the steering wheel turned from left to right and the car bounced up and down whilst checking the brake hose to make sure it cannot come near other parts of the front suspension.
- Remove the nut securing the track rod ball joint (6) to the steering lever and separate the ball joint with a suitable puller. Immediately check the rubber dust cap and the ball joint for damage or excessive clearance. Fit new nuts during installation and tighten the nut to 5.5 kgm (40 ft.lb.).
- On vehicles with Xenon-type headlamps there is a link rod connected between the level controller and the lower suspension arm at the point shown by the arrow on the R.H. side. Disconnect it.
- Detach the upper transverse control arm (4), also referred to as suspension arm. Remove the bolt (5) and the nut on the other side. Note during installation: The nut is initially tightened hand-tight and must be tightened when the vehicle is back on its wheels, ready as used on the road. The nut/bolt attachment is tightened to 12.0 kgm (86.5 ft.lb.).

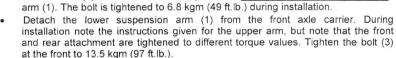

Fig. 5.2 – Removal of a front axle shaft.

- Press the front axle out of the front axle shaft flange. You will need a puller, working on the principle shown in Fig. 5.2. The extractor is bolted to the flange.
- Place a mobile jack underneath the lower suspension arm, lift it up and detach the tension bar (7) from the lower suspension arm (1). The bolt is tightened to 6.8 kgm (49 ft.lb.) during installation.
- Detach the lower suspension arm (1) from the front axle carrier. During installation note the instructions given for the upper arm, but note that the front and rear attachment are tightened to different torque values. Tighten the bolt (3) at the front to 13.5 kgm (97 ft.lb.).
- Loosen the clamped joint at the rear of the lower suspension arm and fold down the bearing shell (2) at the position shown by the pointer. New nuts must be tightened as described above for the upper suspension arm. Tighten new nuts to only 3.0 kgm (22 ft.lb.).
- All parts can now be lifted out.

Installation is carried out in reverse order. Follow the instructions given during the removal. Bleed the brake system.

5.2. Front Springs (torsion bars) – Removal and Installation

A depth gauge is required to measure the spring pre-load of the torsion bar spring before removal, as the spring pre-load must be restored during installation. Not an easy operation.
- Place the front end of the vehicle on secure chassis stands.
- The initial operations are carried out by referring to Fig. 5.3. Measure the spring pre-load of the torsion bar (1) with the depth gauge as shown on the R.H. side,

inserting the gauge into the hole of the counter plate (2). For the remaining operations we refer you to Fig. 5.4.

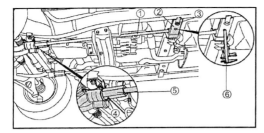

Fig. 5.3 – Details for the removal of a torsion bar spring. View from underneath the vehicle with location of some of the parts.
1   Torsion bar spring
2   Counter plate, 2 in Fig. 5.4
3   Bolt, 3 in Fig. 5.4
4   Bolt, 6 in Fig. 5.4
5   Sleeve, 5 in Fig. 5.4
6   Depth gauge

- Unscrew the bolt (3) and then release the tension of the torsion bar (1). Note that the bolt (3) must be greased during installation and the rubber bellows (9) in Fig. 5.4 must be filled with grease.

Fig. 5.4 – Installation details of a torsion bar spring. Refer to text.

- Remove the bolt (6) in Fig. 5.4 in the profile sleeve (5). In Fig. 5.3 you can see where the bolt is located, identified with (4). Slide back the sleeve (5) The bolt is tightened to 2.3 kgm (16.5 ft.lb.) during installation.

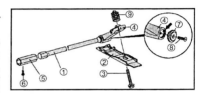

- Remove the torsion bar. To do this, remove the bolt (8) in Fig. 5.4 (tightened to 2.3 kgm/16.5 ft.lb.) and remove the end cover (7). Then remove the torsion bar (1) from the clamping lever (4). Note that the position of the torsion bar spring and the clamping lever (4) is indicated at the position shown by the arrow on the R.H. side in Fig. 5.4. Observe the marking during installation. The tooth profile must be greased.

The installation is a reversal of the removal procedure, noting the points given above.

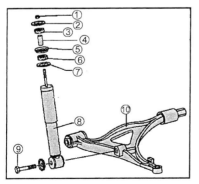

Fig. 5.5 – View of a shock absorber with the mounting details.
1   Nut
2   Mounting plate
3   Upper rubber mount
4   Spacer sleeve
5   Lower plate
6   Lower rubber mount
7   Lower mounting plate
8   Shock absorber
9   Mounting bolt
10   Lower suspension arm

5.3. Front Shock Absorbers – 163 Models

The shock absorbers are fitted between the body and the lower suspension arms. The attachment at the upper end is by means of a self-locking nut and other mounting parts, as shown in Fig. 5.5. Fig. 5.6 shows in detail the arrangement of the various items. The lower end is secured with a bolt, nut and a washer.

Fig. 5.6 – Arrangement of the various parts of the upper shock absorber mounting. The numbers refer to the parts shown in Fig. 5.5.

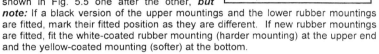

As the piston rod may rotate when the upper nut is slackened you can use an open-ended spanner to counterhold the end of the shock absorber. Also note that the vehicle must be on its wheels when the nut at the upper end is slackened and when the lower mounting bolt is tightened.

- Slacken the nut (1) in Fig. 5.5, counterholding the piston rod as described.
- Place the front end of the vehicle on chassis stands and remove the panel (liner) inside the front wing.
- Fully remove the nut and take off the parts shown in Fig. 5.5 one after the other, *but note:* If a black version of the upper mountings and the lower rubber mountings are fitted, mark their fitted position as they are different. If new rubber mountings are fitted, fit the white-coated rubber mounting (harder mounting) at the upper end and the yellow-coated mounting (softer) at the bottom.
- Detach the lower shock absorber mounting from the suspension arm and take out the unit.

The installation is a reversal of the removal procedure. The following points must be observed as you proceed:

- Place the parts over the upper end of the damper in the order shown in Fig. 5.6 and insert the shock absorber from below. Fit the bolt and washer to the lower end. Tighten the bolt to 13.5 kgm (97 ft.lb.) when the wheels are resting on the ground.
- Fit the rubber bush and the dished washer to the upper end and fit and tighten the nut to 3.0 kgm (22.lb.).

5.4. Front Axle – Removal and Installation – 163 Models

The complete front axle can be removed as described below, very unlikely, but possible. Fig. 5.7 shows a view of the complete front axle and will help you. The front end of the vehicle must be resting on secure chassis stands. **270 CDI and 400 CDI**.

- Remove the front wheels after the upper shock absorber mounting nuts has been removed (see section 5.3). The shock absorber is now removed as described.
- Locate and unplug both connectors from both wheel speed sensors.
- Disconnect the brake hose from the brake pipe. Follow the instructions in section 5.1.
- Detach the propeller shaft from the flange on the front axle transmission. Bolts are tightened to 4.0 kgm (29 ft.lb.).
- Remove both front springs (section 5.2).
- Remove the lower engine compartment panelling and detach the torsion bar (8) from the vehicle frame. Tighten the retaining brackets to 10.0 kgm (72 ft.lb.).
- Remove the upper suspension arm (3) from the vehicle frame as described during the removal of the front axle half (section 5.1). Note the instructions during installation and the tightening torque.

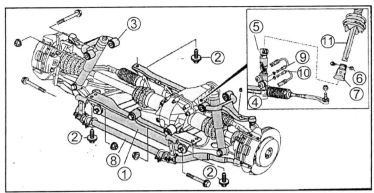

Fig. 5.7 – View of the front axle of a 163 model with details of the removal. See text.

- Detach the bracket securing the oil lines between the transmission and the oil cooler from the front axle carrier (1).
- Unclip the brake line at the rear of the front axle cross member.
- On vehicles with Xenon-type headlamps there is a link rod connected between the level controller and the lower suspension arm at the point shown in Fig. 5.1 by the arrow on the R.H. side. Disconnect it.
- Extract the fluid from the fluid reservoir for the power steering in a similar manner as shown in Fig. 2.11.
- Turn the steering wheel to the centre position and secure it in position by removing the ignition key and locking the steering.
- Detach the plug connector for the speed-sensitive power steering from the timing case (if fitted).
- Remove the nut (6) and the bolt from the steering coupling (5) and pull the lower steering shaft (11) up and out of the steering coupling. The clamping groove can be enlarged with a screwdriver to facilitate the removal. Do not damage the coupling shield (7). During installation the rack and pinion steering (4) must be set to the centre position before the steering coupling (5) is fitted. The self-locking nut (6) must be replaced and tightened to 2.6 kgm (19 ft.lb.).
- Disconnect the return pipe (10) and the high-pressure hose (9) from the steering. Close off the open ends. The connections are either by end fittings or banjo bolts. Replace the sealing rings. Banjo bolts are tightened to 3.0 kgm (22 ft.lb.), end fittings are tightened to 1.5 kgm (11 ft.lb.).
- Detach the bleeding and venting hose from the differential.
- Place a mobile jack underneath the front axle carrier (1) until under tension and remove the bolts (2) from the carrier. The bolts must be replaced. Make sure that the threads have engaged before the bolts are tightened to 20.0 kgm (144 ft.lb.).
- Slowly lower the front axle carrier on the jack, pushing all hoses away fom the carrier during the removal. The front axle carrier has guide pins which must be inserted into holes in the side member during installation.

Installation is carried out in reverse. Steering and brake systems must be bled after installation.

5.5. Torsion Bar – Removal and Installation – 163 Models

The attachment of the torsion bar is shown in Fig. 5.8. The upper attachment is marked with (A) and (B). Version (B) is fitted from August 1998 onwards. The bar can be removed and installed as follows:

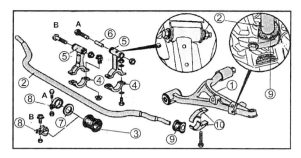

Fig. 5.8 – Details for the removal and installation of the torsion bar (163 models). See text.

- Place the front end of the vehicle on secure chassis stands and remove the bottom engine compartment panelling or the noise encapsulation (270 CDI).
- Remove the bracket (10) securing the torsion bar (2) from the lower suspension arm (1) and also remove the retaining bracket (4). The bolt for bracket (10) is tightened to 10.0 kgm (72 ft.lb.) during installation. The bolt or nut securing the bracket (4), depending on the version (A) or (B) are tightened to 5.0 kgm (36 ft.lb.).
- The torsion bar (2) can now be removed. Make a note of the installation position of the bar before you take it out.
- Pull the rubber mounts (9) and (3) off the torsion bar, again noting the fitted position.
- On models before August 1998 remove the washers (7)
- Undo and remove the bracket (8), referred to as anti-shift device. During installation centre the torsion bar before tightening the bolt and nut to 1.5 kgm (19 ft.lb.).
- Remove the retaining bracket (5) at the upper end. Note that the L.H. and R.H. bracket are not the same and must be marked accordingly. The bolt of each version (A or B) is tightened to 10.0 kgm (72 ft.lb.). The sleeve (6) must be pressed out of the retaining bracket, but note that a repair kit will contain the version fitted as of August 1998.

5.6. Upper Suspension Arms – 163 Models

A two-arm puller/extractor is required to remove the ball joint from the steering knuckle. Removal and installation are straight-forward. The front end of the vehicle must be on chassis stands, the shock absorber removed (see earlier on) and the brake line bracket removed from the steering knuckle. The suspension arm bolts/nuts must be tightened with the wheels resting on the ground.

Remove the ball joint nut and separate the ball joint from the steering knuckle. Remove the bolts and nuts securing the suspension arm to the vehicle frame and remove it. The steering knuckle should be tied to the shock absorber with a piece of wire to prevent it from tilting downwards.

Installation is carried out in reverse order. Fit the ball joint stud and tighten the nut to 5.0 kgm (36 ft.lb.). The suspension arm nuts/bolts are tightened finger-tight and tightened to 12.0 kgm (86 ft.lb.) when the wheels are resting on the ground, vehicle in "ready-to-drive" condition.

5.7. Lower Suspension Arms – 163 Models

Most of the operations have already been described in the earlier sections. To remove a suspension arm, remove the front springs and the steering knuckle (section 5.8) and detach the torsion bar from the lower control arm. Disconnect the linkage if Xenon

headlamps are fitted. Then detach the lower control arm from the front subframe. At the rear of the arm remove the clamped joint and fold down the bearing shell.
Installation is a reversal of the removal procedure. Note during installation: The nut is initially tightened hand-tight and must be tightened when the vehicle is back on its wheels, ready as used on the road. The nut/bolt attachment is tightened to 13.5 kgm (97.5 ft.lb.), clamped joint 3.0 kgm (22 ft.lb.). The torsion bar to 6.8 kgm (49 ft.lb.).

5.8. Steering Knuckle – 163 Models

With the vehicle on secure chassis stands remove the front wheel. Slacken the collar nut securing the axle drive shaft to the steering knuckle.
Follow the cable connections and unclip the cables for the wheel speed sensor and the brake pad wear indicator from the guides. The speed sensor bracket must be removed from the steering knuckle. Then proceed as follows:

- Remove the brake disc as described in section "Brake System".
- Remove the nut securing the track rod ball joint to the steering lever and separate the ball joint with a suitable puller. The nut is tightened to 5.5 kgm (40 ft.lb.) during installation.
- Also with a suitable puller separate the upper ball joint from the steering knuckle after removal of the nut (5.0 kgm/36 ft.lb.) and the lower ball joint after removal of the nut (8.5 kgm/61 ft.lb.). Note the difference in the tightening torques. Attention: The steering knuckle can fall down after removal of the ball joint.
- Remove the steering knuckle towards the front.

Installation is a reversal. Check the upper and lower ball joints for wear and the rubber caps for damaged before refitting the parts. The axle shaft nut is tightened to 49.0 kgm (353 ft.lb.).

5.9. Front Struts – Removal and Installation – 164 Models

The removal of any part of the front suspension of 164 models on models with all-round level control system is not possible under DIY conditions as the AIRmatic system must be drained and re-charged with special equipment. In general the removal and installation is a complicated operation but can be carried out on models without level control system. Some items mentioned in the description are only fitted to models with level control system – ignore them. Take care to follow the tightening torques for the specified nuts and bolts – can be confusing.

- Place the front end of the vehicle on secure chassis stands and remove the wheel on the side in question.
- At the upper end of the spring strut (damper) remove the three nuts securing the strut to the body. The nut are tightened in three stages during installation. First tighten to 3.0 kgm (22 ft.lb.), then slacken them by half a turn and then tighten to 2.7 kgm (19.5 ft.lb.).
- Remove the front section of the wing panel (liner) on the inside of the front wing in question.
- Cut a cable tie on the steering knuckle. Must be replaced. Next to the cable tie you will find the brake hose bracket. Remove it to free the brake hose. Do not damage the brake hose. Near the lower end of the strut there is another cable tie (neat the drive shaft connection) which must also be cut and removed (again replace).
- Locate and unscrew a nut from the tie rod from the steering knuckle and take off the rod. Tighten the nut to 4.5 kgm (32.5 ft.lb.) and then a further quarter of a turn.
- At the upper end of the spring strut remove a nut and disconnect the connecting link from the spring strut. The nut is tightened to 20.0 kgm (144 ft.lb.).

- At the lower end of the spring strut remove a nut and remove the spring strut from the suspension arm. This nut is tightened to 26.5 kgm (191 ft.lb.).
- disconnect the connecting link from the spring strut. The nut is tightened to 20.0 kgm (144 ft.lb.).
- At the upper end of the spring strut remove the nut securing the upper control arm to the steering knuckle and separate the ball joint with a suitable puller. The ball joint nut is tightened to 2.0 kgm (14.5 ft.lb.) and from the final position a further quarter of a turn. Check the ball joint and rubber cap before installation-
- Pull the suspension arm downwards until the front suspension strut can be removed.

Installation is carried out in reverse order, but note the different tightening torques. If parts have been replaced have the front wheel alignment checked.

Replacing the Coil Spring and/or Spring Strut

A spring compressor is necessary to remove the front springs. As the special compressor used in a workshop may not be available you can use a standard compressor, the claws of which are placed over three to four of the coils. Make sure the compressor has adequate strength for the springs. Remove a spring as follows, noting that the spring strut must be removed.

- Clamp the suspension strut into a vice and place the spring compressor over the spring coils until the upper end lower ends are free of their spring seats.
- At the end of the spring strut upper end remove a cap and remove the nut below to remove the shock absorber. The piston rod will rotate and must be prevented from rotating.
- Remove the parts from the top end of the strut. These are the top spring retainer, the upper spring seat, the stop damper, the rubber bellows and the clamped coil spring. Make a note how each part is fitted. The spring clamp can remain in position if the same spring/strut is to be fitted.
- Replace any components with oil contamination, cracks or deformation.

Release the spring compressor slowly, checking that the spring is fitted properly at the upper end lower ends and that all parts are fitted in their original order before tightening the piston rod nut to 3.0 kgm (22 ft.lb.).

The front wheel alignment and the headlamp adjustment must be checked after the completed installation.

5.10. Suspension Arms – Removal and Installation – 164 Models

L.H. upper suspension arm

Bolts and nuts must only be tightened when the vehicle is resting on its wheels, ready to drive. Note that slightly different instructions apply to the L.H. and R.H. arms. First remove the engine cover in the centre of the engine.

- Remove the air filter housing.
- Remove the nut securing the ball joint to the upper suspension arm and separate the joint with a suitable ball joint puller. The nut is tightened to 2.0 kgm (14.5 ft.lb.) and from the final position a further quarter of a turn.
- Remove a bolt and detach the L.H. front level sensor bracket from the suspension arm (only with level control system).
- Locate and remove two nuts and two bolts from the front end and detach the suspension arm from the front end of the vehicle. Bolts and nuts are tightened to 6.1 kgm (44 ft.lb.).

Install in reverse order.

R.H. upper suspension arm

Removal is carried out as described above, but the air plenum chamber must be removed instead of the air cleaner housing. The same tightening torques apply.

Lower suspension arms

Bolts and nuts must only be tightened when the vehicle is resting on its wheels, ready to drive. Self-locking nuts and bolts must be replaced.

- Place the front end of the vehicle on secure chassis stands and remove the wheel.
- Detach the bottom engine compartment panelling or the sound proofing (CDI engine).
- Remove the two bolts securing the stabiliser bar (anti-roll bar) brackets on each side and move the bar downwards. Careful – the stabiliser bar is under tension. The bracket bolts are tightened to 5.0 kgm (26 ft.lb.).
- Mark the installation position of the rear bearing bracket of the lower suspension arm in relation to the front axle carrier and remove the mounting bolts at both sides to detach the suspension arm from the front axle carrier. If new parts are fitted transfer the marks to the new parts to ensure that the suspension arm is fitted to its original position. The bolts are tightened to 25 kgm (180 ft.lb.).
- Remove the bolt and nut securing the suspension arm to the front axle carrier. A spacer washer is fitted underneath the bolt head and must be fitted to the inside. Note the direction of fitting before removal. The bolt/nut is tightened to 2.7 kgm (199.5 ft.lb.).
- Remove the bolt securing the suspension strut to the suspension arm, located immediately next to the drive shaft bellow. Tighten this bolt to 26.5 kgm (191 ft.lb.).
- Remove the ball joint stud nut at the outside of the suspension arm and separate the ball joint and detach the suspension arm from the steering knuckle. The nut is tightened to 23.0 kgm (165.5 ft.lb.).

The installation is carried out in reverse order. Study the tightening torques given above to avoid mistakes. Insert the spacer washer the correct way round to the inside the suspension arm. The wheel alignment must be checked if parts have been replaced (workshop operation).

5.11. Stabiliser Bar – Removal and Installation – 164 Models

The stabiliser bar is fitted across the front of the vehicle, attached with clamps to the front axle carrier and connected with link rods to the suspension (shock absorber) struts. The front end of the vehicle must be supported on secure chassis stands. Nuts and bolts must be tightened when the vehicle is on its wheels.

- Detach the lower engine compartment panelling or the noise encapsulation (CDI models).
- Remove the nuts securing the link rods to the stabiliser bar. If the link rods must be removed detach them from the suspension struts. Nuts are tightened to 20 kgm (144 ft.lb.) in both cases.
- On each side of the bar remove the mounting clamp bolts and remove the clamps. The stabiliser bar is pre-loaded. Take care when the clamps are removed. The bolts are tightened to 11 kgm (79 ft.lb.).
- The stabiliser is also fitted with a so-called torsional bearing on each end, also retained with mountings clamps. If the stabiliser bar is to be replaced remove the clamp bolts and take out the bearing after markings its fitted position. The bolts are tightened in this case to 3.5 kgm (25 ft.lb.).

The installation is carried out in reverse order, noting the following points and order of tightening:
- If the torsional bearing has been replaced transfer the previously made marks to the new stabiliser bar. Do not tighten the nuts securing the mounting clamps.
- Position the stabiliser bar on the front axle carrier, fit the retaining clamps and insert the bolts at both ends. The angled ends of the bar must face downwards, the bar must be centred. Do not tighten the mounting clamp bolts at this stage.
- Fit the link rods to the stabiliser bar and the front struts. Again do not tighten the nuts.
- Check the correct position of the bar and the torsional bearing (if removed) and tighten all bolts and nuts to the torques given during the removal, in the order: torsional bearing clamps, stabiliser bar retaining clamps, link rod nuts.

5.11. Front Axle Shafts/Front Axle Drive – Removal and Installation

163 Models
- Place the front end of the vehicle on secure chassis stands and remove the front wheel. Remove the collared nut (1) in Fig. 5.9. A helper should apply the brake pedal.

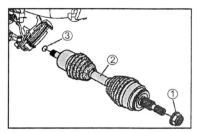

Fig. 5.9 – Removal of a front drive shaft. 163 model shown.

- Remove the front brake caliper without disconnecting the brake hose. Suspend the caliper with a piece of wire to the front suspension.
- Disconnect the track rod ball joint from the steering knuckle, using a suitable puller. In the same manner disconnect the upper suspension arm from the steering knuckle.
- Press the front axle shaft (2) out of the front axle shaft flange as already shown in Fig. 5.2. Push the steering knuckle to one side and attach it with wire.
- Lever the axle shaft out of the front axle drive gear without damaging the protective shield and withdraw the shaft.

Installation is carried out in reverse order. The slot in the retaining circlip (3) must face downwards when the shaft is inserted. Tighten the upper suspension arm ball joint nut to 5.0 kgm (36 ft.lb.), the track rod ball joint nut to 5.5 kgm (40 ft.lb.) and the axle shaft nut to 49 kgm (353 ft.lb.).

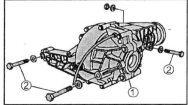

Fig. 5.10 – Front axle drive – 163 models.

Removal of front axle drive – 163 models

Fig. 5.10 shows the attachment of the front axle drive case on these models. Remove the two axle shafts as described above, disconnect the propeller shaft from the axle drive flange and drain the axle case oil. Disconnect a vent hose and remove the bolts, nuts and washers (2), as applicable and remove the axle case (1). Support the assembly on a mobile jack to lower it.

Installation is carried out in reverse order. Tighten the axle bolts to 13.5 kgm (97 ft.lb.) and the propeller shaft connection to 4.0 kgm (29 ft.lb.).

164 Models

The instructions apply to the R.H. axle shaft as the L.H. shaft remains attached to the L.H. front axle shaft flange. The front axle drive gear is removed to free the L.H. shaft. Proceed as follows:

- Place the front end of the vehicle on secure chassis stands and remove the front wheel. Remove the collared nut (1) in Fig. 5.9. A helper should apply the brake pedal.
- Remove the bottom engine compartment panelling or the sound-proofing (CDI models).
- Locate the electrical cables on the spring strut and free them from their brackets. Near the brake hose bracket cut a cable tie (replace) and remove the brake hose from the brake hose bracket.
- Press the front axle shaft out of the front axle shaft flange as already shown in Fig. 5.2. Push the steering knuckle to one side and attach it with wire.
- Disconnect the R.H. track rod ball joint from the steering knuckle, using a suitable puller. In the same manner disconnect the R.H. upper suspension arm from the steering knuckle. Move the steering knuckle to one side to create more space. Track rod ball joint nut = 4.5 kgm (32.5 ft.lb.) + 90°, upper suspension arm ball joint nut = 2.0 kgm (14.5 ft.lb.) + 90°.
- Pull the R.H. shaft out of the front axle drive gear and remove. Some oil may run out.

Remove the L.H. drive shaft as follows:

- Remove the brake hose from the brake hose bracket on the L.H. side and near the brake hose cut a cable tie.
- Disconnect the L.H. track rod ball joint from the steering knuckle, using a suitable puller. In the same manner disconnect the L.H. upper suspension arm from the steering knuckle. Move the steering knuckle to one side to create more space. Tightening torques are the same as given for the R.H. assemblies given above.
- Pull the L:H. axle shaft out of the front axle drive gear. The shaft remains attached to the axle shaft flange.
- Mark the installation position of the propeller shaft flange and the front axle drive flange in suitable manner and detach the propeller shaft flange from the axle case.
- Detach the hose from the front axle case (protect the hose end against entry of dirt).
- Place a mobile jack with a suitable support plate underneath the front axle case and remove the mounting bolts securing the case to the L.H. front axle carrier and the R.H. front axle carrier. The axle case can now be lowered on the jack. Note the tightening torques of the front axle bolts: Bolts on the L.H. side = 9.3 kgm (67 ft.lb.), bolts on the R.H. side = 5.0 kgm (36 ft.lb.).
- Remove the L.H. shaft from the axle shaft flange.

Installation is a reversal of the removal procedure, noting the points given above. The axle shaft nuts are tightened to 52 kgm (374 ft.lb.) on these models.

5.12. Oil Change in Front Axle

The front axle has a capacity of 1.2 litres. To remove the oil drain plug and the oil level/oil filler plug an Allen key of 14 mm A/F is required. Hypoid oil SAE 90 is used to fill the axle. Fig. 5.11 shows the location of the filler and oil drain plugs (163 model shown). Change the oil as follows:

- Drive the vehicle a short distance to warm up the oil.

Fig. 5.11 – Location of the oil filler plug (1) and the drain plug (2).

- Place a suitable container underneath the axle and remove the oil drain plug at the bottom of the axle. The oil level/filler plug can be removed from the axle cover to speed up the draining of the oil.
- Wait until the oil has drained, clean the drain plug and refit the plug to the axle and tighten it.
- Fill the axle housing with the oil and amount given above until the oil level can be seen at the lower edge of the filler hole. Clean the plug, fit it and tighten it. Both plugs are tightened to 5.0 kgm (36 ft.lb.).

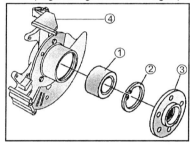

Fig. 5.12 – Wheel bearing components on one side.
1   Wheel bearing
2   Bearing circlip
3   Axle drive flange
4   Steering knuckle

5.13. Wheel Bearings

We strongly recommend to have the wheel bearings replaced in a workshop. The steering knuckle can be removed as described earlier on and taken to the dealer to have the bearings replaced. If you want to attempt the replacement, with the steering knuckle removed, remove the circlip on the outside of the knuckle and replace the double-row angular wheel bearing under a press. The workshop has, however, a special tool set to replace the bearing. Fig. 5.12 shows the fitting of a bearing.

5.14   Front Suspension/Axle – Tightening Torques

The main tightening torques are given for the 163 models in kgm. Multiply by "7.2" to obtain "ft.lb.". The values in brackets apply to the 164 models, if applicable. Most tightening torques are given during removal/installation of the component parts. Note the differences, avoid mistakes.

Nuts/bolts, upper suspension arms to front axle carrier (163) ....12.0 kgm
Nuts/bolts, upper suspension arms to front axle carrier (164) ....6.1 kgm
Nuts/bolts, lower suspension arms at front to front axle carrier..13.5 kgm
Nut, upper suspension arm ball joints to steering knuckle (163) ....5.0 kgm
Nut, upper suspension arm ball joints to steering knuckle (164) ....2.0 kgm + 90°
Bolts, lower suspension arms at front to front axle carrier...3.0 kgm
Nuts, lower suspension arms at front to steering knuckle (164): ....23.0 kgm
Nut, lower suspension arms at front to front axle carrier (164):...27.0 kgm
Nut, lower suspension arms at rear to front axle carrier (164):..25.0 kgm
Bolt, torsion bar to control arm: ....6.8 kgm
Nut, front axle shaft to axle shaft flange (163): ....49.0 kgm (164 = 52.0 kgm)
Nut, track rod ball joint to steering knuckle (163):................................. 5.5 kgm (4.5 kgm+90° - 164)

Brake hose to brake pipe: ....1.8 kgm
Bolt, front axle case to front axle carrier:...13.5 kgm
Oil filler plug/oil drain plug, front axle case:...5.0 kgm
Propeller shaft flange to front axle case flange:..4.0 kgm
Stabiliser bar clamp bracket to front axle carrier (163): ....10.0 kgm
Stabiliser bar to suspension arm (163): ....6.8 kgm
Stabiliser bar retaining bracket to bar (163):...5.0 kgm
Stabiliser bar clamp (bolt) to bar (163):...1.8 kgm
Stabiliser bar clamp bracket to front axle carrier (164): ....11.0 kgm
Torsion bearing clamp bracket (164): ....3.5 kgm
Connecting rods to shock absorber and torsion bar (164):...20.0 kgm
Shock absorber to suspension arm (164) ....26.5 kgm
Shock absorber to front end (164).....................3.0 kgm, slacken, ½ a turn and tighten to 27.0 kgm

6   Rear Axle and Rear Suspension

The rear suspension is fitted with coil springs, upper and lower suspension (control) arms, a stabiliser bar and telescopic shock absorbers. Although not identical, the suspensions in series 163 and 164 are in general of similar construction. The following information are in general based on the earlier 163 models. 6.1 shows a view of the assembled rear suspension on one side. A similar arrangement is used on the 164 vehicles.

6.0.   Spring Struts – Removal and Installation

The shock absorbers act as rebound stop for the rear wheels. The operations can be carried out with the help of Figs. 6.1 and 6.2. The rear end of the vehicle must be on secure chassis stands and the wheels removed. Proceed as follows:

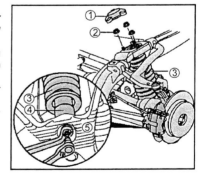

Fig. 6.1 – View of the assembled rear suspension on one side with details of the removal. See text. See also Fig. 6.2.

- Pull off the cover (1) in Fig. 6.1. During installation make sure it is fitted in correct position.
- Remove the nuts (2) from the upper spring strut mounting (nuts 13 in Fig. 6.2). Tighten the nuts equally to 2.0 kgm (14.5 ft.lb.) during installation.
- Remove the lower spring strut mounting nut (5) from the lower suspension arm. Fig. 6.2 shows details of the attachment. This is nut (14) in Fig. 6.2. The threaded end of the strut must be prevented from rotating by inserting an Allen key is shown in the circle of Fig. 6.1. The nut is tightened to 8.5 kgm (61 ft.lb.).
- Place a mobile jack underneath the lower suspension arm and lift up the arm until under tension, i.e. the drive shaft must be in horizontal position. Refer to Fig. 6.2 to proceed.
- Remove the connecting rod (1) between the lower suspension arm (2) and the torsion bar, i.e. stabiliser bar (3) by removing the bearing with the nut (8). The bearing (4), the bearing (5), the distance sleeve (6) and the bearing (7) can be removed. Tighten the nut (8) to 2.8 kgm (20 ft.lb).

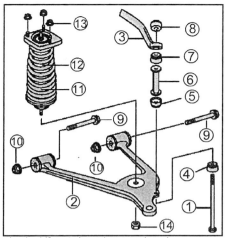

Fig. 6.2 – Removal of a rear spring strut. See text.

- Detach the lower control arm (2) from the rear axle carrier. Bolts (9) and nuts (10) must be removed. Tighten to 13.5 kgm (97 ft.lb.).
- Lower the control arm on the jack, pull it out of the guide and swing it downwards. The suspension strut is now pulled upwards until free of the suspension arm. If necessary use a plastic or rubber mallet and knock the strut (12) out the suspension arm. The strut is removed together with the coil spring (11).

Installation is a reversal of the removal procedure, noting the tightening torques given above. The headlamp adjustment must be checked if parts have been replaced.

Note: The removal of the rear springs of a 164 models is described in Section 6.2. It is not combined with the spring strut.

6.1. Shock Absorbers – Removal and Installation

The shock absorbers of a 163 model is removed after the spring strut has been taken out as described in the last section. The shock absorber of a 164 model is not a part of the spring strut, i.e. the removal is easier, but access is more difficult (see below) and it may be better to have the removal and installation carried out in a workshop.

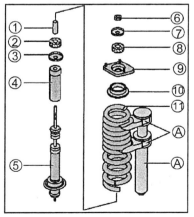

Fig. 6.3 – Details for the removal and installation of a shock absorber together with the coil spring (163). The spring compressor is identified with (A).
1   Sleeve
2   Upper spring mount
3   Metal plate
4   Spacer sleeve
5   Shock absorber
6   Nut, 3.0 kgm
7   Metal plate
8   Rubber mounting
9   Support bearing
10 Spring seat
11 Coil spring

To remove the shock absorber compress the coil spring as described for the front coil springs (refer to page 125) and remove the nut (6) in Fig. 6.3. Remove the parts shown in the illustration and remove the spring together with the compression tool, if the same coil spring is fitted.

The installation is a reversal of the removal procedure. Tighten the self-locking nut at the upper end to 3.0 kgm (22 ft.lb.).

164 Models

Although the removal and installation of the shock absorber is fairly easy, the preliminary operations are not. The trim panel inside the rear compartment must be removed. Underneath there is a sound-deadening mat which must be cut in the area of the upper shock absorber mounting, i.e. you will have to know where to cut. The wing liner inside the rear wing must also be removed. Therefore a workshop operation. Otherwise the shock absorber is attached at the upper end by a self-locking nut (2.1 kgm/15 ft.lb.) and at the lower end with a nut to the suspension arm (26.5 kgm (19 ft.lb.). The suspension arm must be lifted until the nuts are removed and then lowered until the shock absorber can be compressed and taken out.

6.2. Rear Springs – Removal and Installation

A rear spring of a 163 model is removed together with the spring strut as described above, i.e. the spring must be compressed. As described on page 125. Fig. 6.3 shows details of the items to be removed. If a new spring is fitted, quote the model, engine, model year, etc. to make sure the correct spring is fitted.

A rear spring of a 164 model can be removed with the wheel removed and the rear end of the vehicle on secure chassis stands. Each spring is fitted with various parts, i.e. a rubber insert, the upper spring plate, two spacers, a plastic ring and a rubber boot and all parts should be marked to ensure correct installation.

The removal of a spring requires, as for the front springs, a spring compressor or suitable compressor hooks. Compress the spring in a suitable manner until it is free of the upper and lower spring seats and remove it.

Rear springs must always be replaced in pairs. Note during installation: The lower cup has been modified. If the spring has been removed always fit a new cup, which will, however, have a different shape. The one you receive will have a tap which must engage into the groove of the lower suspension arm. The upper spring cup and the rubber insert must be checked for signs of damage and replaced if necessary.

Installation is carried out in reverse order. When releasing the spring compressor, observe the correct engagement of the spring into its upper and lower seats.

6.3. Stabiliser Bar – Removal and Installation

The stabiliser bar (1) in Fig. 6.4, shown on a 163 model, is fitted by means of a connecting link (5) between the lower suspension arm (11) and the frame floor. Removal and installation can be carried out by referring to the illustration.

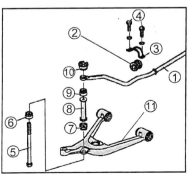

Fig. 6.4 – Details of the stabiliser bar installation.
1 Torsion bar
2 Rubber mount
3 Retaining clamp
4 Mounting bolts, 2.8 kgm
5 Link rod
6 Bearing
7 Bearing
8 Spacer sleeve
9 Bearing
10 Bearing with nut, 2.1 kgm
11 Suspension arm

All types have a similar arrangement. During removal (rear end of vehicle on secure chassis stands) make a note of the order of part installation. The securing nut (10) is at the same time a rubber bearing and it

tightened to 2.1 kgm (15 ft.lb.). The two bolts (4), on each side of the bar, are tightened to 2.8 kgm (20 ft.lb.) when tightened to the rear axle carrier.
The removal of the stabiliser (torsion) bar of a 164 model is carried out in a similar manner, but different tightening torques apply. The torsion bar retaining clamp bolts are tightened to 11.0 kgm (79 ft.lb.), and the nuts securing the link rods to the suspension arms (track control arms) and to the ends of the torsion bar are tightened to 18.0 kgm (130 ft.lb.).

6.4. Rear Suspension Struts/Arms

6.4.0. UPPER WISHBONES – REMOVAL AND INSTALLATION

The operations described apply to the model series 163. The rear end of the vehicle must be resting on secure chassis stands and the wheels removed. Fig. 6.5 shows some details of the removal operations. (5) indicates where the lower wishbone is connected.

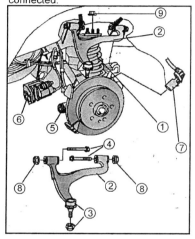

Fig. 6.5 – Details for the removal of an upper wishbone, shown on a 163 model. See text.

• Remove the L.H. or R.H. wheel speed sensor (7).

• Remove the brake caliper (6) and suspend it with a piece of wire to the rear suspension. Must not hang down on the brake hose.

• Remove the spring strut (1) from the longitudinal frame member after unscrewing the nuts (9) – 2.0 kgm (14.5 ft.lb.).

• Remove the nut securing the ball joint (3) to the wheel carrier and separate the joint with a suitable ball joint puller. The nut is tightened to 5.0 kgm (36 ft.lb.) during installation.

• Jack up the rear axle until the rear axle shaft is in horizontal position and remove the nuts (8) securing the upper suspension arm (2) to the frame member. The heads of the mounting bolts (4) must be marked in relation to the frame member (arrows in Fig. 6.5).

• Remove the mounting bolts (4). When removing the bolt you will have to press down the mounting of the lower wishbone to guide the bolts passed the top of the spring strut. Bolts/nuts are tightened to 12.0 kgm (86.5 ft.lb.) with the axle shaft in horizontal position.

Installation is carried out in reverse order. The rubber mounts of the suspension arm (wishbone) can be replaced, but we recommend to consult a workshop (dealer). Note the tightening torques.

6.4.1. LOWER WISHBONES – REMOVAL AND INSTALLATION

The operations described apply to the model series 163. The rear end of the vehicle must be resting on secure chassis stands and the wheels removed. Fig. 6.6 shows some details of the removal operations. The illustration shows two versions, i.e. the earlier version, marked (A) and the later version, marked (B). Note that washers (10) are fitted to the early version. If a new arm is fitted, quote the vehicle type, the engine type and the model year when purchasing the arm.

133

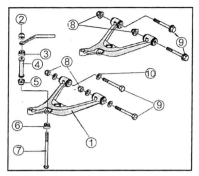

Fig. 6.6 – Details for the removal of a lower wishbone, shown on a 163 model. See text.

- Remove the spring strut from the lower wishbone (1). The nut is tightened to 8.5 kgm (61 ft.lb.) during installation.
- Remove the bearing with the nut (2) and the bolt (7), i.e. the connecting link, from the lower wishbone (1) after the axle assembly has been jacked up to bring the axle shaft to a horizontal position. Otherwise the torsion bar bearings will be damaged. Remove the rubber bearing (3) and (5).
- Detach the lower wishbone (1) from the rear axle carrier by removing the nuts (8) and bolts (9), axle shaft still in horizontal position.
- Swivel the lower wishbone on the rear axle carrier downwards.
- Remove the nut securing the ball joint to the lower wishbone. The ball joint stud can be held with a Tory-head insert of suitable size. The nut is tightened to 12.5 kgm (90 ft.lb.) during installation. The wishbone can now be removed.

Installation is carried out in reverse order. The rubber mounts of the suspension arm (wishbone) can be replaced, but we recommend to consult a workshop (dealer). Note the tightening torques.

6.5. Rear Suspension – 164 Models

The rear suspension of these models consists of the upper and lower suspension arms, the spring struts, coil springs, torsion (stabiliser) bar and various rods and struts. Removal and installation of some of the items is described below. The terminology is based on the manufacturer.

Radius Rod

This is the strut (1) in Fig. 6.7 in the L.H. view, also referred to as "tension arm". The strut is fitted between the rear axle carrier and the wheel carrier and is secured with a nut and a bolt on each end. The rear of the vehicle must be on secure chassis stands or a garage lift and the wheel removed. A mobile jack must be placed underneath the suspension ball joint of the lower suspension arm to retain the suspension in position when the rod is removed.

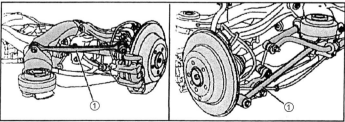

Fig. 6.7 – The radius rod (1), also tension arm and the track rod (1) on the R.H. side (164 model).

Remove the bolt and self-locking nut on one end and the self-locking nut, bolt and a washer on the opposite end and take out the rod. The rubber mountings can be replaced (workshop).

During installation insert the bolt and screw on a new nut and with the washer on one side. On the side without the washer the bolt head must face into the direction of travel, on the side with washer into the direction opposite the direction of travel. Both nuts must be tightened hand-tight. Lift the rear suspension on the jack until it is in its normal position and tighten both bolt/nut combinations to 11.0 kgm (77 ft.lb.). Refit the wheel and lower the vehicle to the ground.

Track Rod
This is the strut (1) in Fig. 6.7 in the R.H. view. The track rod, also referred to as tie rod, is fitted between the rear axle carrier and the wheel carrier. The rod is attached with a bolt and nut on each end. To remove the rod, first remove the torsion bar clamp from the rear axle carrier (11.0 kgm/77 ft.lb.). The head of the bolt on the inside must be marked with a coloured pencil in relation to an eccentric disc to ensure installation in the original position.
Remove the bolt and nut on the other end (a washer is used) and remove the rod. The rubber mountings can be replaced (workshop).
Removal and installation of the bolts is identical as described for the radius rod, but the tightening torques are different. The self-locking nut (new) on the rear axle carrier is tightened to 9.3 kgm (67 ft.lb.), the nut of the wheel carrier to 11.0 kgm (77 ft.lb.). Make sure that the marks made in bolt head and eccentric disc on one side are aligned before bolt and nut are tightened.

Camber Strut
The camber strut is inserted between the rear axle carrier and the wheel carrier. The removal is carried out in the same manner as described for the radius rod, but a wiring harness bracket must be removed from the strut and pulled slightly forward. Again the strut is attached on one side with an eccentric disc and disc and bolt head must be marked before removal.
Note the different tightening torques. The self-locking nut (new) on the rear axle carrier is tightened to 9.3 kgm (67 ft.lb.), the nut of the wheel carrier to 11.0 kgm (77 ft.lb.). Make sure that the marks made in bolt head and eccentric disc on one side are aligned before bolt and nut are tightened.

6.6. Rear Axle Drive Shafts
Remove as follows, noting the different operations on the two versions:

163 Models
- Slacken the wheel bolts, jack up the rear end of the vehicle and remove the large axle shaft nut. A helper must depress the brake pedal. A new nut must always be fitted and is tightened to 49 kgm (353 ft.lb.) after installation of the shaft.
- Locate the wheel speed sensor on the wheel carrier (upper end) and remove the bracket securing bolt from the from the sensor and remove the sensor. The bolt is tightened to 1.0 kgm (7.2 ft.lb.).
- Remove the upper suspension arm ball joint nut from the wheel carrier and separate the ball joint, using a suitable puller. The nut is tightened to 5.0 kgm (36 ft.lb.) during installation. In the same manner disconnect the ball joint of the track rod joint (at the lower end, below the stabiliser bar) out of the wheel carrier. This nut is tightened to 5.5 kgm (40 ft.lb.) during installation.
- Using a puller, of the type shown in Fig. 5.2 and press the rear axle shaft out of the axle shaft flange. The rear axle shaft must be pressed as far as it will go towards the rear axle centre and swing the wheel carrier towards the outside.
- The axle shaft must now be pressed out of the rear axle centre assembly. A tyre lever is required. Apply the lever behind the axle shaft joint and press it away from

the rear axle centre. Take care not to damage the rubber boot. The retaining snap ring at the end of the shaft must be removed and replaced.
The installation is a reversal of the removal procedure. Arrange the new retaining snap ring with the opening at the bottom. Note the tightening torques given above.

164 Models
The removal and installation is carried out in a similar manner as described above, with the difference that the tie rod (track rod), the camber strut and the torque strut must be detached from the wheel carrier. Removal and installation details are given earlier on in section 6.5 together with the tightening torques. The brake cable must be unclipped from the bracket on the rear axle carrier and another brake cable bracket from the camber strut. Different is the tightening torque of the collar nut at the end of the drive shaft (must be replaced), as in this case it is tightened to 52 kgm (375 ft.lb.).

6.7. Wheel Bearings

We strongly recommend to have the wheel bearings replaced in a workshop. The wheel carrier can be removed as described earlier on and taken to the dealer to have the bearings replaced. If you want to attempt the replacement, remove the circlip on the outside of the wheel carrier and replace the double-row angular wheel bearing under a press. The workshop has, however, a special tool set to replace the bearing. Fig. 5.12 shows the fitting of a bearing in the case of a front axle shaft. The same arrangement will be found on the rear axle shafts. The brake disc must be removed.

6.8. Oil Change in Rear Axle

The rear axle has a capacity of 1.65 litres in the case of a 163 model. The capacity in the case of a 164 model is 1.1 litres if no differential lock is fitted or 1.8 litres if a differential lock is fitted. To remove the oil drain plug and the oil level/oil filler plug an Allen key of 14 mm A/F is required. Hypoid oil SAE 90 is used to fill the axle. Fig. 6.8 shows the location of the filler and oil drain plugs (163 model shown). To check the oil level unscrew the oil filler plug and check that the oil reaches the bottom edge of the filler hole. Change the oil as follows:

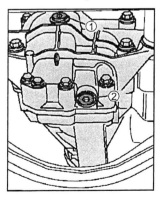

Fig. 6.8 – Location of the oil filler plug (1) and the drain plug (2) in the rear axle (163 shown).

• Drive the vehicle a short distance to warm up the oil.

• Place a suitable container underneath the axle and remove the oil drain plug (2) at the bottom of the axle. The oil level/filler plug (1) can be removed from the axle cover to speed up the draining of the oil.

• Wait until the oil has drained, clean the drain plug and refit the plug to the axle and tighten it.

• Fill the axle housing with the oil and amount given above until the oil level can be seen at the lower edge of the filler hole. Clean the plug, fit it and tighten it. Both plugs are tightened to 5.0 kgm (36 ft.lb.).

6.9. Rear Wheel Alignment

The checking and adjusting of the rear wheel alignment requires the use of special equipment and special wrenches and we recommend to have the alignment checked in a workshop. If you have removed parts of the suspension which will alter the alignment and have followed the advise to mark the eccentric bolts and washers there will be no problems to drive the vehicle to the wheel alignment centre to have the settings checked.

6.10. Rear Axle/Suspension – Tightening Torques

The main tightening torques are given in kgm. Multiply by "7.2" to obtain "ft.lb.". Most tightening torques are given during removal/installation of the component parts. Note the differences, avoid mistakes.

163 Models
Nut, link rods to torsion bar: ....2.2. kgm
Bolt, torsion bar rubber mounts/mounting clamps to rear axle carrier:................................2.8. kgm
Nut, shock absorber to lower suspension: ....8.5 kgm
Nut, shock absorber to frame side member: ....2.0 kgm
Nut, shock absorber to rear spring (piston rod): ....3.0 kgm
Nut, lower suspension arm to rear axle carrier: ....13.5 kgm
Nut, lower suspension arm ball joint stud to suspension arm:...12.5 kgm
Nut, upper suspension arm to frame:...12.0 kgm
Nut, upper suspension arm ball joints to wheel carrier: ....5.0 kgm
Nut, track rod ball joint to wheel carrier: ....5.5 kgm
Nut, wheel speed sensor to wheel carrier: ....1.0 kgm
Collar nut, axle shaft to axle shaft flange: ....49.0 kgm
Oil filler and drain plugs:..5.0 kgm

164 Models
Nut, shock absorber to spring control arm: ....26.5 kgm
Nut, shock absorber to frame floor:..2.1 kgm
Bolt, torsion bar rubber mounts/mounting clamps to rear axle carrier:..............................11.0. kgm
Nut, tie rod to rear axle carrier:...9.3 kgm
Nut, linkage rod to rear axle carrier and torsion bar:..18.0 kgm
Nut, tie rod (tension arm) to rear axle carrier and wheel carrier: ....11.0 kgm
Nut, camber strut to rear axle carrier: ....9.3 kgm
Nut, camber strut to wheel carrier: ....11.0 kgm
Collar nut, axle shaft to axle shaft flange: ....52.0 kgm
Oil filler and drain plugs:...5.0 kgm

7 Steering

7.0. Technical Data
Type:..Rack and pinion with power assistance
Filling capacity of steering system: ....1.2 litre (all models)
Fluid type: ....As for automatic transmissions

7.1. Checks on the Steering

Checking the Steering Play
Excessive play in the steering can be adjusted, but this should be left to a Mercedes dealer who has the necessary special tools. The steering can, however, checked as follows:
- Place the front wheels in the straight-ahead position and reach through the open window and turn the steering wheel slowly to and fro.
- The front wheels must move immediately as soon as you move the steering wheel.

- If there is no play in the straight-ahead position but the steering wheel is more difficult to move as you rotate the steering wheel further you can assume that the steering gear is worn and must be replaced.

Checking the track rod ball joints for excessive play
With the wheel fitted grip the track rod ball joint and move it up and down with a considerable force.
A worn track rod ball joint can be recognised by excessive "up and down" movement. If this exceeds 2 mm, replace the ball joint.

Checking the steering rubber gaiters
Check the rubber gaiter over its entire length and circumference for cuts or similar damage. Also check that the gaiters are securely fastened at both ends. Track rods with worn ball joints or damaged rubber gaiters must be replaced as described earlier on.

7.2. Steering Repairs

7.2.0. REMOVAL AND INSTALATION

The removal and installation of the steering is a complicated operation, as amongst other operations the front axle drive gear must be removed (all models). As it will be very rare to remove the steering, we recommend that the work is carried out in a workshop. A brief description of the removal follows below.
The following precautions must be followed if any work on the steering system is necessary:

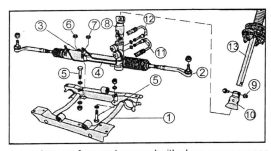

Fig. 7.1 – Details for the removal and installation of the power steering (163).

- All operations must be carried out under the cleanest of conditions.
- After disconnecting any pipes or hoses from the steering system clean the connecting points immediately. All removed parts must be placed onto a clean surface and covered with clean paper or rags.
- Never use fluffy rags to clean any parts of the steering system.
- If fitting new parts take them out of the packing just before they are fitted. Only fit original parts.
- Never re-use fluid drained from the steering system.

The steering can be removed as follows, applicable to all 163 model. Front of vehicle on secure chassis stands, front wheels removed. Fig. 7.1 shows details of a 163 model. Remove the front axle gear as described earlier on and then proceed:

- On a 163 model with speed-sensitive power steering unplug a connector for the power steering from the timing case. Some 164 models have a so-called memory package (driver seat, steering column, mirrors) which must be deactivated. Your Owners Manual will give you the instructions.
- Extract the fluid from the steering fluid reservoir as shown in Fig. 2.11 in the case of the brake fluid reservoir.

- Detach the lower engine compartment panelling or the bottom section of the sound-proofing capsule (for example 270/320 CDI 164 models).
- Disconnect the track rod ball joints (2) in Fig. 6.1 from the lever on the steering knuckle, using a suitable ball joint puller after removal of the stud nut. A new nut must be fitted, 5.5 kgm /40 ft.lb. in the case of a 163 model or 5.0 kgm (36 ft.lb.) + 60° in the case of a 164 model.
- Position the steering wheel in the centre position, i.e. front wheels in straight-ahead position and remove the ignition key (steering locked).
- In the case of a 164 model there is a connector near the steering pinion. Disconnect it.
- Detach the fluid return pipe (11) and the high pressure expansion hose (10). Either fittings or banjo bolts are used. Protect the disconnected pipe/hose to prevent entry of dirt. The sealing rings must be replaced during installation, but note the tightening torques: If a screw joint fitting is used, tighten the return pipe and high pressure hose to 1.5 kgm (10 ft.lb.), if a banjo (hollow) bolt is fitted tighten both fluid lines to 3.0 kgm (22 ft.lb.).
- Remove the nut (9) from the steering coupling (8) and pull the lower steering shaft (13) upwards and out of the coupling. Do not damage the coupling shield (10) during removal. The nut (9) must be replaced. Tightened to 2.8 kgm (20 ft.lb.). Remember that the steering must be in the centre position during installation.
- Detach the rack-and-pinion steering (4) from the front axle carrier (1) by removing the bolts (5). Note the position of the shims (6) and (7) on the R.H. side, inserted between the rubber mount and the front axle carrier as they are different in thickness. The bolts are tightened to 5.0 kgm (36 ft.lb.) during installation in the case of a 163 model. The bolts of a 164 model are tightened in four stages: First tighten to 5.0 kgm (36 ft.lb.), then slackened by half a turn, then tightened to 5.0 kgm once more and from the final position a further quarter of a turn (90°).
- After removal of the steering check the rubber mount (3) for damage and replace if necessary.

Installation is a reversal of the removal procedure, adhering to the torque values given above. The steering must be filled and bled of air after installation. The front wheel alignment should be checked in a workshop if any of the parts have been replaced.

7.2.1. TRACK RODS – REPLACEMENT

Before you decide to have a track rod ball joint or a track rod replaced, you can carry out the following checks:
- Check the track rod ball joints rubber dust caps for cuts or other damage,
- Have the steering wheel turned into one lock (helper required), grip the track rod ball joint with one hand and ask the helper to move the steering wheel to and fro. The engine should be started to facilitate the steering wheel movements. Excessive play requires the fitting of a new track do ball joint.
- Place the front end of the vehicle on chassis stands and grip the track rod with one hand. Move the track rod up and down. Excessive play in the ball joints requires the replacement of the joint.
- Similar checks can be carried out on the inner ball joint. In this case the rubber gaiter must be detached from the steering rack. Excessive clearance at the inner joints requires the replacement of the track rod. As the steering must be removed to replace a track rod we recommend a dealer as the only solution.

7.2.2. TRACK ROD BALL JOINTS - REPLACEMENT

The ball joints at the ends of the track rods can be replaced with the steering fitted. The operations are similar on all models but the tightening torques are not the same. After disconnecting the ball joint from the steering lever undo the locknut securing the ball joint end to the track rod and unscrew the end piece from the track rod, at the same time counting the number of turns necessary.

When fitting the new ball joint screw it onto the track rod by the same number of turns (also half-turns) and provisionally tighten the locknut. If the operations have been carried out properly there should be no need to check the toe-in setting.

Tighten the locknut to 5.0 kgm (36 ft.lb.) in the case of model series 163 or 6.0 kgm (43 ft.lb.) in the case of model series 164. Also different is the torque for the ball joint stud nut. Either 5.5 kgm/40 ft.lb. (163) or 4.5 kgm+90°/32.5 ft.lb.+90° (164).

Have the front wheel alignment checked if possible or if not sure.

7.3. The hydraulic System

7.3.1. FILLING THE SYSTEM

If the steering system has been drained for any reason it must be refilled and bled of air. Fluid drained from the system must not be re-used to fill the reservoir. The filter must be replaced if the system has been completely drained or the fluid is changed for any reason. The following sequence must be adhered to:

- Remove the screw cap from the fluid reservoir. There is a seal inside the cap which could drop out.
- Fill the reservoir to the upper edge.
- Start the engine a few times and immediately switch it off again. This will fill the complete steering system. During this operation the fluid level in the reservoir will drop and must be corrected immediately. Never allow the reservoir to drain as otherwise fresh air will be drawn into the system. A helper is obviously required to start and switch off the engine.
- When the fluid level in the reservoir remains the same the system is filled and the fluid level must be within the markings on the fluid dipstick. As already shown the dipstick has an upper and a lower mark. The total capacity of the system is given as 1.2 litre.
- Push the seal into the screw cap and refit the cap to the reservoir.

We recommend to check the fluid level during each check of the engine oil level. This will assure you not to overlook the check. During the level check or topping-up of the reservoir make sure that no foreign bodies or dirt can enter the system.

7.3.2. BLEEDING THE HYDRAULIC SYSTEM

After the fluid level remains the same after the engine has been started and switched off a few times bleed the system as described below. A helper is required to turn the steering wheel:

- Have the steering wheel moved from one lock to the other and back again to eject the air out of the steering cylinder. The steering wheel must be moved slowly, just enough for the piston inside the steering cylinder to contact its stop.
- Observe the fluid level in the reservoir during this operation. If the level drops, fill in additional fluid, as it must remain on the MAX mark. No air bubbles must be visible during the bleeding operation.

7.3.3. CHECKING THE SYSTEM FOR LEAKS

Sometimes it is possible that fluid is lost for some unknown reason. A quick check may establish where the fluid is lost:

- Ask a helper to turn the steering wheel from one lock to the other, each time holding the wheel in the maximum lock.

This will create the max. pressure in the system and any obvious leaks will be shown by fluid dripping on the floor.
- From below the vehicle (on chassis stands) check the area around the steering pinion. Slacken the rubber gaiters on the steering rack and check the ends of the rack. The rack seals could be leaking.
- Check the hose and pipe connections. These must be dry.

8 Brake System

8.0. Technical Data

Type of system   See description below

Front Brakes
All possible versions listed. Differences will apply between 163 and 164 models. Also covers petrol models. Data given as available:
Caliper piston diameter, front brakes: 60.00 mm
Thickness of brake pads, incl. back plate: Inner pad – 163 models 16.5 mm
                                                            Outer pad – 163 models 15.5 mm
                                                            Both pads – 164 models 19.75 mm
Min. thickness of linings: 2.0 mm (without metal plate)
Brake disc thickness: 26.0 mm (163), 32.0 mm (164)
Brake disc diameter: 303, 330 or 345 mm, depending on model
Min. thickness of brake disc: 24.0 mm (163). 30,0 mm (164)
Max. run-out of brake discs   0.10 mm
Wear limit of brake discs, per side   max. 0.05 mm

Rear Disc Brakes
Caliper piston diameter: Depending on fitted version 38.0 or 40.0 or 42.0 mm
Brake disc diameter: 285 or 331 mm
Brake disc thickness: Between 10 and 22 mm (depending on version)
Min. brake disc thickness: 8.0 mm or 20.0 mm

Min. thickness of brake pads, incl. metal plate: 16.0 mm (163), 19.8 mm (164)
Min. thickness of pad linings   2.0 mm

Handbrake
Min. width of brake linings: 1.00 mm (0.04 in.)
Number of notches required for fully engaging
  handbrake, using average force: 5 – 8
Number of notches until handbrake becomes effective: 1

8.1. Short Description

All models covered in this manual are fitted with a hydraulic dual-circuit brake with vacuum-operated brake servo unit. The brake servo unit is supplied with vacuum from the inlet manifold (petrol models) or a separate vacuum pump (diesel models). Sliding (floating) calipers or fixed calipers are fitted to the front wheels. Disc brakes, working on the same principle as the fixed front brake calipers are used on the rear wheels. The brake calipers are not the same on all models and again you can consult the technical data section for details. Otherwise enquire at your parts supplier, quoting the exact model identification number, model year, etc. if new parts are required

The brake system is diagonally split, i.e. one circuit serves one of the front brake calipers and the diagonally opposed rear brake caliper. The other circuit operates the other two brake assemblies accordingly. If one brake circuits fails, the brakes will operate as normal, but more brake force will be required. The information and instructions in the following description will try to cover all possible versions.

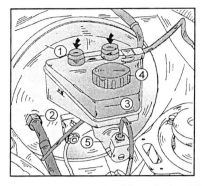

Fig. 8.1 – The brake fluid reservoir is fitted to the master brake cylinder. Note the "min" and "max" marks on the outside of the cylinder. The two buttons shown with the arrows can be depressed to check the brake fluid level.
1 Brake servo unit
2 Vacuum hose
3 Fluid reservoir
4 Screw cap
5 Master brake cylinder

Checking the Brake Fluid Level

The brake fluid reservoir is fitted above the master brake cylinder in the position shown in Fig. 8.1. At all times make sure that the brake fluid is between the "Min" and "Max" marks on the outside of the cylinder. If the brake fluid level sinks below the "Min" mark there are other reasons which must be investigated.

Fig. 8.2 – Brake fluid can be removed from the fluid reservoir as shown, when it is necessary to drain the brake system.

Brake fluid must sometimes be removed from the reservoir. If this is necessary we recommend the method shown in Fig. 8.2.

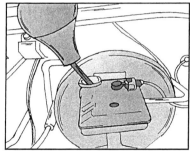

8.2. Front Disc Brakes

As already mentioned, sliding brake calipers with one piston are fitted to the front wheels. The assemblies consist of a caliper mounting bracket bolted rigidly to the front axle steering knuckle and a separate caliper cylinder. When the brake is operated, the piston pressed first with its brake pad against the brake disc. The caliper cylinder then slides on glide bolts and moves against the direction of the pressure, until the other brake pad is pressed against the brake disc on the other side. Only the caliper cylinder must be removed to replace the brake pads, the mounting bracket remains on the steering knuckle.

8.2.0. FLOATING CALIPERS

Floating caliper are fitted to model series 164 and models in the 163 range. Fig. 8.3 shows this type of caliper. Note that floating calipers on the rear axle are fitted in a similar manner.

Checking and Replacing the Brake Pads – 163 Models

To check the pad thickness without removing the pads, but the wheels must be removed (front or rear). Use a torch and shine through the opening in the caliper. You will have a view as shown in Fig. 8.4. If the thickness of the pad material appears to be less than 3.5 mm (0.14 in.), replace the brake pads on both sides. The min. permissible thickness is 2.0 mm (0.08 in.).

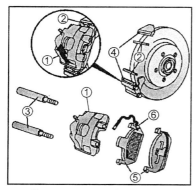

Fig. 8.3 – Fitted brake caliper with the location of some of the parts. Refer to text.

Important: If it is possible that the brake pads can be re-used, mark them in relation to the side of the car and to the inside or outside position of the caliper. Never interchange brake pads from left to right or visa versa, as this could lead to unequal braking.

To remove the brake pads, either for examination or replacement, first jack up the front end of the vehicle and remove the wheel. Then proceed as follows:

- Unplug the contact sensor connector from the L.H. caliper. Fig. 8.6 shows where the connector can be found.

Fig. 8.4 – The thickness of the pad material (1) can be checked through the opening in the caliper.

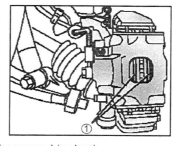

- Remove the guide bolts (3) on the wheel carrier (4). Always use new bolts.
- Remove the floating caliper (1) from the wheel carrier and with a piece of wire or cord suspend the caliper from some part of the front suspension. Do not allow to let it hang down on the brake hose. Do not disconnect the hose. Remove the caliper (1) upwards in direction of the arrow together with the brake pads. The slide rails (2) must be removed (replace).
- Remove the brake pads (5) from the sides of the caliper. The pads are not the same on both sides. Press out the L.H. brake pad contact sensor (6) out of the metal plate of the brake pad (5). The sensor for the brake pad wear indicator is fitted to the inner brake pad as shown. The connector tab of the sensor can be withdrawn from the pad if new pads are fitted.

Measure the thickness of the pad material. If the thickness is around 3.5 mm, fit new pads. Although the pad material can be worn down to 2.0 mm, you will find that the pad wear indicator lights up when a thickness of 3.5 mm is reached. Never replace one pad only even if the remaining pads look in good order.

The sensors for the brake pad wear indicator should be replaced if the insulation shows signs of chafing or other damage.

- Check the thickness of the brake disc and compare the dimensions given in Section 8.0. Replace the discs if the thickness is below the minimum permissible. Although different thicknesses apply you will be able from the thickness given which value applies to your particular model.

Before fitting the new pads clean the caliper opening with a brush and clean brake fluid or methylated spirit. Wipe off any spirit remaining and lubricate the exposed part of the piston with rubber grease. Fit the pads as follows:

- Open the fluid reservoir and draw off some of the fluid as shown in Fig. 8.2.

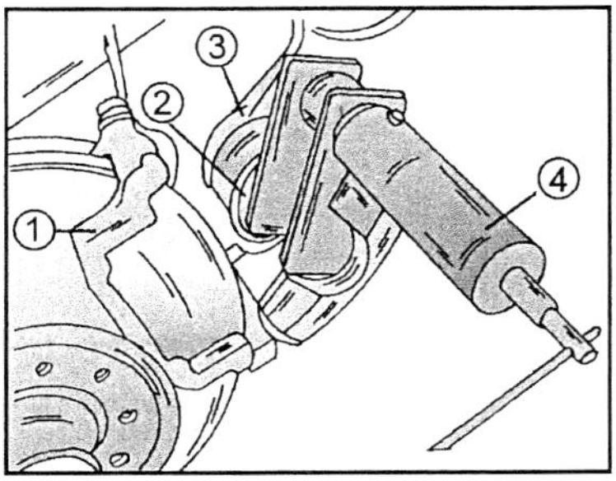

Fig. 8.5 – Using the special tool (clamp) to push the piston back into its bore.
1   Brake caliper
2   Piston
3   Cylinder housing
4   Special tool

- Push the piston back into its bore. Either use the special pliers available for this purpose (see Fig. 8.5) or place a wooden block in position and lever back the piston carefully with a large screwdriver blade.

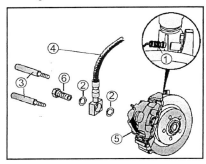

Fig. 8.6 – Details for the removal of a brake caliper. See text.

- Insert both brake pads into the caliper carrier slide rails and carefully lower the caliper housing carefully over the pads. First insert the inner brake pad into the caliper piston and then insert the outer brake pad. Use new self-locking bolts and tighten the bolts to 3.0 kgm (22 ft.lb.).
- Coil the brake pad wear indicator cable and connect to the terminal on the brake caliper. Fit the connector protective cover.
- Apply the foot brake several times after installation of the brake pads. This is an essential requirement to allow the new pads to take up their position. Bleed the brake system if necessary and check and if necessary correct the fluid level in the master cylinder reservoir.

Removal and Installation of a Brake Caliper
The front end of the vehicle must be resting on chassis stands and the wheel removed. Removal details are shown in Fig. 8.6.
- Place a bleeder hose over the bleeder screw (remove the rubber cap first) and insert the other end of the hose into a container (glass jar). Open the bleeder screw and pump the brake pedal until all fluid has been drained from the system.
- Unplug the contact sensor connector (1) at the position shown.
- Unscrew the banjo bolt (6) for the brake hose (4) from the caliper (5). The sealing rings (2) must be replaced during installation. The bolt is tightened to 3.0 kgm (22 ft.lb.).
- Unscrew the two guide bolts (3) from the brake caliper. Always replace the bolts.
- Swivel the caliper upwards in the direction of the arrow and remove it together with the brake pads.

The installation of the caliper is a reversal of the removal procedure. First insert the inner brake pad into the caliper piston and then insert the outer brake pad. Tighten the new caliper guide bolts to the torque given above. Finally bleed the brake system as described later on.

Brake calipers - Overhaul
Remove the caliper from the steering knuckle and have it overhauled at a dealer or a workshop dealing with brake system.

Checking and Replacing the Brake Pads – 164 Models

The instructions given for the 163 models also apply to the 164 models, but the attachment of the brake caliper is different. A retaining spring, as shown in Fig. 8.7 is fitted and must be removed by inserting a screwdriver into the retaining spring as shown and disengage it from the brake caliper housing.

On the inside of the caliper you will find two protective rubber caps (one at the upper end, one at the lower end). Remove the caps and unscrew the guide bolts (replace them).

The remaining operations follow the description for the 163 models. After the guide bolts have been fitted push the rubber caps in position. Fit the retaining spring to the anchoring points.

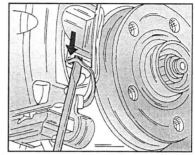

Fig. 8.7 – Removal of the retaining (tensioning) spring from the caliper.

Removal and Installation of a Brake Caliper – 164 models

The front end of the vehicle must be resting on chassis stands and the wheel removed.

- Place a bleeder hose over the bleeder screw (remove the rubber cap first) and insert the other end of the hose into a container (glass jar). Open the bleeder hose and pump the brake pedal until all fluid has been drained from the system.
- Disconnect the brake pipe from the brake hose at the inside of the wheel arch housing by unscrewing the union nut. Knock out the spring plate to free the hose. Suitably close the hose and pipe ends to prevent entry of dirt. The brake line connection is tightened to 1.8 kgm (13 ft.lb.).
- Lift the two lugs for the cover of the brake pad wear connector with a small screwdriver and pull off the plug. The brake hose can be unscrewed from the brake caliper, if desired, whilst the caliper is still fitted.
- Unscrew the brake caliper mounting bolts and lift off the unit. Discard the bolts as new bolts must be used during installation. The brake pads can now be removed from the caliper.

The installation of the caliper is a reversal of the removal procedure. Tighten the new caliper mounting bolts to 20 kgm (144 ft.lb.). Finally bleed the brake system as described later on.

8.2.1. FRONT BRAKE CALIPERS – Fixed Calipers

Checking and Replacing the Brake Pads – 163 Models

When the thickness of the brake pad linings has reached 3.5 mm, a warning light in the dashboard will light up, signalling that new brake pads must be fitted.

- Place the front end of the vehicle on chassis stands and remove the front wheels. The caliper will now have the appearance shown in Fig. 8.8. First withdraw the contact sensor connectors (7).
- Using a drift of suitable diameter drive the retaining pins out of the caliper from the outside towards the inside in the manner shown in Fig. 8.9. Remove the retaining spring in the centre.
- Remove the brake pads. The workshop used a special tool to withdraw the pads.
- Otherwise hook a piece of wire through the two brake pad holes and withdraw the pads one after the other with a short, sharp pull.

Fig. 8.8 – View of a brake caliper after removal of the wheel.
1 Brake caliper
2 Cross spring
3 Brake pads
4 Cable
5 Cable connector plug
6 Retaining pins
7 Contact sensor, brake pad wear indicator

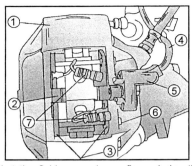

- Push the pistons back into their bores, using a re-setting pliers as shown in Fig. 8.10. Otherwise use a piece of wood and carefully push the piston into the bore. It may be that the fluid reservoir overflows during this operation. Keep an eye on it. If necessary remove the fluid (Fig. 8.2).

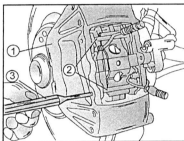

Fig. 8.9 – The retaining pins are removed from the outside towards the inside when the pads are removed.
1 Brake caliper
2 Retaining pins
3 Drift

- Withdraw the contact sensor out of the metal plate of the brake pad. The sensor must be replaced if the insulating layer on the contact plate is worn or any other part of the sensor or its cable is damaged.
- Measure the thickness of the pad material. If the thickness is around 3.5 mm, fit new pads. Although the pad material can be worn down to 2.0 mm, you will find that the pad wear indicator lights up when a thickness of 3.5 mm is reached. Never replace one pad only even if the remaining pads look in good order.

Fig. 8.10 – Piston can be pushed into their bores using a pair of re-setting pliers. Brake fluid could overflow from the fluid reservoir.

- Check the thickness of the brake disc and compare the dimensions given in Section 8.0. Replace the discs if the thickness is below the minimum permissible. Although different thicknesses apply you will be able from the thickness given which value applies to your particular model.

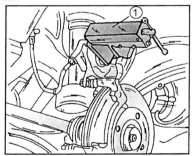

Before fitting the new pads clean the caliper opening with a brush and clean brake fluid or methylated spirit. Wipe off any spirit remaining and lubricate the exposed part of the piston with rubber grease. Fit the pads as follows:

- Coat the brake pad metal plates and their sides with Molycote paste and insert the pads into the brake caliper mounting brackets.
- Place the tensioning spring over the brake pads and insert the two retaining pins from the inside towards the outside into the caliper and through the brake pads. The pins have a clamping shape on one side which will keep them in position. Carefully drive them in position to their stop.

- Operate the brake pedal a few times to set the brake pads against the brake disc.
- Check the fluid level in the fluid reservoir and correct if necessary. Treat the new brake pads with feeling at the beginning before they are fully bedded in.

Removal and Installation of a Brake Caliper – 163 Models
The removal and installation of the caliper is carried out as described for the other type. One fitted bolt and a normal bolt are used to secure the caliper. Both are tightened to 18 kgm (130 ft.lb.) during installation.

Brake calipers - Overhaul
Refer to the points to be observed for the other caliper type. Additionally note that the two halves of a caliper must not be separated. A caliper should be overhauled by a specialist.

8.3. Rear Disc Brakes
8.3.0. BRAKE PADS - REPLACEMENT
Floating calipers with four pistons or fixed calipers are fitted (see below). The rear wheels must be removed to check the pad thickness. The remaining pad material can be checked by inspecting the thickness as shown in Fig. 8.4. If the thickness is less than 2.0 mm (0.8 in.), replace the brake pads of both rear calipers.
A view of a rear floating caliper and its attachment is shown in Fig. 8.11. Two bolts are used to attach the caliper. The instructions refer to the illustration.

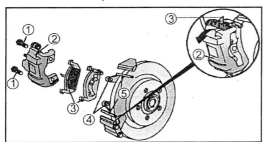

Fig. 8.11 – View of the rear brake caliper of a 163 model. Similar on a 164 model. See text.

ATTENTION: If it is possible that the brake pads can be re-used, mark them in relation to the side of the car and to the inside or outside position of the caliper. Never interchange brake pads from the inside to the outside, or visa versa, as this could lead to uneven braking.
- Place the rear of the vehicle on chassis stands and remove the rear wheels.
- Remove the bolts (1) and tilt the caliper in the direction of the arrow to remove it together with the brake pads (3). Remove the brake pads. The pads are different, make a note of the installation position.

Before fitting clean the caliper opening with a brush and clean brake fluid or methylated spirit. Wipe off any remaining spirit and lubricate the exposed parts of the piston with rubber grease. Push the pistons back into their bores. Either use the method described above (re-insert one of the old brake pads) or use a wooden block in position and lever back the piston carefully with a screwdriver blade. Note that one pad must be placed into the caliper as the other piston is pushed into the bore,. Otherwise the opposite piston will be pushed out when one of the pistons is pushed in. As this is done the level in the master cylinder reservoir will rise so either empty some of the fluid or alternatively release the bleeder screw to allow some fluid to escape as the piston is pushed in. The bleeder screw is only opened a little, and only whilst the piston is moved. It should not be necessary to bleed the brake system.

- Push the piston back into its bore. Either use the special pliers available for this purpose (see Fig. 8.5) or place a wooden block in position and lever back the piston carefully with a large screwdriver blade.
- Replace the two slide rails (5) for the brake pads (3) in the wheel carrier (4).
- Insert both brake pads into the caliper carrier slide rails (5) and carefully lower the caliper housing carefully over the pads. First insert the inner brake pad into the caliper piston and then insert the outer brake pad. Use new self-locking bolts and tighten the bolts to 2.3 kgm (16.5 ft.lb.).
- Apply the foot brake several times after installation of the brake pads. This is an essential requirement to allow the new pads to take up their position. Bleed the brake system if necessary and check and if necessary correct the fluid level in the master cylinder reservoir.

164 Models – with Fixed Calipers

The brake pads can be replaced after the calipers have been removed as described below. The fixed calipers are, however, fitted to petrol models and after a certain vehicle number to 163 models with CDI engine.

8.3.1. BRAKE CALIPERS – REMOVAL AND INSTALLATION

The removal of a brake caliper is a simple operation. The following operations are valid for all models, but note that a different tightening torque must be observed when the caliper is fitted. Figs. 8.12 and 8.13 show the attachment of a caliper.

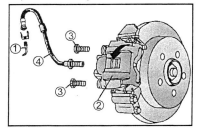

Fig. 8.12 – Rear brake caliper in fitted position (163 shown). Refer to text.

- Jack up the rear end of the vehicle, place chassis stands in position and remove the wheel on the side in question.
- Place a bleeder hose over the bleeding screw in the caliper (remove the rubber dust cap first) and insert the other end of the hose into a container (glass jar). Open the bleeder screw and pump the brake pedal (helper) until the fluid has been drained from the system.

Fig. 8.13 – Fitted floating caliper to a 164 model.
1 Caliper mounting bracket
2 Brake hose
3 Guide bolt
4 Floating caliper
5 Spring clip

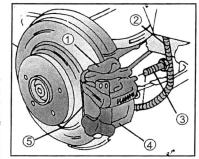

- Refer to Fig. 8.12 and disconnect the brake pipe from the brake hose (4) from the brake pipe (1) and free the brake hose from its bracket. Suitably close the hose and pipe ends to prevent entry of dirt. Slacken the brake hose connection at the caliper whilst the caliper is till fitted. Then unscrew the caliper mounting bolts (3) and lift off the caliper (2). Discard the bolts as new ones must be fitted during installation. The brake pads can now be removed from the caliper.

The installation is a reversal of the removal procedure. Use new bolts (3) and tighten them to 2.3 kgm (16.5 ft.lb.). In the case of a 164 model the bolts to 15.0 kgm (108 ft.lb.). Tighten the brake hose-to-brake pipe union nut with 1.8 kgm (13 ft.lb.), if it has been disconnected from the caliper. The brake system must be bled of air after installation of the caliper.

163 and 164 Models – with Fixed Calipers

Removal and installation is carried out in a similar manner as described above, but the connector plug must be disconnected from the wheel speed sensor und the sensor securing bolt removed (if fitted). The bolt is tightened to 0.9 kgm (7 ft.lb.). The items shown in Fig. 8.12 also apply to the 164 models, but the bolts (3) securing the brake caliper(s) to the wheel carrier are tightened to 11.5 kgm (83 ft.lb.).

8.4. Brake Discs

Brake discs can be re-machined, but not below the thickness given in Section 8.0. As discs are sometimes changed we advise you to obtain the latest information from your dealer, quoting the model, engine, etc. Remove a brake disc as follows (in general for all models):

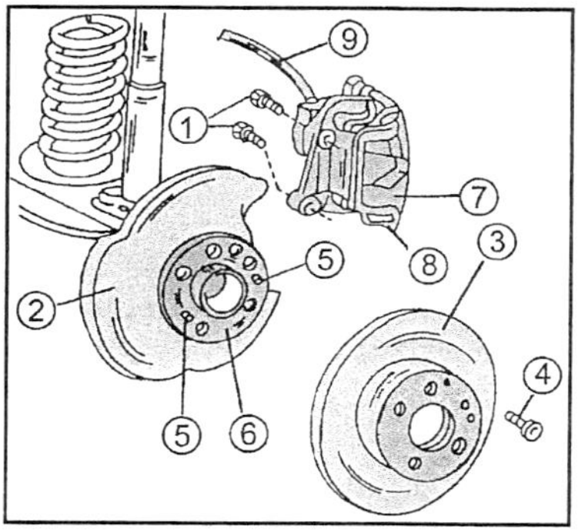

Fig. 8.14 – Details for the removal and installation of a front brake disc.
1   Caliper bracket bolt
2   Splash guard
3   Brake disc
4   Screw
5   Clamping sleeve
6   Front drive shaft flange
7   Cylinder housing
8   Brake caliper bracket
9   Brake hose

- Place the front or rear end of the vehicle on chassis stands and remove the wheel. If the rear disc is removed release the handbrake.
- Remove the two bolts securing the brake caliper (bolts must be replaced) and lift off the caliper. Attach the caliper with a piece of wire to the chassis. Do not allow the caliper to hang down on the brake hose.

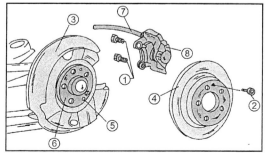

Fig. 8.15 – Details for the removal and installation of a rear disc brake (general view).
1   Brake caliper bolts
2   Disc securing screw
3   Splash guard
4   Brake disc
5   Dowel pin (not fitted)
6   Axle flange
7   Brake hose
8   Brake caliper

- The brake disc can now be removed after unscrewing the small securing screw.

Use a rubber or plastic mandrel to knock off a sticking disc. Figs. 8.14 and 8.15 show general views how the discs are fitted.

New disc are coated for protection and s suitable solvent must be used to clean them. Refit the disc as follows:

- In the case of the front discs, fit the disc and tighten the securing screw to 2.3 kgm (16.5 ft.lb.) in the case of a 163 model, but only to 1.0 kgm (7.2 ft.lb.) in the case of a 164 model. Tighten the caliper mounting bolts as described during the installation of the brake calipers, again noting the difference in the tightening torques.
- In the case of the rear discs, fit the disc and tighten the securing screw to 2.3 kgm (16.5 ft.lb.) in the case of a 163 model, but only to 1.0 kgm (7.2 ft.lb.) in the case of a 164 model. Tighten the caliper mounting bolts as described during the installation of the brake calipers, again noting the difference in the tightening torques, mainly as there are differences between floating calipers and fixed calipers which must not be overlooked.

Fig. 8.16 – Checking a brake disc for run-out.
1   Brake disc
2   Dial gauge bracket
3   Dial gauge

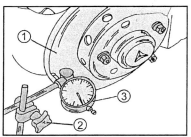

- After installation of the disc, place a dial gauge against the brake disc as shown in Fig. 8.16. Slowly rotate the disc and observe the reading of the dial gauge. If the run-out of the disc is more than specified in section 8.0, there could be two reasons:
- The brake disc is not fitted correctly to the hub. In this case remove the disc, move it around to the next fitting position and refit the disc.
- The brake disc is distorted (overheated for example).

Before driving off operate the brake pedal several times to establish the correct clearance between the brake pads and the brake disc. Check the fluid level in the reservoir and top-up if necessary.

8.5. Master Brake Cylinder

All vehicles use a tandem master cylinder with a twin reservoir, enabling the supply of brake fluid to the two circuits to the dual-line brake system. The brake pipes are split between the front and rear brakes. The piston nearest to the push rod operates the front brakes, the intermediate piston operates the rear brakes. The master cylinder should not be overhauled. Fit a new unit if the original one is worm beyond use.

The fluid level in the reservoir is monitored by means of a warning light in the instrument panel. The operation of the light must be checked when the reservoir is topped-up. To do this, switch on the ignition, release the handbrake and, using the thumb, press down the two rubber caps, shown by the arrows in Fig. 8.1.

The following information are given for the master cylinder fitted to 163 models, but one of two different versions can be fitted. Fig. 8.17 shows the later version. The two ESP brake pressure sensors 1 and 2 (12 and 13) are not fitted to earlier versions. Also not fitted is the heat shield (3).

The removal and installation of 164 models is more complicated and cannot be recommended. Amongst the difficult operations is the detachment of the left partition wall from the bulkhead inside the engine compartment. Only one ESP brake pressure sensor is fitted to the bottom the cylinder instead of the two shown in Fig. 8.17.

To remove the cylinder of a 163 model proceed as follows. The engine cover must be removed on certain engines:

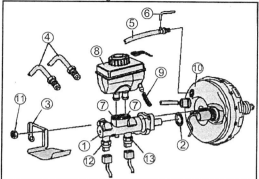

Fig. 8.17 – Details for the removal and installation of the master cylinder.
1 Brake master cylinder
2 Sealing ring
3 Heat shield
4 Brake pipe, 2.0 kgm
5 Vacuum pipes
6 Vacuum pipe (diesel only)
7 Rubber grommets
8 Fluid reservoir
9 Hose, with M/T
10 Brake servo unit
11 Cylinder securing nut
12 ESP pressure sensor 1
13 ESP pressure sensor 2

- Place a bleeder hose over one of the bleeder screws of one of the front calipers and another one over a bleeder screw of one of the rear calipers (remove the rubber dust cap first). Insert the other end of the hoses into a container (glass jar). Open both bleeder screws and operate the brake pedal until the system is empty.
- Remove the fuse and relay module covers. There are 2 covers, 5 bolts on the rear cover.
- Unplug the connector from the fluid reservoir (8).
- Disconnect the vacuum pipe (5) from the brake servo unit (10) and in the case of a diesel engine the vacuum pipe (6) from the splash wall. In the latter case also remove a vacuum hose from the vacuum pump and separate two hoses from a bracket.
- Detach hoses from the side of the fuse and relay module and place them to one side.
- Unscrew the brake linen (4) from the master cylinder. Make a note where the pipes are connected, if not sure. The union nuts are tightened to 2.0 kgm (14.5 ft.lb.) during installation. Plug up the open brake pipes to avoid entry of dirt.
- If fitted, unplug the connectors of the two ESP brake sensors (12) and (13). A release catch at the underside of the plugs must be pressed to release them.
- Remove the nuts (11) securing the cylinder. New nuts must be used during installation and tightened to 2.0 kgm (14.5 ft.lb.). If fitted, remove the heat shield (3).
- Remove the cylinder by pulling it out straight towards the front. The sealing ring (2) must be replaced during installation. Note that the reservoir of a 164 model is attached with a screw.
- If a manual transmission is fitted remove the hose (9) from the fluid reservoir and plug up the opening.
- To remove the reservoir (8) place it on a bench, make sure it is empty and withdraw the reservoir. Install new rubber grommets (7) if necessary.

The installation is a reversal of the removal procedure. The "O" sealing ring must always be replaced as the connection must be vacuum-tight. Insert the sealing ring into the groove of the cylinder. Tighten the cylinder securing nuts to 2.0 kgm (14.5 ft.lb.). There is no need to adjust the master cylinder push rod. Fill the brake system and bleed the complete system as described later on.

Note: If the cylinder of a 164 model is removed, note different tightening torques: Brake pipes to master cylinder = 1.8 kgm (13 ft.lb.), master cylinder to brake servo unit = 1.0 kgm (7.2 ft.lb.), screw for fluid reservoir = 0.4 kgm.

8.6. Parking Brake

The parking brake (handbrake) is a "duo-servo-type" brake shoe system. "Duo" indicates that the brake is effective in both directions of brake disc rotation, "servo" indicates the transmission of the brake shoe movement from one shoe to the other.

8.6.0. PARKING BRAKE SHOES – REMOVAL AND INSTALLATION

Although similar in operation, the arrangement of the individual parts is not the same on 163 and 164 models. The main difference is, however, the location of the thrust piece with the adjusting wheel. On 163 models it is fitted as shown in Fig. 8.18, on the 164 models it is located at the upper end of the brake shoe assembly.

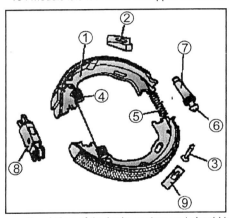

Fig. 8.18 – Component parts of the handbrake brake shoes as fitted to 163 models.
1 Brake shoes
2 Retaining spring
3 Adjuster
4 Retracting spring
5 Retracting spring
6 Thrust piece
7 Thrust pin
8 Expanding lock
9 Retaining spring

The special installation tool 116 589 01 62 00 is required to remove the brake shoes with the rear wheel hub fitted. Otherwise the rear hub must be removed to gain access to the hold-down springs. Fig. 8.19 shows a sectional view of the brake system and should be referred to locate the individual parts. 163 vehicles are fitted with an automatic handbrake cable compensating mechanism which must be tensioned before the following operations can be carried out and must de-tensioned after the operations are completed. The operation is described later on. Remove the brake shoes as follows. The description is valid for 163 models. Similar operations are carried out on 164 models with the difference that the items mentioned are arranged differently:

- Place the rear end of the vehicle on secure chassis stands and remove the wheels.
- Tension the automatic handbrake cable compensator (Section 8.6.2).
- Remove the brake caliper and the brake disc as already described. You will now have the view shown in Fig. 8.20. The special tool mentioned above is now necessary. The shape of the tool is shown in Fig. 8.21. It may be necessary to make up a similar handle with a hook at the end. Insert the tool into the retracting spring (4) in Fig. 8.18 and disconnect it. During installation make sure that the spring is correctly engaged.

Fig. 8.19 – Removal and installation of brake shoes.
1 Hold-down spring
2 Brake shoes
3 Thrust piece
4 Adjuster wheel
5 Brake back plate
6 Cover plate
7 Thrust sleeve
8 Upper shoe return spring
9 Lower shoe return spring
10 Brake carrier
11 Expanding lock

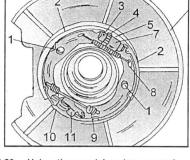

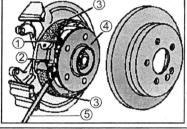

Fig. 8.20 – Using the special spring removal tool.
1 Retracting spring
2 Expanding lock
3 Brake shoes
4 Rear axle drive flange
5 Spring removal tool

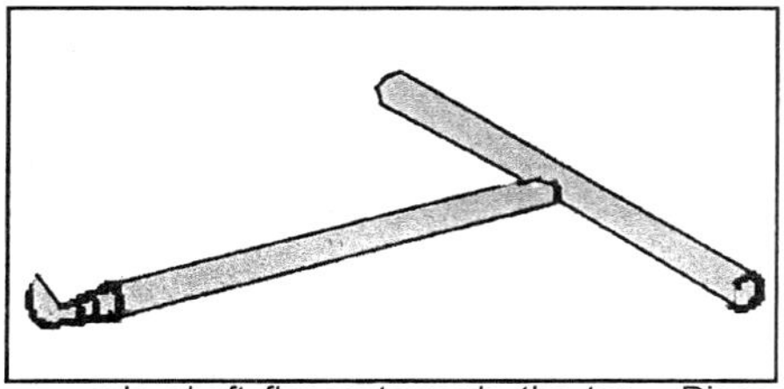

Fig. 8.21 – The special spring removal tool.

- Remove the retracting spring (2) and the pin (7). Again make sure that the spring is correctly seated during installation.
- Remove the brake shoes. To do this, pull the two brake shoes apart until they can be lifted over the axle shaft flange towards the top. Disconnect the upper return spring (5) and remove the expanding lock (8).

The installation of the new brake shoes is carried out as follows:

- Coat all bearing and sliding faces on the expanding lock with Molykote paste and fit the expanding lock. Then push the expanding lock against the cover plate.
- Coat the threads of the thrust piece and the cylindrical portion of the adjuster wheel (6) with long-term grease and assemble the adjusting device. Turn the adjuster completely back.
- Insert the adjuster between the two brake shoes, with the adjuster wheel pointing in the direction shown in Fig. 8.18. Fit the upper return spring (5) to the two brake shoes.
- Pull the brake shoes apart at the bottom, lift them over the drive shaft and attach them to the expanding lock.
- Fit the retracting spring (4) to one of the brake shoes, insert the installation tool, compress the spring slightly and then turn it by 90° to attach it to the cover plate. Check that the spring is correctly fitted and fit the other hold-down spring in the same manner.

153

- Fit the lower return spring with the smaller hook to one of the brake shoes and expand the spring until it can be engaged into the other brake shoe. This can be accomplished by means of a wire hook and a screwdriver to guide the spring into the anchor hole.
- Finally fit the brake disc and the caliper as described earlier on and adjust the braking brake as described in the next section.

8.6.1. PARKING BRAKE - ADJUSTMENT

The parking brake must be adjusted if it can be operated by more than 5 "clicks" of a total of 6 without locking the rear wheels. To adjust the handbrake proceed as follows, noting the difference between 163 and 164 models:

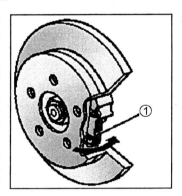

Fig. 8.22 – Adjusting the parking brake. The location of the adjusting wheel (1) of a 163 model. The threaded hole must be opposite. The arrow shows the direction of adjustment.

- Operate the parking brake pedal and check the pedal travel. Adjust if outside the limit given above.
- Place the rear end of the vehicle on chassis stands. **In the case of a 164 model** remove the rear wheels and on the outside of the brake discs locate the rubber plugs and remove it.
- **In the case of a 163 model** remove one of the wheel bolts on each wheel and turn one of the wheels until the threaded hole (where the wheel bolt was fitted) is in the approximate position shown in Fig. 8.22. The wheels can, however, be removed to facilitate the adjustment.

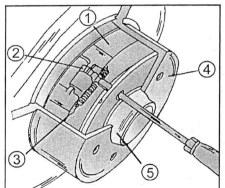

Fig. 8.23 – Adjusting the parking brake.
1 Brake shoe
2 Adjuster wheel
3 Upper return spring
4 Brake disc/drum
5 Wheel shaft flange

163 Models

- Insert a screwdriver blade of suitable diameter into the hole. The screwdriver will pass through the brake disc/drum and the drive shaft flange and engages with the adjuster wheel inside the brake drum. Fig. 8.23 shows where the engagement takes place. The drum has been cut-away to give a better view and the screwdriver is of course, inserted on the other side.
- Operate the screwdriver in the correct direction, referring to the arrow in Fig. 8.22 until the wheel is locked. The adjusting wheel must be moved from left to right in the case of both wheels.

- With the wheel locked, turn back the screwdriver by 5 to 6 "clicks" of the adjuster wheel until the wheel once more is free to rotate. Refit the rear wheels (if removed) and re-check the adjustment. De-tension the brake compensator.

164 Models
- Insert a screwdriver blade of suitable diameter into the hole where the rubber insert was located. The screwdriver will pass through the brake disc/drum and the drive shaft flange and engages with the adjuster wheel inside upper end of the brake drum.
- Operate the screwdriver in the correct direction until the wheel is locked. In the case of the L.H. adjusting wheel turn it from the top to the bottom, in the case of the R.H. adjusting wheel turn it from the bottom to the top.
- With the wheel locked, turn back both adjusting wheels by the same number of turns. It must be possible to rotate the rear wheels or the brake disc completely free, using the hands only. Refit the rear wheels and push the rubber inserts into the brake discs.

8.6.2. THE AUTOMATIC PARKING BRAKE COMPENSATOR

As already mentioned the compensator must be pre-tensioned bore the removal of the parking brake shoes and de-tensioned after installation. Fig. 8.24 shows the compensator. Read the instructions carefully as it is rather complicated.

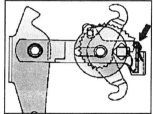

Fig. 8.24 – View of the handbrake compensating mechanism.

To de-tension the compensator after completing the work on the brake shoes use a screwdriver and lift the spring clip shown by the arrow. The compensator will then be de-tensioned and the length of the handbrake cable will be automatically compensated. Operate the handbrake a few times to set the mechanism into operation.

8.6.3. PARKING BRAKE CABLES – REPLACEMENT

The replacement of the front handbrake cable and the rear handbrake cables is a very complicated operation, which we cannot recommend to carry out under DIY conditions. If the front cable or the rear cables require replacement you will have to seek the help of a Mercedes dealer.

8.7. Brake Servo Unit

Brake servo units should not be dismantled, as special tools are required to dismantle, assemble and test the unit. Different servo units are fitted to Mercedes-Benz models, manufactured by either Teves, Bendix or Girling. Always make sure to fit the correct part if the servo unit is replaced. Remember that a failure of the servo unit to act will not affect the efficiency of the braking system but, of course. additional effort will be required for the same braking distance to be maintained.

ATTENTION! If you coast downhill, for whatever reason, with a vehicle equipped with a brake servo unit, remember that the vacuum In the unit will be used up after a few applications of the brake pedal and the brake system will from then onwards operate without power-assistance. Be prepared for this.

8.8. Bleeding the Brakes

Bleeding of the brake system should be carried out at any time that any part of the system has been disconnected, for whatever reason. Bleeding must take place in the order left-hand rear side, right-hand rear, left-hand front and right-hand front. If only one of the brake circuits has been opened, either bleed the front or the rear circuit. The procedure given below should be followed and it should be noted that an assistant will be required, unless a so-called "one-man" bleeding kit is available.

Always use clean fresh brake fluid of the recommended specification and never re- use fluid bled from the system. Be ready to top up the reservoir with fluid (a brake bleeding kit will do this automatically) as the operations proceed. If the level is allowed to fall below the minimum the operations will have to be re-started.

Obtain a length of plastic tube, preferably clear, and a clean container (glass jar). Put in an inch or two of brake fluid into the container and then go to the first bleed point. Take off the dust cap and attach the tube to the screw, immersing the other end of the tube into the fluid in the container.

Open the bleed screw about three quarters of a turn and have your assistant depress the brake pedal firmly to its full extent while you keep the end of the tube well below the fluid level in the container. Watch the bubbles emerging from the tube and repeat the operation until no more are seen. Depress the brake pedal once more, hold it down and tighten the bleed screw firmly.

Check the fluid level, go to the next point and repeat the operations in the same way. Install all dust caps, depress the brake pedal several times and finally top up the reservoirs.

8.9. Tightening Torques – Brakes

The tightening torques for the individual items for 163 and 164 models are given in the individual sections, dealing with the parts in question. When referring to the torque values, make sure to read for values (kgm or ft.lb.) applicable to the model in question. All data are given to the best of our knowledge. We would like to point out that torque values are sometimes changed without prior publications. Therefore latest values, if changed, are only available immediately to Mercedes-Benz dealers.

9 Electrical System

9.0. Battery

Voltage: .... 12 volts
Polarity: .... Negative earth (ground)
Condition of Charge:
    Well charged: 1.28
    Half charged : 1.20
    Discharged: 1.12

To check the voltage of the battery, use an ordinary voltmeter and apply between the two battery terminals. A voltage of 12.5 volts or more should be obtained.

If a hydrometer is available, the specific gravity of the electrolyte can be checked. The readings of all cells must be approximate by the same. A cell with a low reading indicates a short circuit in that particular cell .Two adjacent cells with allow reading indicates a leak between these two cells.

A battery can be re-charged, but the charging rate must not exceed 10% of the battery capacity, i.e.7.2 amps. The battery must be disconnected from the electrical system.

Charge the battery until the specific gravity and the charging/voltage are no longer increasing within 2 hours. Add distilled water only. Never add acid to the battery.
The level of the battery electrolyte should always be kept above the top of the plates.

9.1. Alternator
9.1.0. ROUTINE PRECAUTIONS
The vehicle covered in this manual employs an alternator and control unit. This equipment contains polarity-sensitive components and the precautions below must be observed to avoid damage:
- Check the battery polarity before connecting the terminals. Immediate damage will result to the silicon diodes from a wrong connection—even if only momentarily.
- Never disconnect the battery or alternator terminals whilst the engine Is running.
- Never allow the alternator to be rotated by the engine unless ALL connections are made.
- Disconnect the alternator multi-pin connector before using electric welding equipment anywhere on the vehicle.
- Disconnect the battery leads if a rapid battery charger is to be used.
- If an auxiliary battery is used to start the engine. take care that the polarity is correct. Do not disconnect the cables from the vehicle battery.

9.1.1. DRIVE BELT TENSI0N
Always tension the drive belt whenever the alternator, water pump or drive belt have been removed or slackened for any reason. The single drive belt is properly tensioned when the operations described in Section "Cooling System" are followed. The alternator runs at higher speed than the older D.C. dynamo generators and the belt tension should be maintained accurately for the best results. When a new belt has been fitted, it is as well to re-check the tension after a few hundred miles have been covered.

9.1.2. ALTERNATOR – REMOVAL AND INSTALLATION
The alternator is rigidly attached to the engine. Remove as follows, noting that some differences will be found within the engine range. The alternator is either water-cooled (163 – 270 CDI), can be water-cooled or air-cooled (163 – 400 CDI) or has no cooling (164 – 280 and 320 CDI). Follow the instructions for the engine/model in question.

628 Engine – 163 Model – 400 CDI – with water-cooled alternator
Removal and installation is a complicated operation as various parts must be removed as specified. The difficult parts is to locate the individual items. If you attempt the removal (not recommended) proceed as follows:
- Disconnect the battery earth cable and drain the cooling system.
- Remove the sound-proofing underneath the engine.
- Remove a nut from the coolant expansion reservoir and from the windscreen washer fluid reservoir, lift the fluid reservoir out of the catches and remove.
- Remove the air cleaner and the charge air cross-pipe.
- .Disconnect the coolant hoses in front of the alternator to facilitate access to the various parts.
- Remove the Poly V-belt as described in section "Cooling System" for the 612 engine.

- Locate a bracket securing the glow plug output stage, remove a bolt securing a coolant line in the immediate area and remove the bracket. Two types of bolts are used. The M7 bolt is tightened to 1.4 kgm, the M6 bolt to 0.9 kgm.
- Unscrew the nut securing one of the cable connectors on the alternator from circuit "30" (1.3 kgm) and disconnect the cable connector from the other terminal, circuit "61".
- Unscrew the bolt securing the oil dipstick guide tube and remove the guide tube. During installation make sure the tube is correctly inserted.
- Remove the bolts securing the alternator at the top and bottom of the cooling housing. This is the part covering the alternator. The bolts are tightened to 2.0 kgm (14.5 ft.lb.) during installation.
- Press the alternator with the cooling housing towards the R.H. side and remove it from the engine compartment.

The installation is a reversal of the removal procedure. Alternator and cooling housing must be fitted with new "O" sealing rings. After installation start the engine and run it until warm and check the cooling system for leaks.

628 Engine – 163 Model – 400 CDI – with air-cooled alternator

Removal and installation is a complicated operation as various parts must be removed as specified. The difficult parts is to locate the individual items. If you attempt the removal (not recommended) proceed as follows:
- Disconnect the battery earth cable and remove in the following order the complete air cleaner, the charge air cross pipe and the Poly V-belt.
- Unlock an electrical connector and detach it from the pressure sensor downstream of the air cleaner (located above the alternator).
- On the R.H. side of the sensor you will find the glow plug output stage. Remove the upper bolt from the bracket (immediately above the alternator). During installation this bolt must be tightened after the glow plug output stage bracket has been tightened as given below.
- Remove the bolt securing the coolant line bracket across the alternator.
- Next to the alternator remove two bolts securing the glow plug output stage bracket and push the glow plug stage and the bracket together to one side. Two types of bolts are used. The M7 bolt is tightened to 1.4 kgm, the M6 bolt to 0.9 kgm.
- Remove the lower and upper alternator mounting bolts and lift off the alternator. Swivel the alternator towards the front until the electrical connections can be disconnected. One of them is secured by means of a nut (1.3 kgm). During installation tighten the upper and lower alternator bolts to 2.0 kgm (14.5 ft.lb.) after the bracket for the glow plug output stage has been refitted and tightened.

Installation is carried out in reverse order.

612 Engine – 163 Model – 270 CDI – with water-cooled alternator

Again the operations are complicated. If attempted (not recommended) proceed as follows:
- Disconnect the battery earth cable and remove the inner panel of the R.H. front wing (refer to Fig. 9.1) and the sound encapsulation underneath the engine compartment.
- Disconnect a coupling and unscrew the electrical cable from the alternator. Next to the coupling and at the upper end of the hose disconnect a cable (terminal "30" connection) and remove a bolt at the bottom of the hose.
- Drain the cooling system, the air cleaner housing and the Poly V-belt.
- Two oil lines must be disconnected. One is connected to the turbo charger and a

bolt must be removed to free it. The other one is the feed line and is sealed off with "O" sealing rings. The connections are either with a screw socket (3.0 kgm/22 ft.lb.) or a banjo bolt (1.8 kgm/13f ft.lb.).

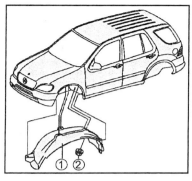

Fig. 9.1 – Attachment of the liner (1) inside a front wing is secured by screws (2).

- At the upper end of the alternator, i.e. the cooler housing, remove two bolts and take off a bracket. The item covering the alternator is the cooler housing which must be removed. Remove two bolts at he lower end and one bolt at the upper end. The bolts are tightened to 2.0 kgm (14.5 ft.lb.) during installation. At the upper end of the cooler housing there is a bolt. Remove it.

- The alternator is now removed towards the bottom together with the cooler housing. A new gasket must be fitted between the cooler housing flange and the engine connection. If a new alternator is to be fitted (or a new cooling housing) separate the parts and refit them with a new "O" sealing ring.

Installation is carried out in reverse order.

642 Engine – 164 Model – 280/320 CDI

Again the operations are complicated. If attempted (not recommended) proceed as follows:

- Disconnect the battery earth cable and remove the engine trim panel.
- Remove the R.H. intake air duct, the charge air hose downstream of the charge air cooler and the Poly V-belt.
- Remove the alternator securing bolts (4 in total), disconnect the electrical cablew connections and remove the alternator in a downward direction. The oilk dipstick may have to be removed if it appears to be in the way. The alternator bolts are tightened to 2.0 kgm (14.5 ft.lb.).

Installation is carried out in reverse order. Tighten the terminal nut to 1.5 kgm (10 ft.lb.).

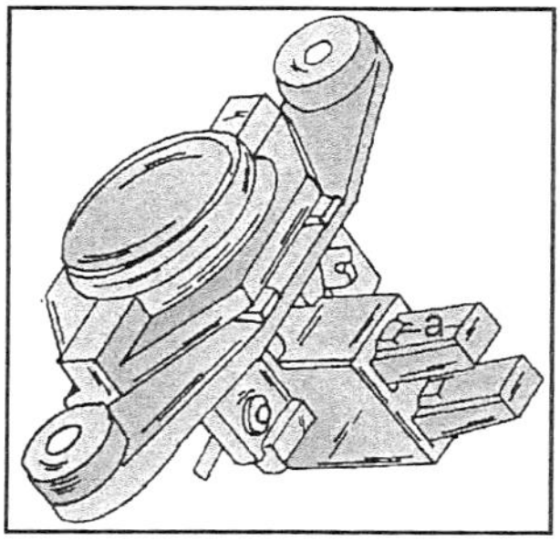

Fig. 9.2 – Th dimension "a" gives the remaining brush length.

9.1.3. SERVICING

A Bosch alternator is used on the engines dealt with in this manual, having a different output, depending on the engine. Remember that alternator are sometimes changed. Always check the applicable part number when a new alternator is fitted.

We do not recommend that the alternator or control unit should be adjusted or serviced by the owner. Special equipment is required in the way of test instruments and the incorrect application of meters could result in damage to the circuits.

The alternator is fitted with sealed-for-life bearings and no routine attention is required for lubrication. Keep the outside of the alternator clean and do not allow it to be sprayed with water or any solvent.

The alternator brush gear runs in plain slip rings and the brushes have a long life, requiring inspection only after a high mileage has been covered. To inspect the brushes, we recommend the removal of the alternator. Take out the two screws from the brush holder assembly and withdraw for inspection.

Measure the length of the brushes, shown by a in Fig. 9.2. If the protruding length is less than 5.0 mm (0.2 in.) or approaching this length, replace the brushes. New brushes will have to be soldered in position. We would like to point out that it is not an easy operation to guide the brushes over the slip rings when the slip ring cover is being fitted.

9.2. Starter Motor

9.2.0. REMOVAL AND INSTALLATION

Disconnect the battery earth (ground) cable. Again we try to separate the different models. Read the instructions before you commence with the job – Complicated on some of the models:

612 engine in model series 163 – 270 CDI: Remove the wing liner (see Fig. 9.1) inside the L.H. wing. Locate and disconnect the electrical cables from the rear of the starter motor. Tighten the upper nut to 1.4 kgm and the lower one to 0.6 kgm.

Remove the starter motor mounting bolts and remove the starter motor downwards and out.

Install in the reverse sequence to removal. Tighten the starter motor bolts to 4.2 kgm. Make sure that the mating faces are clean before bolting up. Re-connect the wires and the battery terminal.

628 engine in model series 163 – 400 CDI: Remove the engine compartment panelling at the bottom. Remove the bottom right charge air pipe, but do not disconnect it from the charge air hose. Instead push the pipe to one side.

Remove the protective cap and disconnect the cables from the starter motor terminals. Tighten the nuts as given above during installation.

Remove the starter motor securing bolts and remove the starter motor downwards and out.

Install in the reverse sequence to removal. Tighten the starter motor bolts to 4.2 kgm. Make sure that the mating faces are clean before bolting up. Re-connect the wires and the battery terminal.

642 engine in model 164 (280/320 CDI): The vehicle must be raised to gain access from below. First detach the lower engine compartment panelling. The starter motor is protected by a heat shield which must be removed. A dome nut secures the shield (0.9 kgm/7 ft.lb.).

Unclip the electrical cable from the engine mounting shield and remove the bolt securing the R.H. engine mounting and remove the protective shield towards the top. The bolt is tightened to 5.3 kgm (38 ft.lb.) when attaching the mounting to the engine support bracket.

Remove a protective cap from one of the terminals, remove the nut and disconnect the cable (terminal 30). Tighten the nut to 1.4 kgm. The second cable at the lower end can now be disconnected (terminal 50). Tighten the nut to 0.6 kgm.

Remove the two starter motor bolts and take out the starter motor towards the bottom, rotating and tilting it to pass the engine support.. The two bolts are tightened to 4.0 kgm (29 ft.lb.) during installation.

9.2.1. SERVICING

It may be of advantage to fit an exchange starter motor if the old one has shown fault. Exchange starter motors carry the same warranty as a new unit.

9.3. Headlamps - Replacement

As the replacement of a headlamp requires the adjustment of the headlamp beams, which should be carried out at a Mercedes dealer or a workshop dealing with headlamp adjustments we will not describe the operations for the removal and installation of the units. Fig. 9.3 shows the individual parts of a headlamp as fitted to a 163 model, which can be referred to when you intent to remove a lamp unit. The location of the bulbs on the same model range can be seen in Fig. 9.4. Removal of the headlamps on a 164 model is similar, but under no circumstances do we recommend to carry out any work if Xenon headlamps are fitted. On these models it will be necessary to remove the front bumper. Remember, always have the headlamp alignment checked after a headlamp is replaced.

With some knowledge it will be possible to replace a headlamp unit as follows, but remember that the information is given for the 163 model:

- With the bonnet open, unlock the cover (1) in Fig. 9.3 at the clip (arrow A) under the lamp unit and unhook it. During installation of the headlamp make sur that the clip is locket correctly.
- Unscrew the bolt (2) at the upper end of the headlamp unit.
- Remove the three nuts (3) at the lower end of the headlamp unit. Again note during installation: The distance of the cover to the bumper must be even. Check before the nuts are tightened.
- Unhook the L.H. or R.H. headlamp unit (5) from the hole (arrow B) using a drift (4) and pull the headlamp unit forwards.
- Disconnect the headlamp harness connector (6) and remove the headlamp towards the front.

Installation is carried out in reverse order.

9.4. Bulb Table

Main and dipped beam:	Halogen H4, 60 & 55 watts, ECE H4
Fog lamps:	Halogen H3, 55 watts, ECE H3
Indicator lamps, front end rear:	ECE P, 21 watts
Reversing light, rear fog lamp:	ECE P, 21 watts
Parking lamps:	ECE T, 4 watts
Tail lights:	ECE R, 10 watts
Number plate lights:	5 watts
Luggage compartment, interior lamps:	10 watts

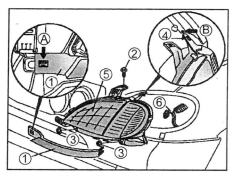

Fig. 9.3 – The component parts of a headlamp unit (163 model). The arrow (A) shows where a clip under the lamp unit must be unhooked. (B) shows where the lamp unit must be unhooked.
1 Cover
2 Securing bolts
3 Securing nuts
4 Retaining pin
5 Lamp unit
6 Headlamp wiring harness

Fig. 9.4 – The location of the bulbs at the rear of the headlamps (163 model).
1   Lamp cover
2   Bulb cover
3   Catch lever
4   Electrical connector plug
5   Retaining clip
6   High beam bulb
7   Low beam bulb
8   Fog lamp bulb
9   Headlamp unit

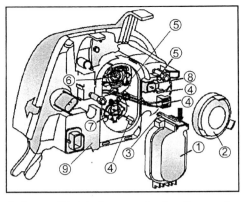

9.5   Headlamp Bulb Replacement

Fig. 9.4 shows where the headlamp bulbs are fitted to the rear of a headlamp unit. Bulbs can be replaced as follows:

- Remove the cover (1) by pressing on the catch lever (3) in the direction of the arrow and remove.
- Remove the cover (2).
- Disconnect the electrical connections (4) for the bulbs.
- Open the retaining clip (5) for the bulbs and remove the bulbs as given in Fig. 9.4. Do not touch the bulbs with the fingers only. Use a paper towel or similar.

During installation make sure that the bulbs are correctly installed.
Make sure that the correct bulb for the light in question is used.

10   Automatic Transmission

Different types of automatic transmissions are fitted to the model range, however, all transmissions are of type „722" with different end numbers. Models 280 CDI, 320 CDI (164 series) and 400 CDI (163 series) are only available with automatic transmission. Model series 163 are fitted with a 5-speed transmission, model series 164 with a 7-speed transmission. Only the 270 CDI can have a manual or automatic transmission. The petrol models have similar transmissions.

10.0.   Technical Data

Fitted transmission:
– 270 CDI (163): 722.661
– 400 CDI (163): .... 722.666 or 722.673
– 280 CDI (164): 722.902
– 320 CDI (164): 722.902

Transmission Ratios (only CDI models given):	ML 270 CDI	ML 400 CDI
- First gear:	3.59 : 1	3.59 : 1
- Second speed	2.19 : 1	2.19 : 1
- Third speed	1.41 : 1	1.41 : 1
- Fourth speed	1.00 : 1	1.00 : 1
- Fifth speed	0.83 : 1	0.83 : 1
- Reverse speed	3.16 : 1	3.16 : 1
- Axle ratio	3.46 : 1	3.09 : 1

Series 164:	ML 280 CDI	ML 320 CDI
- First gear:	4.38 : 1	4.38 : 1
- Second speed	2.56 : 1	2.56 : 1
- Third speed	1.92 : 1	1.92 : 1
- Fourth speed	1.37 : 1	1.37 : 1
- Fifth speed	1.00 : 1	1.00 : 1
- Sixth speed	0.82 : 1	0.82 : 1
- Seventh speed	0.73 : 1	0.73 : 1
- Reverse speed	3.42 : 1	3.42 : 1
- Axle ratio	3.45 : 1	3.45 : 1

Filling Capacity:
– 270 CDI (163) – Initial filling: .... 7.5 litres
– Other models – Initial filling: .... 9.0 litres

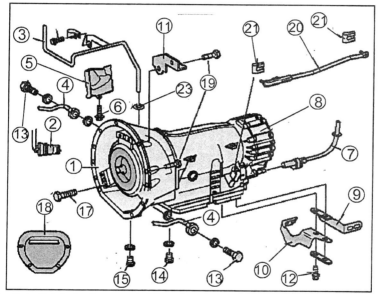

Fig. 10.1 – Details for the removal of the automatic transmission in the case of a 163 model (270 and 400 CDI). Refer to text.

10.1. Removal and Installation

As the engine can be removed without the transmission there may be no need to remove the transmission except when an exchange transmission is to be fitted. The following operations describe the removal and installation of the transmission as fitted to 163 models, followed by a summary of the operations in the case of a 164 model. Fig. 10.1 shows details of the location of the various parts to be disconnected or removed. The following numbered items refer to the illustration. A mobile jack will be required to lower the transmission.

- Disconnect the battery and place the vehicle on secure chassis stands..
- Remove the transfer case as described in section 3.1 commencing on page 115 from the adapter end (8) of the transmission.

163

- Detach the oil filler pipe (3) from the crankcase. Secured by bolts (22). Note the "O" sealing rings (23) on the pipe ends.
- Remove the heat shield (5) after removal of the bolt (6) and disconnect the 13-pin connector (2). The bolt (6) is tightened to 0.8 kgm6 ft.lb.).
- Remove the shift rod (20). The securing clip (21) must be removed with a pair of pliers.
- From the rear end of the transmission remove the L.H. exhaust bracket (9) and the R.H. exhaust bracket (10) after removal of he bolt (12).
- Place a suitable container underneath the transmission and remove the fluid drain plug (14) from the transmission oil sump. Allow the fluid to drain and immediately refit the plug. Tighten the plug to 2.0 kgm (14.5 ft.lb.). Also remove the oil drain plug (15), this time from the torque converter. Note that this plug is tightened to 1.6 kgm (11.5 ft.lb.).
- Detach the cable for the so-called park lock interlock (7) at the transmission. The cable is only fitted to some models. If fitted, position the selector lever or the range selector lever into position "P" and leave it in this position when the cable and transmission are removed.
- Detach the fluid cooling lines (4). The area around the connecting points must be thoroughly cleaned to prevent entry of foreign matter. The banjo bolts (13) must be removed.
- Remove the cover (18) and detach the torque converter from the driven plate. The bolts (17) are tightened to 4.2 kgm (30 ft.lb.) during installation.
- Place a mobile jack with a suitable lifting plate underneath the transmission and unscrew the bolts (19). The retainer (11) is secured with one of the bolts and must be pushed upwards. All transmission to engine bolts are tightened evenly all round to 4.0 kgm (29 ft.lb.). Remember to fit the retainer (11) underneath one of the bolts.
- Remove the transmission from the engine and lower it at an angle on the lifting device. The torque converter can drop out and must be secured in position.

The torque converter can be removed, but the workshop uses special grab handles to pull it out. We would also like to point out that the installed height of the torque converter, i.e. the distance from the transmission housing, is not the same on all transmissions. For example the dimension is 7 mm in the case of a transmission for a 270 CDI and 19.5 mm for a 400 CDI – we would say a job for a workshop.

Installation is a reversal of the removal procedure. Fill the transmission with oil (approx. 5 litres) and then check the oil level as described below. The workshop carries out a transmission check and we advise you to seek the assistance of a dealer if not satisfied with the operation of the unit.

164 Models

The following instructions are given in general. The removal is more complicated as in the case of 163 models. Read through the information below before commencing the removal.

- Disconnect the battery earth cable and place the vehicle on secure chassis stands.
- Remove the complete exhaust system.
- Underneath the propeller shaft you will find some protective shields, secured by four nuts and 10 bolts. Remove them and take off the three-part shields.
- Detach the rear propeller shaft from the flange on the transfer case. Before separating the two flanges mark the outside edges with a coloured pen to refit them in the same position. All bolts must be replaced and are tightened to 5.4 kgm (39 ft.lb.).

- On one side of the transmission remove a heat shield and in the same area unplug a connector. The heat shield bolts are tightened to 0.9 kgm.
- On the torque converter side of the transmission remove a cover and detach the torque converter from the drive plate. The drive plate must be rotated to reach all bolts. The bolts are tightened to 4.2 kgm.
- Remove a bolt securing the oil cooler line from the bracket on the oil sump.
- On the alternator bracket there is a bolt securing a double clamp. Remove it. Tighten to 0.8 kgm (6 ft.lb.).
- On the side of the transmission locate the two oil cooler lines. Remove them from the transmission and the engine oil sump and place them to one side without bending them. Close the open ends in suitable manner. The "O" seals must be replaced during installation. The union nuts are tightened to 0.9 kgm.
- Place a mobile jack with a suitable lifting plate underneath the transmission and lift the unit. The workshop uses, of course, a special lifting device.
- Remove the engine crossmember. Bolts are used at the outer edges and in the centre. The rear engine mounting remains on the crossmember. The bolts must be replaced. The bolts are tightened to 5.5 kgm (40 ft.lb.).
- Detach the front propeller shaft from the transfer case. Before separating the two flanges mark the outside edges with a coloured pen to refit them in the same position. Push the shaft o one side and tie it up with wire or similar. All bolts must be replaced and are tightened to 5.4 kgm (39 ft.lb.).
- Detach the transmission from the engine and the engine oil sump. First the bolt on the vent line bracket and the vent line is removed on one side of the transmission. The starter motor will be free and must be moved to one side and secured with wire to prevent it from falling down (cables connected). All bolts are tightened to 4.0 kgm (29 ft.lb.), including the starter motor bolts.
- Remove the transmission from below. The torque converter must be secured to prevent it from falling out.

The installation is a reversal of the removal procedure, noting the tightening torques given above.

10.2. Fluid Level and Fluid Change

The fluid level in the transmission changes with the temperature of the transmission fluid. The fluid dipstick is marked with two levels, one for a temperature of around 30° C (cold) and one for around 80° C (hot). These are shown in Fig. 10.2 with "A" and "B". On the other side of the dipstick you will find the temperatures in Fahrenheit (F). If the fluid level is correct you will find the fluid between the "Min" and "Max" marks. The transmission is filled with automatic transmission fluid (ATF). Dexron II fluid is recommended. The total capacity is as given in section 10.0, but less fluid will be used during a fluid change..

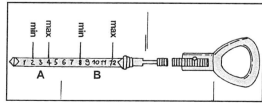

Fig. 10.2 – View of the fluid dipstick as fitted to an automatic transmission. The fluid must be within the area "A" when the fluid is cold or the area "B" when the fluid is hot.

Fig. 10.3 – Break off the lug on the plate (1) and push the pin downwards in the direction of the arrow. The cap (2) can then be removed.

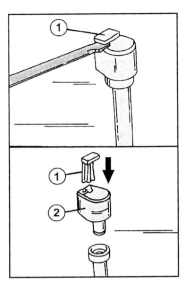

Absolute cleanliness is to be observed during a fluid level check that even small particles entering the transmission can lead to malfunctions. Do not use fluffy cloth to wipe the dipstick. Tissue paper is best.

Filling in additional fluid is not straight forward. As you can see in Fig. 10.3, the upper end of the filler tube is fitted with a locking pin, which must be removed. To do this brake off the plate (1) of the pin with a screwdriver as shown and press out the remaining pin in the cap downwards. Remove the cap (2). The pin must, of course, be replaced.

The engine must be running at idle speed when fluid is filled in through the filler tube (a funnel is required). Apply the handbrake and depress the brake pedal and change through all gears. Finally leave the gear selector lever in position "P" and re-check the fluid level.

Finally refit the cap to the filler tube ands press in a new locking pin until it locks in position.

The fluid can only be changed at a dealer as a diagnostic system is used to carry out the operation.

11   Exhaust System

The exhaust system of a 163 diesel model is shown in Fig. 11.1. It consists of the front and rear section with a three-way catalytic converter fitted as standard. The front exhaust pipe is connected to the rear silencer by means of an exhaust pipe clamp. A sealing ring is fitted between the end of the front pipe and the exhaust manifold.

11.1.   Removal and Installation of the Exhaust System
11.1.1.   ML 270 CDI Models

The operations can be carried out by referring to Fig. 11.1.

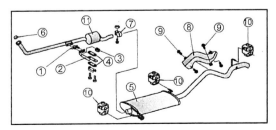

Fig. 11.1 – The exhaust system as fitted to 270 CDI diesel models.

1 Threaded plate
2 Exhaust bracket on transmission
3 Self-locking nut
4 Rubber support
5 Rear exhaust system
6 Sealing cone
7 Exhaust pipe clamp
8 Heat shield
9 Bolts
10 Rubber mounting
11 Catalytic converter

- Jack up the vehicle and place secure chassis stands underneath the body.
- Remove the bottom section of the sound-proofing capsule.
- Remove the protective underbody shield (8) from the exhaust system after removal of the bolts (9).
- Remove the exhaust pipe clamp (7) from the exhaust system and unhook the rear exhaust system (5) from the three rubber mounts (10). Check the rubber mounts for wear and replace if necessary. The mounts must be disengaged from the suspension hooks on the exhaust.
- Disconnect the front exhaust system from the rear system. The clamp nut is tightened to 5.5 kgm (40 ft.lb.) during installation. Some shields on the underbody are in danger of being damaged. Take care during the removal operation. The rear section of the exhaust system can now be lifted out.
- Release the spring connection between the primary catalytic converter and the three-way catalytic converter (11). A water pump pliers must be used to press the spring washers together and the metal tongue must be pressed off with a screwdriver. During installation fit a new sealing cone (6) and use the pliers to press together the spring washers until the metal tongue locks in position.
- Unscrew the nuts (3) from the exhaust bracket (2). New nuts must be used (2.0 kgm/13.4 ft.lb.).
- Unbolt the exhaust bracket (2) from the transmission. The exhaust system is now free and must be supported from below accordingly. Bolts are tightened to 2.0 kgm (14.5 ft.lb.).
- Lift out the three-way converter and the front exhaust system. Again take care no to damage any of the heat shields on the underbody.

Note the following points during installation:
- Check the mounting rubbers and replace them if no longer in perfect condition. Also check the connecting faces of the pipes for corrosion. Slight corrosion can be removed with emery paper.
- All other operations are carried out in reverse order to the removal procedure, noting the tightening torques given during the removal instructions..

Replacement of Rubber Suspension Rings

Three rubber suspension mountings are used in total. To replace the rubber mountings, jack up the rear end of the vehicle, place chassis stands under the sides of the body and unhook the mountings from the pins on exhaust and vehicle underbody. Check that the new rubber mountings are fully engaged when refitting them.

11.1.2. ML 400 CDI Models

As you will know, two catalytic converters are fitted. The vehicle should be lifted on a vehicle lift. As it is also necessary to remove the torsion bar springs and the rear engine crossmember we recommend to have parts of the exhaust replaced in an exhaust centre. Below we give you, however, applicable tightening torques, if you intend to remove one of the converters or the front section of the exhaust system.

Nut of support bracket at transmission = 2.0 kgm (14.5 ft.lb.), pipe clamp, front exhaust pipe to rear exhaust system = 5.5 kgm (40 ft.lb.), rear engine crossmember bolts to body = 4.0 kgm (22 ft.lb.),

11.1.3. ML 280/320 CDI Models

The complete exhaust system is removed as a single unit.

Removal and installation requires the use of a garage-type lift, if possible. Otherwise place the front and rear end of the vehicle on secure chassis stands. After the vehicle is on the chassis stands place a mobile jack with suitable supports (for example a wooden plank) underneath the exhaust system. The catalytic converter is fitted with a Lambda probe and an electrical cable must be disconnected. We strongly recommend to have the exhaust system replaced at an exhaust centre, as the operations are not straight forward as you will see from the description. The system can be removed as follows, but a helper must be available to lower the exhaust system:

- Locate the bracket securing the system to transmission case and remove the two bolts near the silencer. The bolts are tightened to 2.0 kgm (14.5 ft.lb.).
- Near the transfer case remove the nuts and detach the system from the mounting bracket. Tighten the nuts to the torque given above.
- On the side of the silencer box there are some hoses. Loosen the hose clamps and disconnect the hoses.
- Locate the Lambda probe (O2 sensor) and unclip the connector and free the electrical cable from a clip. A further electrical cable is connected to the temperature sensor of the catalytic converter and to the temperature sensor of the so-called diesel particulate filter, which must also be disconnected.
- Remove the bolts securing the outer exhaust rubber mount (1.2 kgm/9 ft.lb.), unhook the rear silencer from the inner rubber mount and remove the exhaust system.
- Remove all remaining attachments and lower the system on the jack. The helper will have to guide the system as necessary.

Installation is carried out in reverse order. Follow the tightening torques given in the text and install the system free of stress or tension.

12. SERVICING AND MAINTENANCE

Most of the maintenance operations can be carried out without much difficulties. In many cases it is, however, better to have certain maintenance operations carried out in a workshop as experience and special equipment, for example test instruments, are required to carry out a certain job. Most important are the regular inspections and checks which are described below. Operations to be carried out after a certain mileage are described later on in this section and the text will advise when specific jobs should be left to a Mercedes Dealer.

12.0. Regular Maintenance

Oil Level Check: Check the engine oil level every 500 miles. With the vehicle standing on level ground, remove the oil dipstick and wipe it clean with a clean rag or a piece of tissue paper. Re-insert the oil dipstick and remove once more. The oil level must be visible between the upper and the lower mark on the dipstick. If the oil level is below the lower mark, top-up with engine oil of the correct viscosity. The oil quantity between the two marks is approx. between 5.0 and 3.5 litre and from the actual level indicated you will be able to tell how much oil is missing. Never overfill the engine - the level must never be above the upper dipstick mark.

Checking the Brake Fluid Level: - The brake fluid reservoir is in the engine compartment on the drivers side. The reservoir is transparent and it is easy to check whether the fluid level is between the "Min" and "Max" mark. If necessary, top-up to the "Max" mark with the correct brake fluid.

Checking the Brake Lights: The operation of the brake lights can either be checked with the help of another person or you can check it by yourself by driving the vehicle backwards near the garage door. Operate the brake pedal and check if the reflection of the brake lights can be seen on the garage door by looking through the rear view mirror.

Checking the Vehicle Lights: In turn check every vehicle light, including the horn and the hazard warning light system. Rear lights and reversing lights can be checked in the dark in front of a garage door, without leaving the vehicle.

Checking the Tyre Pressures: Check the tyre pressures at a petrol station. Pressures are different for the various models. Either your Operators Manual or tyre charts will give you the correct pressures.

If continuous speeds of more than 100 mph are anticipated, increase the tyre pressure by 0.2 kg/sq.cm. (3 psi.).

Checking the Coolant Level: See Section "Cooling System". Never open the radiator filler cap when the engine is hot.

Checking the Fluid Level in the Automatic Transmission: The fluid level should be checked at regular intervals to ensure the correct operation of the transmission:

- Apply the handbrake and place the gear selector lever into the "P" position. Start the engine and allow to idle for 1 to 2 minutes.
- Remove the oil dipstick from the transmission and read off the fluid level. The level must be between the "Min" and "Max" mark when the transmission is at operating temperature; the level may be up to 10 mm (0.4 in.) below the "Min" mark if the transmission is cold.
- If necessary top-up the transmission with ATF fluid through the fluid dipstick tube. A funnel is required. Only use the fluid recommended for the transmission.

12.1. Service every 6000 Miles

Changing the Engine Oil and Oil Filter: Some petrol stations will carry out an oil change free of charge – You only pay for the oil. The same applies to the oil filter (there may be a small extra charge), but not every petrol station will be able to obtain a Mercedes filter. To change the filter yourself, refer to the relevant page.

Lubrication Jobs: Apart from the engine lubrication there are further lubrication points which should be attended to. These include the throttle linkage and shafts (only grease the swivel points), the engine bonnet catch and the hinges (use a drop of engine oil) and perhaps the door mechanism.

10.2. Additional Service Every 12,000 Miles

Checking the Idle Speed: If the engine no longer idles as expected, have the idle speed checked and if necessary adjusted at your Dealer.

Air Filter Service: Remove the air filter element for cleaning.

Checking the Brake System: If no trouble has been experienced with the brake system, there is little need to carry out extensive checks. To safeguard for the next 6000 miles, however, follow the brake pipes underneath the vehicle. No rust or corrosion must be visible. Dark deposits near the pipe ends point to leaking joints. Brake hoses must show no signs of chafing or breaks. All rubber dust caps must be in position on the bleeder valves of the calipers. Insert a finger underneath the master

cylinder, where it is fitted to the brake servo unit. Moisture indicates a slightly leaking cylinder.
The brake pads must be checked for the remaining material thickness as has been described in Section "Brakes" for the front and rear brakes.

Adjusting the Parking Brake: Adjust the parking brake as described in Section "Brakes" under the relevant heading.

Brake Test: A brake test is recommended at this interval. Your will decide yourself if the brakes perform as you expect them to. Otherwise have the brakes tested on a dynamometer. The read-out of the meter will show you the efficiency of the brake system on all four wheels.

Checking the Wheel Suspension and Steering: In the case of the front suspension remove both wheels and check the shock absorbers for signs of moisture, indicating fluid leaks.
Check the free play of the steering wheel. If the steering wheel can be moved by more than 25 mm (1 in.) before the front wheels respond, have the steering checked professionally.
Check the rubber dust boots of the track rod and suspension ball joints. Although rubber boots can be replaced individually, dirt may have entered the joints already. In this case replace the ball joint end piece or the suspension ball joint.
Check the fluid level in the reservoir for the power-assisted steering. Refer to the "Steering" section for details. If steering fluid is always missing after the 12,000 miles check, suspect a leak somewhere in the system - See your dealer.

Tyre Check: Jack up the vehicle and check all tyres for uneven wear. Tyres should be evenly worn on the entire surface. Uneven wear at the inner or outer edge of front tyres points to misalignment of the front wheel geometry. Have the geometry measured at your dealer. Make sure that a tread depth of 1.6 mm is still visible to remain within the legal requirements. Make sure to fit tyres suitable for your model, mainly if you buy them from an independent tyre company.

Re-tighten Wheel Bolts:- Re-tighten the wheel bolts to 9.0 – 11.0 kgm (65 – 80 ft.lb.). Tighten every second bolt in turn until all bolts have been re-tightened.

Checking the Cooling System: Check all coolant hoses for cuts, chafing and other damage. Check the radiator for leaks, normally indicated by a deposit, left by the leaking anti-freeze. Slight radiator leaks can be stopped with one of the proprietory sealants available for this purpose.

Checking the Clutch: Check the clutch operation. The fluid reservoir should be full. If it is suspected that the clutch linings are worn near their limit, take the vehicle to a dealer.

Checking the Anti-freeze: The strength of the anti-freeze should be checked every 12,000 miles. Petrol stations normally have a hydrometer to carry out this check. Make sure that only anti-freeze suitable for Mercedes engines is used.

Checking the Manual Transmission Fluid Level: Refer to Section "Manual Transmission".

Checking the Rear Axle Oil Level: Remove the filler plug at the side of the rear axle centre piece, just above one of the drive shafts (L.H. side). The oil level should be to the lower edge of the filler hole. If necessary top-up with differential oil. Refit the plug.

12.3. Additional Service every 36,000 Miles

Automatic Transmission Oil and Filter Change: These operations should be carried out by a Dealer.

Air Cleaner Element Change: Refer to Section "Diesel Fuel Injection" for details.

Clutch: The wear of the clutch driven plate should be checked by a dealer with the special gauge available.

Propeller Shaft: Check the two shaft couplings for cuts or other damage. The sleeves must not be loose in the couplings. Check the intermediate bearing for wear by moving the shaft up and down in the bearing.

12.4. Once every Year

Brake Fluid Change: We recommend to have the brake fluid changed at your dealer. Road safety is involved and the job should be carried out professionally. If you are experienced with brake systems, follow the instructions in the "Brakes" section to drain, fill and bleed the brake system.

12.5. Once every 3 Years

Cooling System: The anti-freeze must be changed. Refer to Section "Cooling System" to drain and refill the cooling system.

FAULT FINDING SECTION

The following section lists some of the more common faults that can develop in a motor car; both for petrol and diesel engines. For the purpose of this manual, references to petrol engines are of course, first and foremost, as the detection of faults in a petrol engine is a job for a special workshop, dealing with fuel injection systems. The section is divided into various categories and it should be possible to locale faults or damage by referring to the assembly group of the vehicle in question. The faults are listed In no particular order and their causes are given a number. By referring to this number it is possible to read off the possible cause and to carry out the necessary remedies, if this is within the scope of your facilities.

ENGINE FAULTS

Engine will not crank:	1, 2, 3, 4
Engine cranks, but will not start:	5, 6, 7, 8
Engine cranks very slowly:	1, 2, 3
Engine starts, but cuts out:	5, 6, 9, 10
Engine misfires in the lower speed ranges:	5, 6, 9, 11
Engine misfires in the higher speed ranges:	5, 6, 11, 12
Continuous misfiring:	5, 6, 7, 10 to l5, 21, 22
Max. revs not obtained:	5, 6, 12, 22
Faulty idling:	5, 6, 8 to 11, 13, 15, 16, 21 and 22
Lack of power:	3, 5 to 11, I3 to 15, 22
Lack of acceleration:	5 to 8, 12, 14 to 16
Lack of max. speed:	5 to 8, 10, 12, 13 to 15 ,22
Excessive fuel consumption:	3, 5, 6, 15 ,16
Excessive oil consumption:	16 to 19
Low compression:	7, 11 to 13, 16, 20 to 22

Causes and Remedies

1. Fault in the starter motor or its connection. Refer to "Electrical Faults".
2. Engine oil too thick. This can be caused by using the wrong oil, low temperatures or using oil not suitable for the prevailing climates. Depress the clutch whilst starting (models with manual transmission). Otherwise refill the engine with the correct oil grade, suitable for diesel engines.

3. Moveable parts of the engine not run-in. This fault may be noticed when the engine has been overhauled. It may be possible to free the engine by adding oil to the fuel for a while.
4. Mechanical fault. This may be due to seizure of the piston(s), broken crankshaft, connecting rods, clutch or other moveable parts of the engine. The engine must be stripped for inspection.
5. Faults in the glow plug system (diesel only).
6. Faults in the fuel system.
7. Incorrect valve timing. This will only be noticed after the engine has been reassembled after overhaul and the timing belt has been replaced incorrectly. Redismantle the engine and check the timing marks on the timing gear wheels.
8. Compression leak due to faulty closing of valves. See also under (7) or leakage past worn piston rings or pistons. cylinder head gasket blown.
9. Entry of air at inlet manifold, due to split manifold or damaged gasket.
10. Restriction in exhaust system, due to damaged exhaust pipes, dirt in end of exhaust pipe(s), kinked pipe(s), or collapsed silencer. Repair as necessary.
11. Worn valves or valve seats, no longer closing the valves properly. Top overhaul of engine is asked for.
12. Sticking valves due to excessive carbon deposits or weak valve springs. Top overhaul is asked for.
13. Cylinder head gasket blown. Replace gasket and check block and head surfaces for distortion.
14. Camshaft worn, not opening or closing one of the valves properly, preventing proper combustion. Check and if necessary fit new camshaft (s).
15. Incorrect valve (tappet) clearance. There could be a fault in the hydraulic tappets.
16. Cylinder bores, pistons or piston rings worn. Overhaul is the only cure. Fault may be corrected for a while by adding "Piston Seal Liquid" into the cylinders, but will re-develop.
17. Worn valve guides and/or valve stems. Top overhaul is asked for.
18. Damaged valve stem seals. Top overhaul is asked for.
19. Leaking crankshaft oil seal, worn piston rings or pistons, worn cylinders. Correct as necessary.
20. Loose glow plugs, gas escaping past thread or plug sealing washer damaged. Correct.
21. Cracked cylinder or cylinder block. Dismantle, investigate and replace block, if necessary.
22. Broken, weak or collapsed valve spring(s). Top overhaul is asked for.

LUBRICATION SYSTEM FAULTS

The only problem the lubrication system should give is excessive oil consumption or low oil pressure, or the oil warning light not going off.

Excessive oil consumption can be caused by worn cylinder bores, pistons and/or piston rings, worn valve guides, worn valves stem seals or a damaged crankshaft oil seal or leaking gasket on any of the engine parts. In most cases the engine must be dismantled to locate the fault.

Low oil pressure can be caused by a faulty oil pressure gauge, sender unit or wiring, a defective relief valve, low oil level, blocked oil pick-up pipe for the oil pump, worn oil pump or damaged main or big end bearings, In most cases it is logical to check the oil level first. All other causes require the dismantling and repair of the engine. If the oil warning light stays on, switch off the engine IMMEDIATELY, as delay could cause complete seizure within minutes.

COOLING SYSTEM FAULTS

Common faults are: Overheating, loss of coolant and slow warming-up of the engine:

Overheating:
1. ***Lack of coolant:*** Open the radiator cap with care to avoid injuries. Never pour cold water in to an overheated engine. Wait until engine cools down and pour in coolant whilst engine is running.
2. ***Radiator core obstructed by leaves, insects, etc.*:** Blow with air line from the back of the radiator or with a water hose to clean.
3. ***Cooling fan not operating:*** Check fan for proper cut-in and cut-out temperature. If necessary change the temperature switch or see your Dealer.
4. ***Thermostat sticking:*** If sticking in the closed position, coolant can only circulate within the cylinder head or block. Remove thermostat and check as described in section "Cooling".
5. ***Water hose split:*** Identified by rising steam from the engine compartment or the front of the vehicle. Slight splits can be repaired with insulation tape. Drive without expansion tank cap to keep the pressure in the system down, to the nearest service station.
6. ***Water pump belt torn:*** Replace and tension belt.
7. ***Water pump inoperative:*** Replace water pump.
8. ***Cylinder head gasket blown:*** Replace the cylinder head gasket.

Loss of Coolant:
1. ***Radiator leaks:*** Slight leaks may be stopped by using radiator sealing compound (follow the instructions of the manufacturer. In emergency a egg can be cracked open and poured into the radiator filler neck.
2. Hose leaks: See under 5, "Overheating".
3. Water pump leaks: Check the gasket for proper sealing or replace the pump.

Long Warming-up periods:
1. Thermostat sticking in the open position: Remove thermostat, check and if necessary replace.

CLUTCH FAULTS

Clutch slipping:	1, 2, 3, 4, 5
Clutch will not disengage fully:	4, 6 to 12, 14
Whining from clutch when pedal is depressed:	13
Clutch judder:	1, 2, 7, 10 to 13
Clutch noise when idling:	2, 3
Clutch noise during engagement:	2

Causes and Remedies
1. Insufficient clutch free play at pedal.
2. Clutch disc linings worn, hardened, oiled-up, loose or broken. Disc distorted or hub loose. Clutch disc must be replaced.
3. Pressure plate faulty. Replace clutch.
4. Air in hydraulic system. Low fluid level in clutch cylinder reservoir.
5. Insufficient play at clutch pedal and clutch release linkage. Rectify as described.
6. Excessive free play in release linkage (only for cable operated clutch, not applicable). Adjust or replace worn parts.
7. Misalignment of clutch housing. Very rare fault, but possible on transmissions with separate clutch housings. Re-align to correct.
8. Clutch disc hub binding on splines of main drive shaft (clutch shaft) due to dirt or burrs on splines. Remove clutch and clean and check splines.
9. Clutch disc linings loose or broken. Replace disc.
10. Pressure plate distorted. Replace clutch.
11. Clutch cover distorted. Replace clutch.
12. Fault in transmission or loose engine mountings.

13. Release bearing defective. Remove clutch and replace bearing.
14. A bent clutch release lever. Check lever and replace or straighten, if possible.
- The above faults and remedies are for hydraulic and mechanical clutch operation and should be read as applicable to the model in question, as the clutch fault finding section is written for all types of clutch operation.

STEERING FAULTS

Steering very heavy:	1 to 6
Steering very loose:	5, 7 to 9, 11 to 13
Steering wheel wobbles:	4, 5, 7 to 9, 11 to 16
Vehicle pulls to one side:	1, 4, 8, 10, 14 to 18
Steering wheel does not return to centre position:	1 to 6, 18
Abnormal tyre wear:	1, 4, 7 to 9, 14 to 19
Knocking noise in column:	6, 7, 11, 12

Causes and Remedies

1. Tyre pressures not correct or uneven. Correct.
2. Lack of lubricant in steering.
3. Stiff steering linkage ball joints. Replace ball joints in question.
4. Incorrect steering wheel alignment. Correct as necessary.
5. Steering needs adjustment. See your dealer for advice.
6. Steering column bearings too tight or seized or steering column bent. Correct as necessary.
7. Steering linkage joints loose or worn. Check and replace joints as necessary.
8. Front wheel bearings worn, damaged or loose. Replace bearing.
9. Front suspension parts loose. Check and correct.
10. Wheel nuts loose. Re-tighten.
11. Steering wheel loose. Re-tighten nut.
12. Steering gear mounting loose. Check and tighten.
13. Steering gear worn. Replace the steering gear.
14. Steering track rods defective or loose.
15. Wheels not properly balanced or tyre pressures uneven. Correct pressures or balance wheels.
16. Suspension springs weak or broken. Replace spring in question or both.
17. Brakes are pulling to one side. See under "Brake Faults".
18. Suspension out of alignment. Have the complete suspension checked by a dealer.
19. Improper driving. We don't intend to tell you how to drive and are quite sure that this is not the cause of the fault.

BRAKE FAULTS

Brake Failure: Brake shoe linings or pads excessively worn, incorrect brake fluid (after overhaul), insufficient brake fluid, fluid leak, master cylinder defective, wheel cylinder or caliper failure. Remedies are obvious in each instance.
Brakes Ineffective: Shoe linings or pads worn, incorrect lining material or brake fluid, linings contaminated, fluid level low, air in brake system (bleed brakes), leak in pipes or cylinders, master cylinder defective. Remedies are obvious in each instance.
Brakes pull to one side: Shoes or linings worn, incorrect linings or pads, contaminated linings, drums or discs scored, fluid pipe blocked, unequal tyre pressures, brake back plate or caliper mounting loose, wheel bearings not properly adjusted, wheel cylinder seized. Rectify as necessary.
Brake pedal spongy: Air in hydraulic system. System must be bled of air.
Pedal travel too far: Linings or pads worn, drums or discs scored, master cylinder or wheel cylinders defective, system needs bleeding. Rectify as necessary.
Loss of brake pressure: Fluid leak, air in system, leak in master or wheel cylinders, brake servo not operating (vacuum hose disconnected or exhauster pump not

Brake pedal spongy: Air in hydraulic system. System must be bled of air.

Pedal travel too far: Linings or pads worn, drums or discs scored, master cylinder or wheel cylinders defective, system needs bleeding. Rectify as necessary.

Loss of brake pressure: Fluid leak, air in system, leak in master or wheel cylinders, brake servo not operating (vacuum hose disconnected or exhauster pump not operating). Place vehicle on dry ground and depress brake pedal. Check where fluid runs out and rectify as necessary.

Brakes binding: Incorrect brake fluid (boiling), weak shoe return springs, basic brake adjustment incorrect (after fitting new rear shoes), piston in caliper of wheel cylinder seized, push rod play on master cylinder insufficient (compensation port obstructed), handbrake adjusted too tightly. Rectify as necessary. Swelling of cylinder cups through use of incorrect brake fluid could be another reason.

Handbrake ineffective: Brake shoe linings worn, linings contaminated, operating lever on brake shoe seized, brake shoes or handbrake need adjustment. Rectify as necessary.

Excessive pedal pressure required: Brake shoe linings or pads worn, linings or pads contaminated, brake servo vacuum hose (for brake servo) disconnected or wheel cylinders seized. Exhauster pump not operating (diesel). Rectify as necessary.

Brakes squealing: Brake shoe linings or pads worn so far that metal is grinding against drum or disc. Inside of drum is full of lining dust. Remove and replace, or clean out the drum(s). Do not inhale brake dust.

Note: Any operation on the steering and brake systems must be carried out with the necessary care and attention. Always think of your safety and the safety of other road users. Make sure to use the correct fluid for the power-assisted steering and the correct brake fluid.

Faults in an ABS system should be investigated by a dealer.

ELECTRICAL FAULTS

Starter motor failure:	2 to 5, 8, 9
No starter motor drive:	1 to 3, 5 to 7
Slow cranking speed:	1 to 3
Charge warning light remains on:	3, 10, 12
Charge warning light does not come on:	2, 3, 9. 11, 13
Headlamp failure:	2, 3, 11, 13, 14
Battery needs frequent topping-up:	11
Direction indicators not working properly:	2, 3, 9, 13, 14
Battery frequently discharged:	3, 10, 11, 12

Causes and Remedies

1. Tight engine. Check and rectify.
2. Battery discharged or defective. Re-charge battery or replace if older than approx. 2 years.
3. Interrupted connection in circuit. Trace and rectify.
4. Starter motor pinion jammed in flywheel. Release.
5. Also 6, 7 and 8. Starter motor defective, no engagement in flywheel, pinion or flywheel worn or solenoid switch defective. Correct as necessary.
9. Ignition/starter switch inoperative. Replace.
10. Drive belt loose or broken. Adjust or replace.
11. Regulator defective. Adjust or replace.
12. Generator inoperative. Overhaul or replace.
13. Bulb burnt out. Replace bulb.
14. Flasher unit defective. Replace unit.

WIRING DIAGRAMS
Wiring Diagram Index

1a to 1c	Starter motor, alternator, from Sept. 2002, ML 270 CDI	Page 176
2a to 2c	Common rail diesel injection system, ML 270 CDI	Page 180
3a to 3d	Instrument cluster, display instruments, warning system (163)	Page 183
4a to 4b	Signal system (163 models)	Page 187
5a to 5b	Turn signal light and hazard warning lights (163 models)	Page 189
6a to 6c	Exterior mirrors (163 models)	Page 191
7a to 7d	Exterior lights (163 models), except Xenon headlamps	Page 194
8a to 8c	Starter motor, alternator, 400 CDI	Page 198
9a to 9e	Common rail diesel injection system, ML 400 CDI	Page 201
10a to 10b	Transfer case	Page 206
11	Rear window defroster	Page 208
12a to 12b	Horn system	Page 209

Cable Colour Code

bl	=	blue		nf	=	natural colour
br	=	brown		rs	=	pink
ge	=	yellow		rt	=	red
gn	=	green		sw	=	black
gr	=	grey		vi	=	violet
				ws	=	white

Cable identification: a = size, square mm, b = basic colour, c = second colour

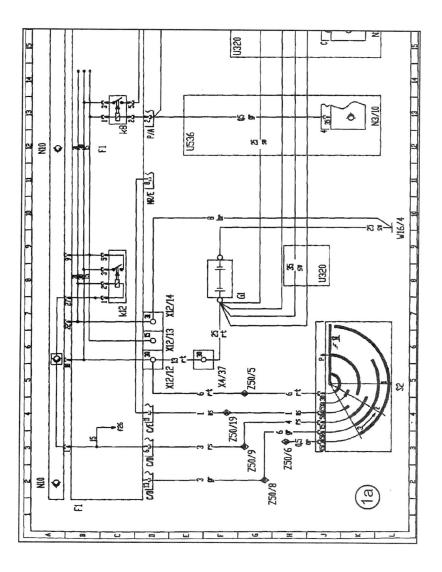

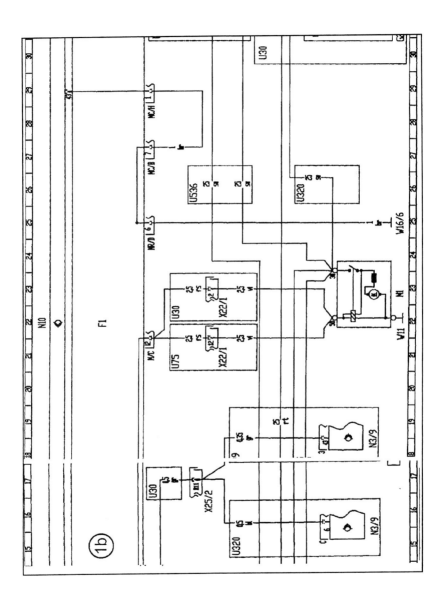

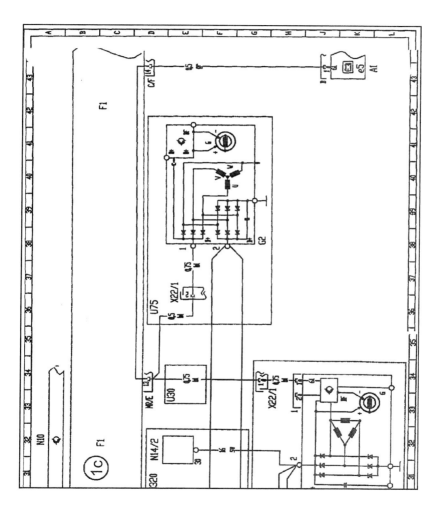

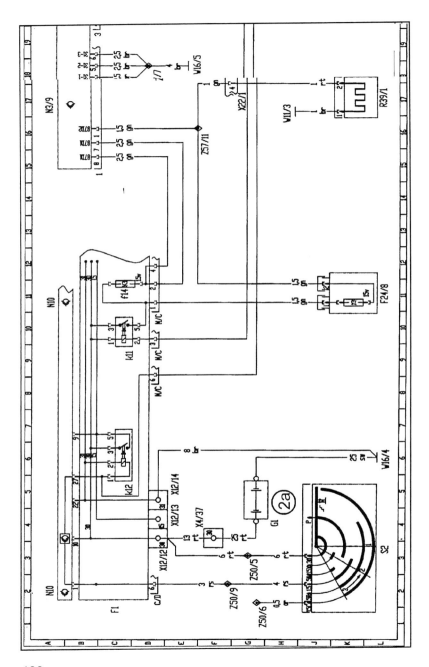

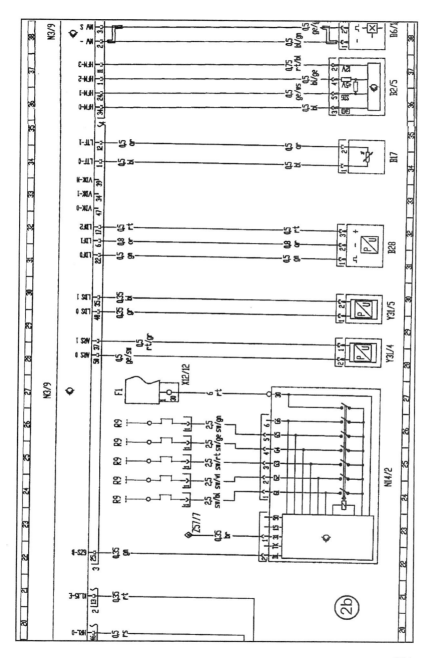

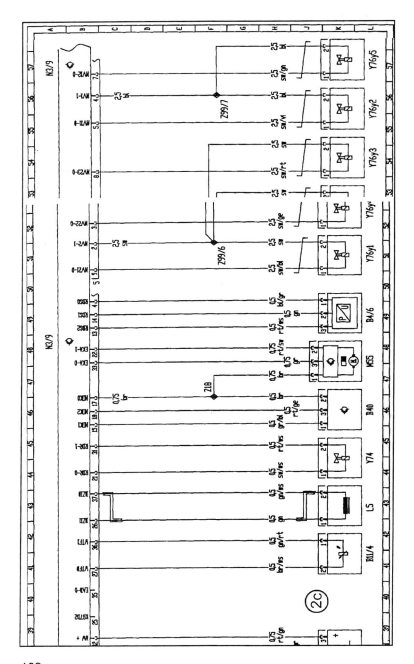

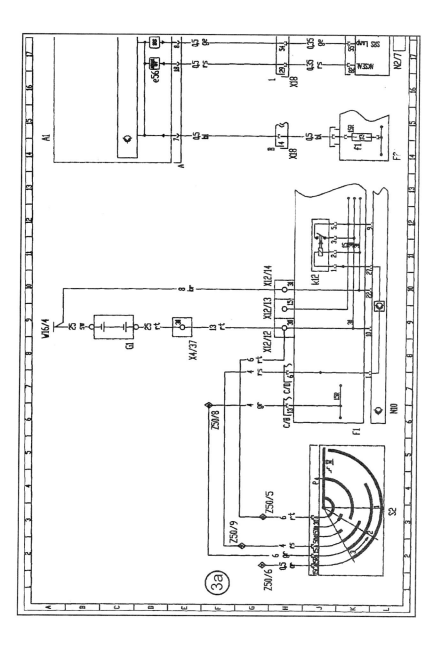

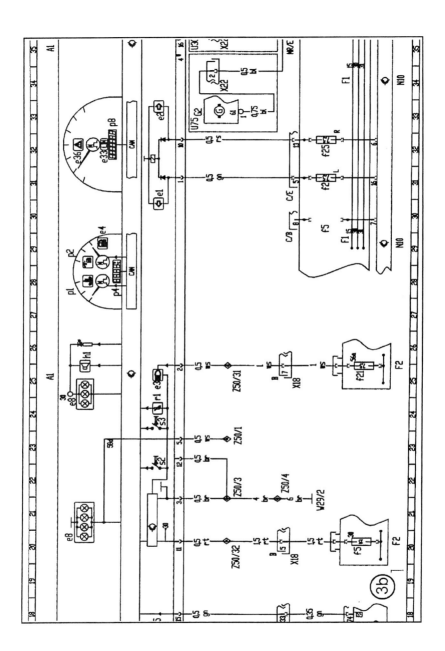

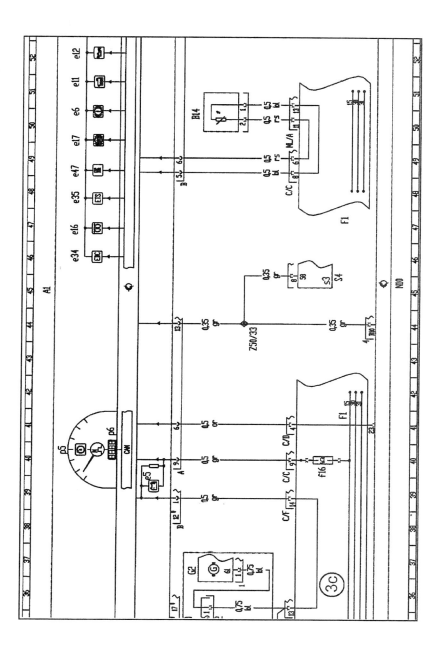

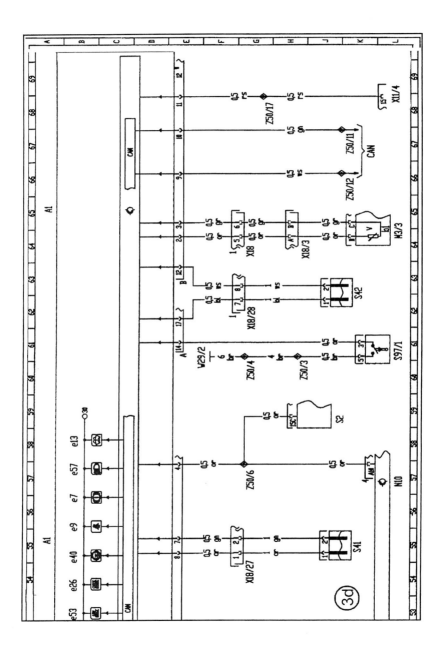

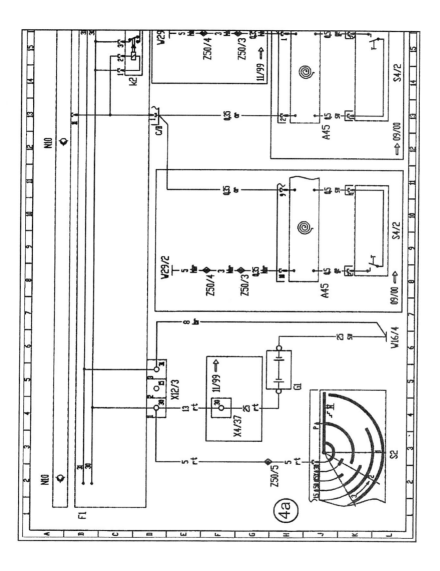

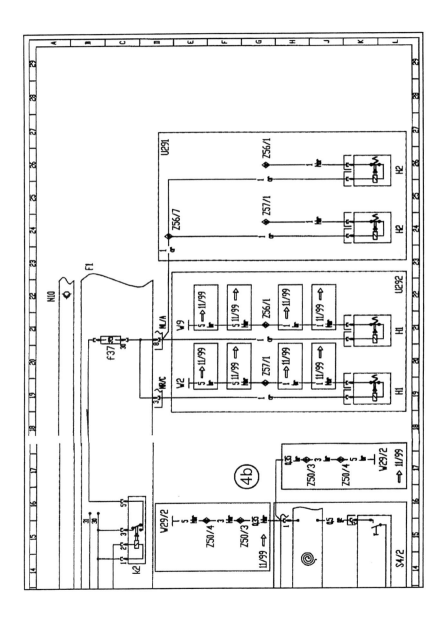

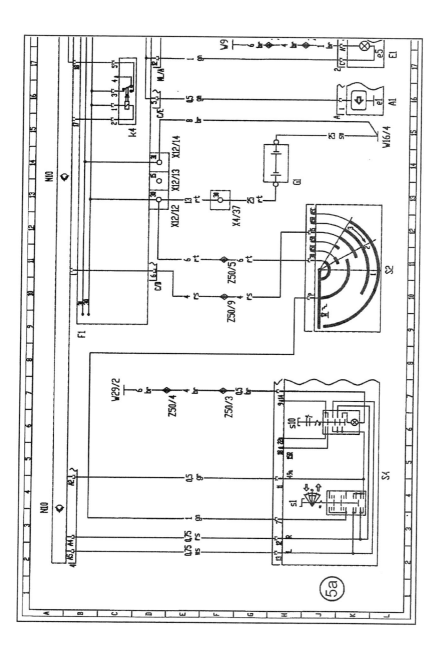

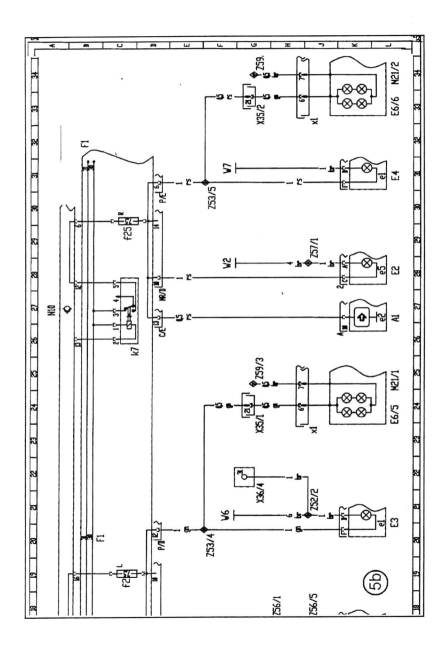

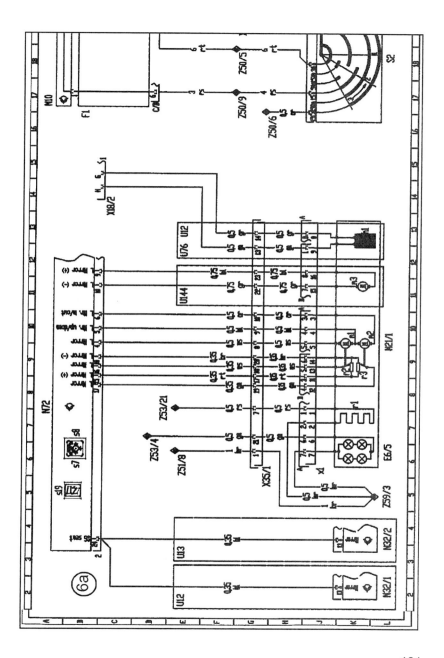

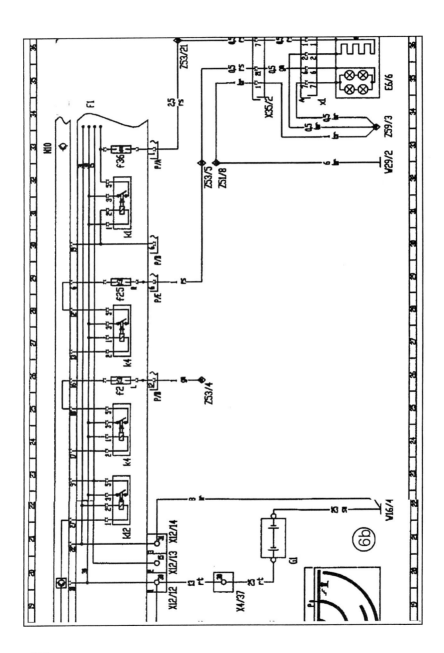

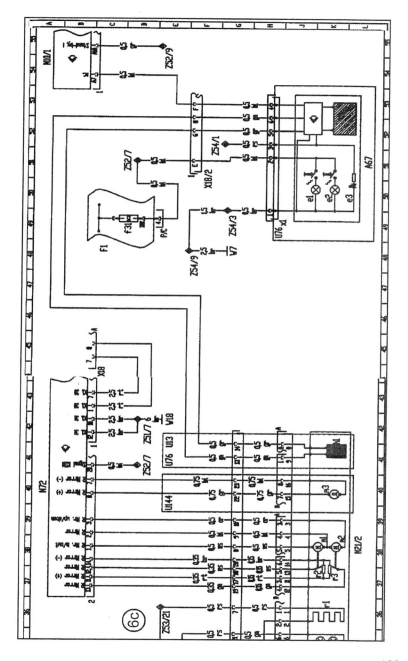

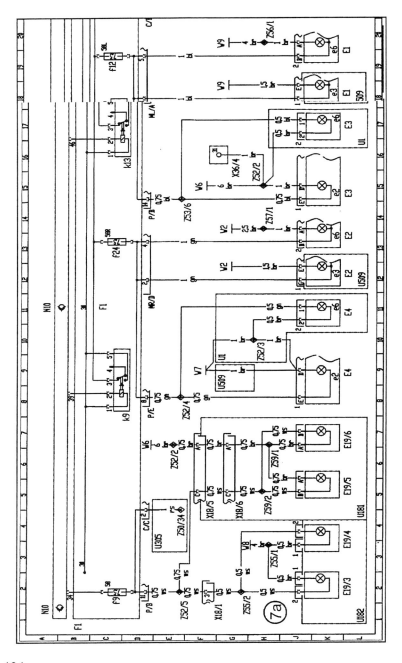

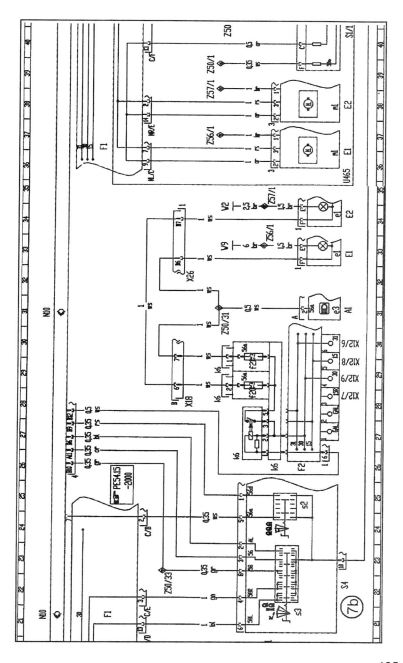

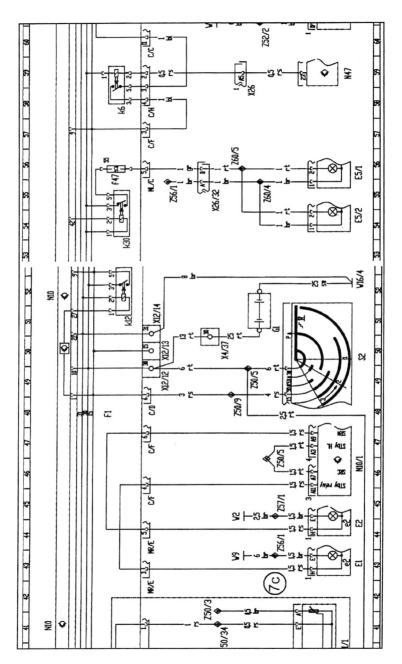

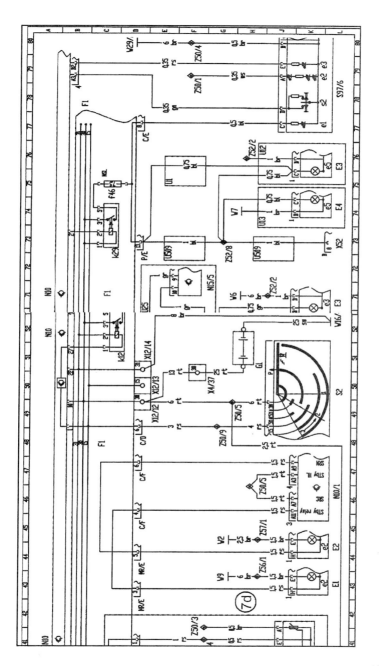

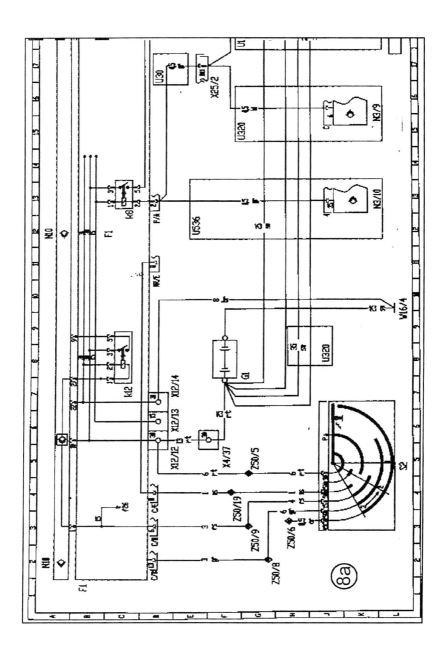

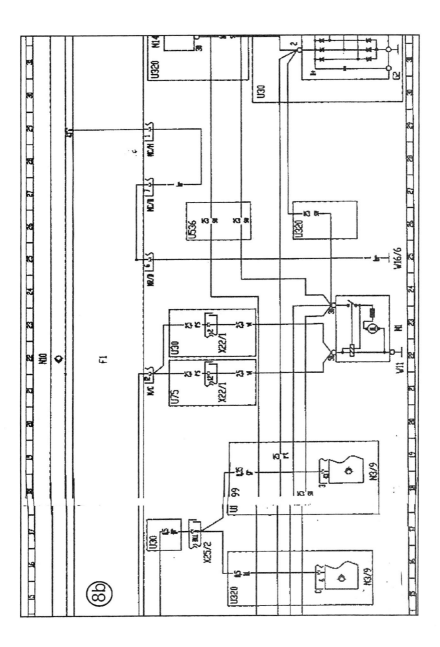

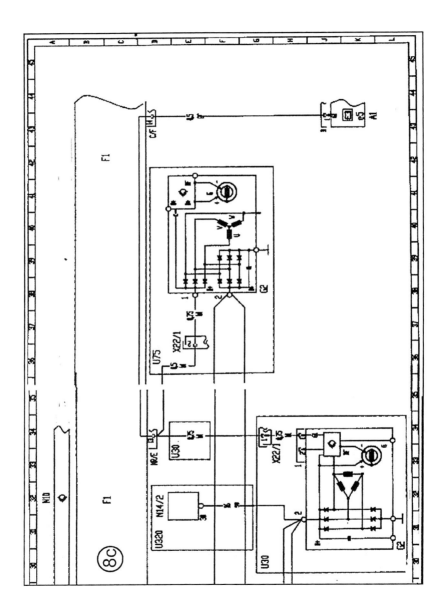

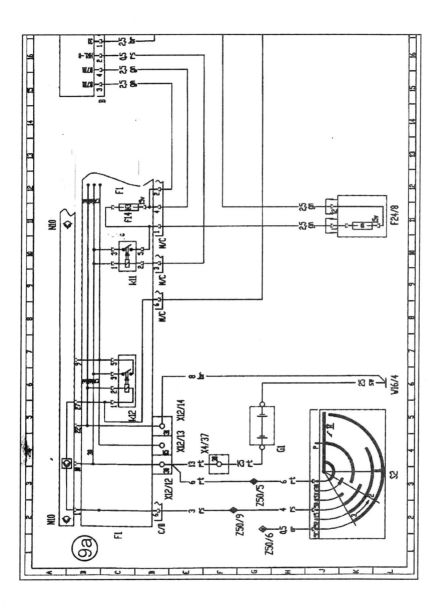

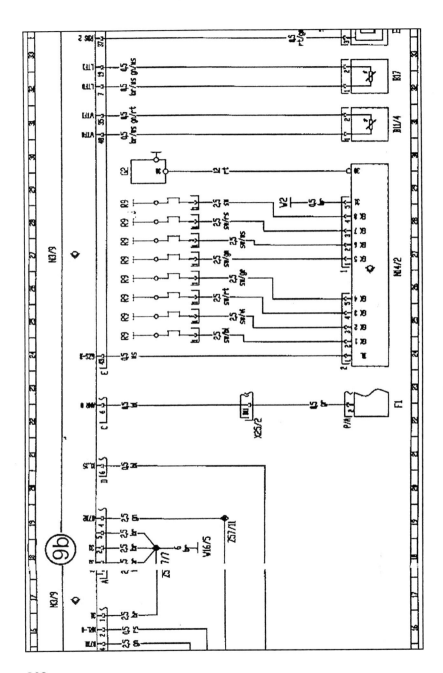

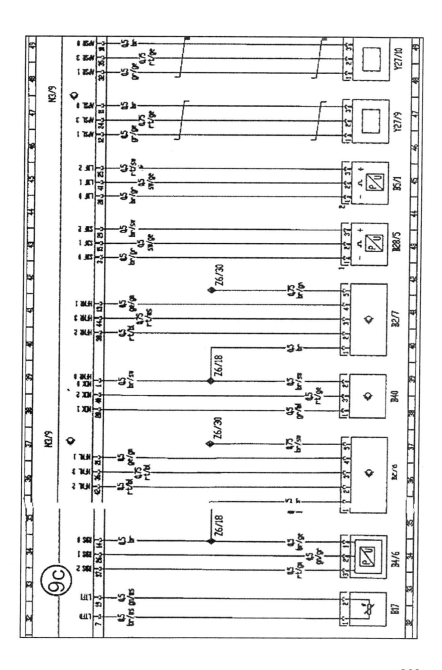

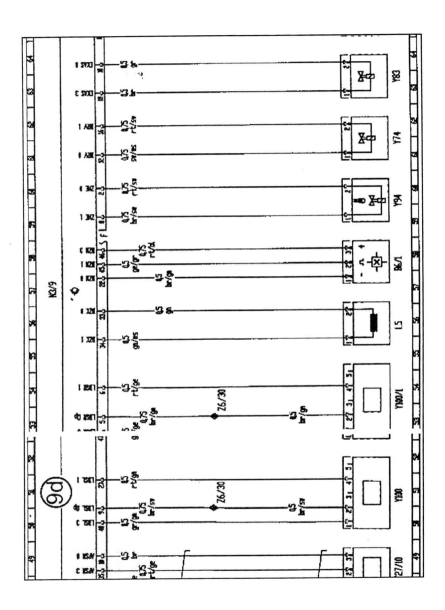

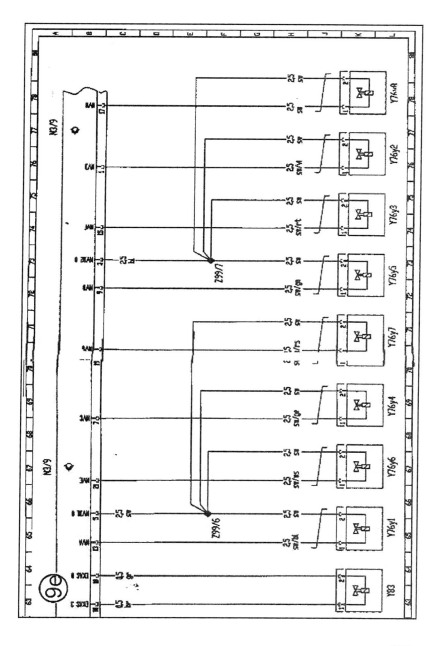

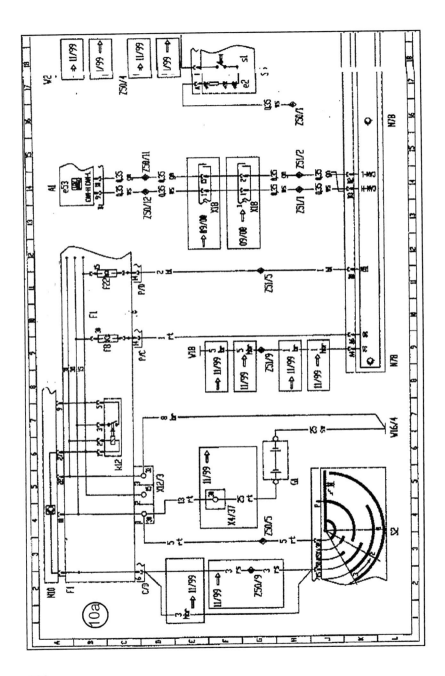

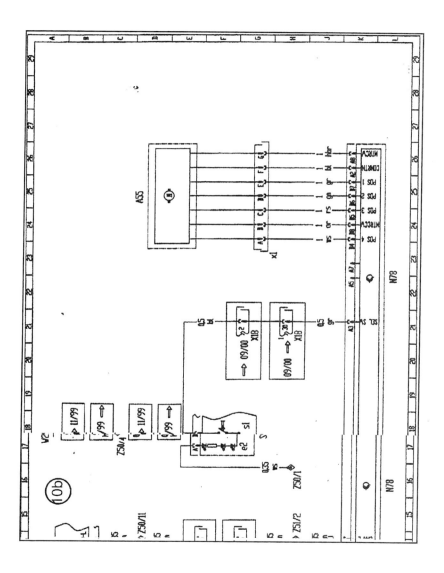

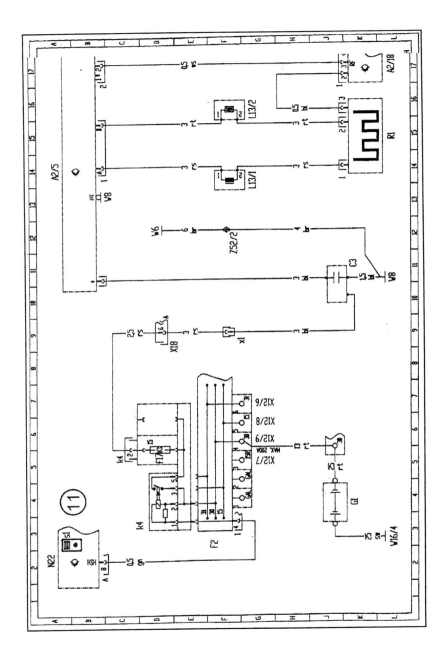

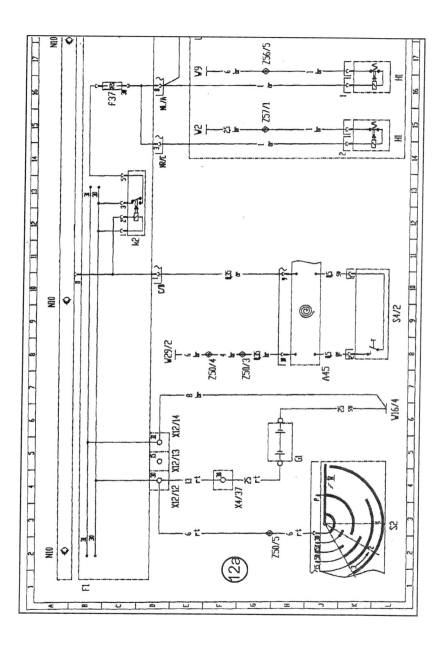

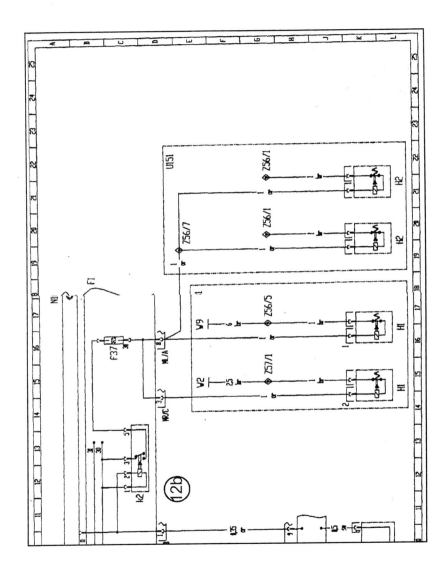

SOCIALIST HISTO

SOCIALIST HISTORY
OCCASIONAL PUBLICATIONS SERIES
No. 29

SETTING AN AGENDA

THOMSON, DOBB, HILL AND THE COMMUNIST PARTY HISTORIANS

WILLIE THOMPSON

2012

Published by the
Socialist History Society
2012

ISBN 978-0-9555138-5-5

Designed and typeset by SHS, November 2011

www.socialisthistorysociety.co.uk

Setting an Agenda:
Thomson, Dobb, Hill and the Communist Party Historians

Introduction

Although the Socialist History Society in its present form is less than twenty years old, that bare fact conceals a very different reality – for the present Society is the successor organisation to, and directly continuous with, the more venerable Communist Party Historians' Group (later the History Group). If that is treated as our origin, as it ought to be, then our seventieth anniversary will fall in 2016.

The Communist Party Historians' Group is now renowned in historiography, which is a striking example of how historical perceptions can alter, for writing in 1982 Bill Schwarz could almost apologetically begin his chapter on the Group by noting that this theme, 'would probably appear as an excessively parochial and antiquarian subject',[1] but since then at least three full-length volumes, together with many articles and chapters, have taken it as their focus, and David Parker can confidently open his admirable introduction to a recent volume of its papers with the statement that, 'The immense contribution to historical studies made by the members of the Historians' Group of the Communist Party of Great Britain is now almost universally recognised'. It was the crucible for new approaches to historical writing and interpretation which went on to have enormous impact. It inspired in the fifties the creation of the greatly respected journal *Past & Present*, which is still going strong, and was also associated with the formation of the Society for the Study of Labour History.[2] Its luminaries became world famous in their intellectual field and beyond – including Eric Hobsbawm, currently the Socialist History Society's Honorary President.

The present Society, even if it cannot hope to emulate the achievements of its mighty predecessors, still produces a significant quantity of historical output both through its own publications and in books and articles written by its members. In that context special mention should be made of the two-volume biography of Arthur Horner by Nina Fishman, our sadly missed late Secretary, who died at the end of 2009 while her *magnum opus*, a major work of historical scholarship, was still in the press.

However, this Occasional Paper is not about the Historians'

Group/Socialist History Society – that is for another time, possibly to celebrate the seventieth anniversary. Instead, my paper sets out to examine and assess three texts produced by the Group's members at the time of, or not long before, its origin, and which were of particular importance to the historical revolution which they initiated. Two of these were written in 1940,[3] while the third was published in the year of the Group's formation, 1946.

The Background

Raphael Samuel in *New Left Review,* issue no. 120, provides an insight into the thirst for historical knowledge and understanding among politically conscious workers at the beginning of the twentieth century. They were concerned with broad themes – the evolution of society through historical stages and modes of production, the emergence of class society and property relations, the significance of religion and suchlike. They showed great interest in the classical world, not least because of the example of Spartacus and slave revolts.

Things changed in the 1920s, when more immediate concerns were on the agenda, and the Communist Party during the first decade-and-a-half of its existence, though alert, as Marxists were bound to be, to historical considerations (for example in the literary essays of T A Jackson), was not strongly attuned to historical research and discussion. Maurice Dobb, though his work was to become absolutely central to the Historians' Group activities, was by profession an economist rather than a historian. And as Christopher Hill noted, before 1938 '… there was hardly any Marxist work on English History'.[4]

As several commentators have observed, the political climate which enabled the Historians' Group to come into existence a decade later, was created at the Seventh Congress of the Comintern in 1935, which saw the abandonment of the 'Class against Class' line and the sectarian postures of the preceding 'Third Period'. Instead, with fascism an increasingly menacing reality, the communist parties were exhorted to form popular fronts with all progressive forces and even not-so-progressive ones so long as they were stoutly anti-fascist. One aspect of this policy was the devotion of closer attention to radical traditions which had preceded the twentieth century and to the social matrix, embracing wider sections of the labouring poor, out of which the modern labour movements had emerged. The bourgeois revolutions and their achievements were also to be treated with greater respect, though not uncritically acclaimed. The Communist Party in Britain began to mount historical pageants to provide visual representations of its historiographical argument, and made a serious effort to identify itself as the authentic inheritor of British, especially English, radical traditions.[5]

At the Comintern's Seventh Congress in 1935, which launched the popular front strategy, Dimitrov remarked that, 'The fascists are rummaging through the entire history of every nation so as to be able to pose as the heirs and continuators of all that was exalted and heroic in the past', and criticised communists who 'do nothing to link up the present struggle with the people's revolutionary traditions and past'. Towards the end of his life, James Klugmann, the official historian of the CPGB, declared that British communists,

> ... became the inheritors of the Peasants' Revolt, of the left of the English revolution, of the pre-Chartist movement, of the women's suffrage movement from the 1790s to today. It set us in the right framework, it linked us with the past and gave us a more correct course for the future.[6]

It was from this background that in 1938 A L Morton produced *A People's History of England*, published by Victor Gollancz, as a Left Book Club choice, the first history of the country written from a Marxist perspective. As well as avoiding oversimplification, integrating various aspects of development – economic, social, political, cultural – in clear and readable prose, it presented a concisely written picture from the prehistoric era to the twentieth century. It became a classic, was reprinted as a paperback in 1965, and has remained continuously in print.

It was, following the trauma of the Second World War, which infinitely reinforced the appropriateness and importance of popular fronts, that in 1946 the Historians' Group was formed – out of meetings in London of communist historians held to discuss the preparation of a new edition of Leslie Morton's work, conceived to be necessary in the changed circumstances which faced the Party in the shape of a Labour Government and communist advance in Europe and Asia. The idea was not completely novel; earlier plans in 1938 to establish a body of this nature had been frustrated by the war.[7] The very fact that there were now British communist historians to undertake the project was significant in itself. Alongside Morton others had emerged and had already published some important texts. In 1940 Christopher Hill's brief *The English Revolution* had appeared, to be followed shortly afterwards by George

Thomson's *Aeschylus and Athens*. Of equal importance was the volume which came out in the year of the Group's formation, Maurice Dobb's *Studies in the Development of Capitalism*.

The three volumes to be considered cover an extensive timespan of European history. George Thomson's, as its title indicates, is concerned with classical Greece, and Christopher Hill's title likewise clearly announces its theme. *Studies in the Development of Capitalism* is wide-ranging in its scope, covering developments from the era of the crusades to the interwar years of the twentieth century (a postscript added in 1962 is entitled 'After the Second World War').

An aside at this point is appropriate in order to note the contemporaneous work of another Marxist, the archaeologist, V Gordon Childe, who was not a CP member and hence not associated with the Historians' Group, though that did not save him from becoming one of the names that George Orwell snitched to the secret services. Childe was concerned, as far as archaeology could do so, to explain within a Marxist perspective the development of prehistoric society through its material remains in the absence of written evidence. His key texts were *Man Makes Himself* (1936) and *What Happened in History* (1942). Childe advanced the now generally accepted concept of the Neolithic revolution, the adoption for the first time of agriculture as the predominant source of food supply, occurring in the area of the present Middle East approximately eight thousand years BCE.

> Childe showed how food production was in fact the significant distinction, making possible the controlled consumption of food, and therefore larger social units and an increased population. Ultimately it brought about fundamental changes in human thought and habits, just as the Industrial Revolution of more recent historical times has done.[8]

George Thomson, *Aeschylus and Athens*

Thomson was concerned to examine and account for the nature of classical Athenian culture in the matrix of the economic and social relations which prevailed in fifth-century BCE Attica, Athens and its rural region, and in particular the violent class conflicts which characterised that era. The subtitle of the volume is 'A Study in the Social Origins of Drama'.

Thomson, who joined the Communist Party in 1936, was primarily a literary scholar rather than a historian (his first book was *Greek Lyric Metre*) a circumstance which unfriendly critics have been at pains to emphasise. The renowned Marxist historian of the classical world, Geoffrey E M de Ste Croix,[9] is very dismissive, writing that,

> ... Thomson presents the development of Greek thought and even of Greek democracy in the sixth and fifth centuries as the consequence of the rise to power of a wholly imaginary 'merchant class'. Thomson even describes the Pythagoreans of Croton as 'the new class of rich industrialists and merchants' ... In my opinion this is little better than fantasy.[10]

Ellen Meiksins Wood's study of the social context of Western pre-modern political thought, *Citizens to Lords*, in its discussion of the Greek tragedians, makes no reference to Thomson, though her analysis does not contradict his in any substantial manner. She notes that,

> The plays of Aeschylus and Sophocles bespeak the rise of the civic community, citizenship and the rule of law, equality and justice ... But their tragedies also manifest the tensions of the democratic polis, the questions it inevitably raises about the nature and origin of political norms, moral values and conceptions of good and evil.[11]

It is in fact not particularly easy to find any contemporary material on Thomson (even Wikipedia is relatively thin), though his book created a notable impression when it was initially published, being the first attempt by a writer in English at a Marxist interpretation of classical Greek society. Bill Schwarz describes it as a '... brilliant study ... which not only raised questions about transitions in the mode of production, but also the social function of drama, issues of democracy, and fascinating investigations into totemic structures, language and ritual'.[12] Eric Hobsbawm mentions that the Historians' Group organised in the early fifties a discussion of this work and another of Thomson's on ancient Greece, with contributions from social anthropologists 'including a now [1978] famous name in the field'.[13] He does not specify whom that was, but Keith Thomas, who was after all Christopher Hill's student, seems a likely candidate.

Admittedly the work is dated and flawed in certain respects. Thomson is explicitly basing his approach on Engels's *Origins of the Family, Private Property and the State*, and on the anthropologist Lewis Morgan, whom Engels regarded as having uncovered the social structures of 'primitive' societies. Thomson also later claimed Christopher Caudwell as an inspiration.[14] The notion of a 'primitive horde' which practiced 'group marriage' – i.e. unregulated sexual behaviour – and out of which clan and tribal societies emerged, could never have existed and was a wholly discredited concept even when Thomson wrote, though to be fair, there was a legend in Attica that in the distant past society had indeed operated in that fashion. His opening chapter, on pre-literate Greek society, is mostly speculative – 'conjectural' as he puts it – and without much evidential basis. He asserts, for instance, that the origin of various cultural forms derives from primitive hunting magic,

> ...the mimetic rite, with its wild cries, abandoned gestures and ecstatic rhythm dissolves into a multiplicity of collateral activities, out of which emerge the arts of poetry, music, and the dance.[15]

It is an interesting hypothesis, but Thomson treats it as an established fact. However, it should be noted that even in these early chapters he has some pertinent points to make. Certainly his examination of the socio-cultural significance of various forms of Indo-European names for family relationships is intriguing and thought-provoking. Elsewhere though, the idea that, 'The view of human progress expressed by Aeschylus is therefore not far removed from the position of modern dialectical materialism ...' (p.306) is not one that can be taken very seriously. Reference to 'primitive materialism' (p.78) can be regarded as absurd,[16] for as Thomson himself had already noted, 'in primitive society everything is sacred, nothing profane'. (p.59) – though it is worth noting that the surviving fragment of a play by Plato's uncle contains the cynical perception that,

> ... although the laws restrained
> Mankind from deeds of open violence
> They still did wrong in secret, until some
> Shrewd and far-sighted thinker had the wit

> To invent gods, that all who did or said
> Or even imagined evil might be afraid.

Thomson's anachronisms and gestures to the communist dogmas of the time do not discredit the volume as a whole or detract from its overall importance. Geoffrey de Ste Croix may or may not be right to dismiss the notion of a 'merchant class' as 'wholly imaginary' (one would hardly dare to argue with his expertise) – yet surely it cannot be denied that with the remarkable growth in the sixth and fifth centuries of trade based on coined money, there did exist a substantial corps of merchants, or traders, as Ste Croix prefers to call them.

Dionysus, Orpheus and Tragedy

The discussion of early Greek society and its relation to tribal structures is interesting and extensive. In fact, Thomson is over half-way through the volume – at Part 4 (chapter 12) – before he begins to concentrate on Aeschylus or the city of Athens in any detail. What he is concerned to do is to trace the emergence of Greek drama, tragedy in particular, out of various forms of religious ritual as these were modified by developments in social relations, particularly class relations. The titles of his chapters up to that point give an idea of the themes he is exploring and his interpretation of their development – Part 1 (Tribal Society); Totemism, Exogamy, Property; Part 2 (from Tribe to State); Monarchy, Aristocracy, Tyranny; Part 3 (Origin of Drama); Initiation, Dionysus, Orphism, Dithyramb, Tragedy.

The god Dionysus, Greek counterpart of the Roman Bacchus, is regarded as being of particular importance. In Thomson's view his worship was initially practised by the hard-pressed lower orders, particularly women, for consolatory purposes, as an escape in fantasy from the cruel reality of their lives, and which was then, like Christianity in future centuries, taken over by the elites but retained certain clues as to its origins, particularly the relatively high profile of women in the ceremonies and myths. Thomson is emphatic that the Dionysian myths, as with those of other gods, grew out of seasonal rituals, *not* that the rituals were devised as illustration of the myths. 'They (the rituals) were very ancient – older in fact than the god to whose name they were attached – and they consisted of a primitive form of agricultural magic'. (p.141)

Dionysus, particularly in his Bacchus manifestation, is in popular memory most associated with wine – which can when consumed in sufficient quantity certainly produce a mental state of ecstasy and abandon – but the key point about him was that with or without alcohol he was the god of orgiastic wildness and indifference to convention – which was also intertwined with human sacrifice. In the sixth century BCE, the Athenian tyrant (in its original meaning a non-traditional ruler, not a cruel despot) Peisistratos, whose power base was among the poor Attic peasantry, promoted Dionysian worship to weaken the aristocracy's control of religion.

Orphism, a religious cult of the mythical musician Orpheus, originating in Thrace, was a further development of Dionysus worship, but with less emphasis on female participation, and, transplanted into the city in the wake of trade and industry, was 'an outgrowth of the urban revolution'. Thomson thinks it likely to have reflected the outlook of a dispossessed peasantry. Their account of the origins of the earth and humanity is derived from Hesiod the eighth-century BCE poet of an independent but hard-pressed and overworked peasantry – he describes his own holding at the foot of Mount Helicon as 'a cursed place, cruel in winter, hard in summer, never pleasant'.

The Orphics treated life as bad news for the living person, a penance which had to be lived through in toil and misery to atone for the sin of the Titans who killed and devoured Dionysus (he was subsequently resurrected) for the human soul is born from the ingested god after Zeus blasted the Titans with his thunderbolt, but the human body from the ashes of the Titans. 'The body is the tomb of the soul ... All life is a rehearsal for death [through which] the soul can hope to escape from its imprisonment'. (p.146) However if the individual has been very evil the soul is damned to eternal torment. If it is salvageable it undergoes reincarnation till after three lives of asceticism and following the correct rituals it is allowed to join the blessed in the Elysian fields. '... man is to God and body to soul what the slave is to his master'. It was a doctrine which, turned upside-down, was at the foundation of Plato's aristocratic and virulently anti-democratic metaphysic and the resemblance to Christian mythology is not accidental. Thomson concludes that, '...the movement drew its initial inspiration from the sufferings of the peasantry, turned off the land and enslaved or driven into industry by the urban revolution'. However it subsequently penetrated into all classes of society, including aristocrats like Plato – and, with modifications, a moderately prosperous Hellenised Jew, Saul of Tarsus.

According to Thomson,

[The Orphics] could not rest content with what they had be-

cause they had nothing, and their hopes were as infinite as
their desires. All life was strife and struggle. And if man would
only run the race with courage, there was none so humble or
debased but he might win the prize of glory and become a god.
In all this the Orphics revealed – in an inverted and mystical
form – the objective potentialities of the democratic movement
... (pp.152-3)

Whether this argument will stand up to investigation might be questionable, given the reality that, like Christianity, Orphism soon came to be adopted by all classes in society including the elite, but given the emphasis on suffering and redemption it is not an unreasonable interpretation of its beginnings.

Bertrand Russell in his *History of Western Philosophy*, written about the same time as Thomson's book, gives considerable space to discussion of Orphism. He is conscious, though naturally not to the same extent as Thomson, of its social context and origins, and quoting a student of the cult writes that,

> They were first of all associations for the worship of Dionysus; but they were distinguished by two features which were new among the Hellenes. They looked to revelation as the source of religious authority, and they were organised as artificial communities. ... the word 'orgy' was used by the Orphics to mean 'sacrament', and was intended to purify the believer's soul and enable it to escape from the wheel of birth. The Orphics ... founded what we may call 'churches', i.e. religious communities to which anybody without distinction of age or sex, could be admitted by initiation ...

The concept of initiation, to which Thomson devotes a chapter, derives from the universal practice, often painful, in clan and tribal societies, by which the youth are admitted to the secrets of the universe as understood by the clan elders, and into adult life. It was seen as a form of rebirth – the child died and the adult was born. The structure of initiation followed certain rules – first purification, then revelation of secret knowledge frequently accompanied by ordeal, and celebration after the ordeal was over and the initiate was supposedly reborn.

Orphic practices imitated those structures and so did Athenian tragedy. The meaning of the word was not what it is in modern English – literally it means 'goat-song', a goat being the prize for the winner of the theatrical competition at the Athenian Dionysian festival when the winning tragedies were presented. These took the form of trilogies, comparable to acts in modern theatre, followed by a 'satyr play' – again the Dionysus reference, for satyrs were his companions.

The best-known fact about Athenian theatre is that the actors wore masks – indeed the combination of tragic and comic mask remains a theatrical icon – and the reason for this is linked to the fact that in the early days there was only a single actor (plus chorus) on stage at any one time, which one source describes as 'animated oratorios'. Aeschylus is credited with having introduced the practice of two actors; his successors expanded this to three, but never a greater number. The Dionysia which included the theatrical performances was a religious event and the single actor was derived from the priest who officiated at Dionysian rituals and wore a mask representing the god. The chorus originally represented the worshippers. Even while there were two actors on the stage plus chorus, Aeschylus's dramas only have two-way dialogues – between the two actors or between either and the chorus, never a three-way one. A further widely-known feature of these plays was what Aristotle termed the 'unities' – the action had to take place in a single setting and cover the events of a single day, again features of the religious rituals from which they were descended. Events taking place off-stage at different times and places were reported rather than performed. For the same reason, the revelation of secret knowledge usually formed a central element of the plot.

Moira and the Erinyes

Moira was not the name of a person. It meant roughly share or portion, and according to Thomson, derived from the lot drawn in tribal agricultural society when the available land was periodically redivided between households (a similar procedure is referred to in the Old Testament book of Joshua). However it assumed in due course a metaphorical significance and came to mean what we would call our ticket in life's lottery, in other words the lot assigned by the Fates (represented as three women, the Moirai, identical to the Norns of Norse mythology) to an individual at birth and 'represented the authority of ancestral custom which determined from birth the part allotted to the individual in the life of the tribe.' (p.46) It fixed an individual's unavoidable destiny – Oedipus's *moira* was to accidentally kill his father and marry his mother, Orestes's to deliberately murder his mother. It is easy to see that this was nothing else than the ideological reflection of an all too material social reality, where the majority had to endure the hard and dangerous station in life that they found themselves in, and the elites could congratulate themselves on their fortunate winning ticket – but nevertheless always faced the possibility of early death through accident, plague, battle or murder.

Nor is it difficult to see how the concept of *moira* could be readily put to use for reconciling tender consciences to the existence of slavery and its great and increasing prevalence in fifth-century BCE Athens, when Aeschylus was writing. Slaves were used in a great number of functions – as a labour force and as domestics on the estates of the landowning elite, in the city again as domestics, also for municipal purposes (even police duties!) and in brothels. Most importantly however was the slave labour force employed in the silver mines at Laurion, on which Athens's commercial power depended.

The conditions in which these centrally important slaves worked were unspeakable. Ste Croix suggests that the Christian image of hell may have been derived from the nature of this forced labour. No contemporary description exists of what the Laurion mines were like, but Thomson quotes an account of the similar Egyptian mines, operated by the Romans in the first century BCE, where conditions were unlikely to have been very different:

> To these mines the Egyptian king sends condemned criminals, captives in war and those who have fallen victim to false accusations or been imprisoned for incurring the royal displeasure, sometimes with all their kinsfolk – both for the punishment of the guilty and the profits which accrue from their labour. There they throng, all in chains, all kept at work continuously day and night. ... Where the daylight is shut out by the twists and turns of the quarry, they wear lamps tied to their foreheads, and there, contorting their bodies to fit the contours of the rock ... [toil] on and on without intermission under the pitiless overseers lash. Young children descent the shafts into the bowels of the earth ... No-one could look on the squalor of these wretches, with not even a rag to cover their loins, without feeling compassion for their plight. They may be sick, or maimed, or aged, or weakly women, but there is no indulgence, no respite. All alike are kept at their labour by the lash, until, overcome by hardships, they die in their torments ... and death is welcomed as a thing more desirable than life.

Thomson comments that it is not for the citizens of an empire which continues to employ children in mines and factories (presumably he is thinking of India) to accuse the Romans, but 'it is necessary for us to remember the blood and tears that were shed on the raw materials of Greek art'. (pp. 149-50)

Aeschylus writes that in its early days, before the ascendancy of the Olympian gods, the world was governed by 'the threefold Moirai and the unforgiving Erinyes'. The latter, also known as the Furies, were the ministers of vengeance who pursued and drove into insanity any person who committed the unforgivable crime of killing a fellow clan member, or more generally, tried to violate their 'established portion or the limits set to human conduct', in other words, their *moira*. 'The Moirai decree what shall be, and the Erinyes see to it that their decrees are carried out'. (p.30) Aeschylus, as we shall see, in his surviving work (most of his dramas are lost) attached great importance to the Erinyes.

The concept of *moira*, however, did also have a more positive result than propounding the notion of an assigned and unalterable fate, for closely related to it was another concept, that of *nomos*, which also in its origins referred to a portion, though in this instance the right to keep a specified number of stock on the common pasture rather than share in arable land. It too developed metaphorical significations, and took on the sense of customary right and hence of great importance to the Athenian democracy in its struggle with the landowning elites.

The Athenian Struggle

Democracy only became embedded in Athenian society following a lengthy and turbulent history of struggle, and though tenacious it was never secure. It was a form of direct instead of representative democracy. All citizens, namely adult males,[17] were expected to attend and participate in the Assembly, with decisions reached by majority vote. Appointments to executive offices however were not voted upon, they were decided by drawing lots and they were time limited. In practice leadership tended to fall to wealthy and well-connected citizens, such as Themistokles and Perikles, who had the leisure to learn and practice the arts of persuasion and public speaking – but these had to satisfy the public or risk seeing themselves indicted and punished by popular vote.

This democracy reached its full expression at the end of the Persian wars early in the fifth century BCE; its achievement coincided with the years in which Aeschylus was writing. During the previous century tyranny (keeping in mind the different meaning of the term) and oligarchic rule had been the norm, but following the wars the ordinary citizens who had served in the fearsome hoplite infantry that won the land battles and crewed the ships that destroyed the Persian fleet, could no longer be disregarded. The aristocracy hated the system, as is evident from the writings of Plato, (whose birth name was Aristokoles) but endured it for a number of reasons. Firstly, if they challenged it head-on they had no guarantee of success; but more importantly they could afford to put up with their relative political subordination since they had plentiful slaves to exploit. Moreover, following its success in the war the Athenians had erected an empire, the Delian League, under the pretence of an alliance, and this they exploited commercially, a further source of wealth for the elites. It was this wealth which enabled the construction of the magnificent public buildings and monuments for which classical Athens is renowned.

Athenian democracy therefore had its downside and was established on the backs of the female half of the population, working immigrants to the city who lacked civic rights, an extensive and growing slave population and the 'allies' under Athenian hegemony. It was this latter relationship which was responsible for the Peloponnesian War which, after a series of frictions, broke out in 431 BCE between Athens and Sparta,[18] the city which dominated the Pelopennese peninsula and feared Athenian ambition. The war lasted several decades with much death and destruction and resulted in Athens's total defeat.

The victorious Spartans during their occupation imposed upon Athens an oligarchy known as the Thirty Tyrants, but that was soon overthrown and the democracy restored. Although Athens had ceased to be a first-rate power the democracy survived until the Macedonian conquest in the fourth century, and for internal affairs even beyond that, until the Roman conquest in the second century BCE. The Romans, as was their custom, imposed, or in Athens's case, reimposed, oligarchic local government, this time for good.

Aeschylus and his Plays
The dramatist himself came from a wealthy background, and was born around 525 BCE, dying in 456. He fought at the victory of Marathon in 490 BCE which repelled the first Persian invasion, and also in the subsequent fighting against renewed invasion.[19] There are differing views regarding his politics. It has been claimed that he was a supporter of oligarchic rule, but there is no direct evidence of that and on the evidence of his plays it seems unlikely. Thomson describes him as a 'moderate democrat', another source as a 'broadminded conservative'. Regularly the winner at the Dionysia contests in which he competed, he is said to have been the author

of around ninety dramas, but of these only seven survive, and the authorship of one of them is uncertain.

Earlier Plays

Although Greek drama tended to concentrate on mythological or legendary themes, as did most of Aeschylus's output, the oldest of his extant works deals with contemporary history, the second Persian invasion and its critical turning point, the naval battle of Salamis, in which Aeschylus himself also took part, and the destruction of the Persian war fleet. None of the action is shown on stage of course, the play, in accordance with the style of Greek drama, consists entirely of dialogue conducted in stable surroundings. Interestingly, the *Persae* is staged from the point of view of the enemy, specifically the family of the Persian monarch, Xerxes. The message of the play however, unapologetically patriotic, is not sympathetic to the Persian viewpoint – it warns, through his mother, of the danger of the hubris (Greek *hybris*) that Xerxes has committed from challenging the gods by his pontoon bridge over the Hellespont (Dardanelles). The ghost of Darius, his predecessor, is then brought on stage to round off the denunciation.

That is straightforward enough, good patriotic propaganda cleverly handled, and it may be of some importance that the play's sponsor was Perikles, later the democratic leader, suggesting that Aeschylus was no supporter of oligarchy.

The next extant play is *Seven against Thebes* (the existing text however is corrupt), based on Greek legend regarding the sons of Oedipus, and focused upon the power of oracles, fratricidal conflict and – an important consideration – the responsibility of a king towards the people under his rule. The lost predecessor play of the trilogy to which *Seven* belongs, dealt with Oedipus' father Laios, and raised the issue, according to Thomson, of 'a conflict between the interests of the state and those of the ruling dynasty'. (p.281)

The next survivor is *The Suppliants*, the opening play of a trilogy dealing with an implausible myth of two brothers, one whom had fifty sons and the other fifty daughters. The brothers agree that the sons of one should marry the daughters of the other; the daughters object vehemently and, now joined by their father Danaos, flee from Egypt to supplicate the King of Argos for refuge and protection from the forcible marriage, hence the title. By Thomson's interpretation (which he does not claim to be novel) and taking into account what is know about the two missing linked plays, there are two significant social issues raised. Firstly, in *The Suppliants*, when the King of Argos has listened to their case he declares that he will have to consult his people before reaching a decision – as a good ruler should.

Even more important though, there is the issue of why the Danaides object to the marriage. They do so not because it is an arranged one, or because they find their suitors repulsive, but because they regard it as incestuous. In exogamous clan society first-cousin marriage is banned. However it is quite different in Attic law, where such marriage is compulsory if a woman is the only heir on her father's death – and even if it involves her divorcing an existing husband. The King of Argos comments, 'if the sons of Aigyptos [Danaos's brother] are your masters by the law of the land, claiming to be your next-of-kin, who would wish to oppose them?' Subsequently he remarks, 'And yet by this means [first-cousin marriage] mortal wealth is multiplied'. Thomson comments, 'Exactly: the way to accumulate wealth is to keep it "in the family" and that can only be done by keeping the heiress "in the family"'.

Thomson then quotes an opponent of his interpretation who writes that, 'The real issue seems to be the right of women to refuse to be forced into marriage ... The crime of the sons of Aigyptos is their determination to force themselves on unwilling brides'. Thomson retorts that,

> If that was the crime ... it was a crime enjoined in democratic Athens by an express provision of the law. ... the moral issue has been isolated from its social context. The influence of private property on the morals of the proprietors raises issues which contemporary critics are instinctively reluctant to explore, and so they 'cannot believe' it is fundamental. To Aeschylus however, living in the heyday of ancient democracy, the subjection of women was not only just, but preferable to the liberty they had formerly enjoyed. (p.293)

However Aeschylus's genius as a dramatist is shown in the fact that even though he rejects it, he has the Danaides state their case eloquently.

The Oresteia

Related issues are explored in the trilogy on which Aeschylus's modern reputation principally rests. It is an even more complex work and its social significance both nuanced and intriguing. *The Oresteia,* produced late in the playwright's life, is the only one of his trilogies which survives complete, and around the bloody drama of Agamemnon and his children he constructs a moral lesson which validates the social structure and cultural norms prevailing in the Athens of his time, the mid-fifth century BCE, when it was at the height of its power, prosperity and cultural magnificence in the years between the defeat of Persia and the outbreak of the Peloponnesian War.

Agamemnon, the king of Mycenae (or Argos in some versions) was in the Homeric epics the Greek leader in the Trojan War. Having angered the gods while the Greek army was assembling at the port of Aulis, he was forced to appease them by making a human sacrifice of his daughter Iphigenia, so that a favourable wind could be obtained, then angered them again by his behaviour at the sack of Troy when the Greeks violated the sacred temples.

Consequently he is doomed when he returns home. His wife Clytemnestra, sister of Helen of Troy, has been planning vengeance for Iphigenia and is further enraged when Agamemnon brings home with him as his sex-slave Kassandra, the captured daughter of the Trojan king. She proceeds to murder them both with the help of Agamemnon's relative, Aegisthus. However her son young Orestes, who had been sent to another part of Greece to get him out of the way, when he reaches adulthood secretly returns, and with the assistance of his sister Elektra, kills both Aegisthus and Clytemnestra. Orestes, then as a matricide, is pursued by the Erinyes, driving him mad with remorse and horror. Taking refuge in the temple of the god Apollo, who had put him up to the killing and indeed threatened him with severe punishment if he refused, proves only a temporary expedient, and, continuing to be tormented by the Erinyes, Orestes flees next to Athens, where the patron goddess of the city, Athena, convenes a court in which Apollo, acting as the spokesperson of Zeus, and the Erinyes upholding mother-right, argue their respective cases and which acquits Orestes – on Athena's casting vote – and integrates the Erinyes into Greek society, changing their name to Eumenides (kindly ones).

Such are the bare outlines of the story, but Aeschylus fills it with moral subtlety and develops the argument not between right and wrong but over different and competing rights. Firstly, Agamemnon's situation when the goddess Artemis demands that he sacrifice his daughter.[20] To be sure, his foolish behaviour and boastfulness have put him in that position, but if he refuses, the fleet will be unable to sail, he will have let down his brother Menelaus, on whose behalf he is leading the expedition to recover Menelaus's abducted wife, Helen, and will have made the Greek warriors preparing to attack Troy look proper fools. Perhaps one person should die for the benefit of a much greater number.

A modern sensibility however would conclude that Agamemnon deserved everything he got, and Aeschylus does not fail to let the audience hear Clytemnestra's justification of her actions, expressing the passionate rage she feels on behalf of her murdered daughter. We then reach the heart of the matter, the contrary forces acting on Orestes. Is he justified in avenging his father by slaughtering his mother? The male-dominated Olympian gods in the person of Apollo insist upon it, the Erinyes take a different point of view. Significantly, they are indifferent to Clytemnestra's killing of Agamemnon – he is not kin, merely a husband. It is not only a case of Agamemnon himself, his ancestors had form, including eating their relatives, and the family is under a hereditary curse. Visiting the iniquities of the fathers upon the children even unto the third and fourth generation was standard practice in clan societies.

It is not difficult to detect the social conflicts underlying the representations of the legendary characters by Aeschylus, in the form stated by Thomson as, 'To which parent does the son owe the prior duty'? – in other words, which is the better form of social structure and relationship, that of the ancient clan society of matrilineal inheritance, relatively equal apportionment, and blood feud when a kinsperson was killed, or the existing patriarchal, hierarchical, judicial and commercial state of affairs? Historically of course the issue had long been settled, Aeschylus's purpose was to justify the outcome ideologically and artistically.

Thomson quotes Athena's judgment,

> With all my heart I commend the masculine
> Wherefore I shall not hold of higher worth
> A woman who was killed because she killed
> Her wedded lord and master of her home. (p.269)

And as Thomson concludes,

> The reason[ing] could not have been more clearly stated ... Athena endorses the attitude of Apollo, thus laying down the cardinal principle of the Attic law of inheritance in which ... the liberty of the wife [was] narrowly circumscribed in the interests of the husband ... And if we ask why the dramatist has made the outcome of the trial turn on the social relation of the sexes, the answer is that he regarded the subordination of woman, quite correctly as an indispensable condition of [Athenian] democracy ... the subjection of woman was a necessary consequence of the development of private property. (ibid)

Thomson argues that the narrative of this trilogy mirrors the growth of law through different stages of development and that in the outcome, 'The conflict between tribal custom and aristocratic privilege has been resolved in democracy'. It also ratifies the principle of male dominance and, 'the emergence of a state in which the [male] common people had recovered in a new form the equality denied to them during the rule of the aristocracy'. (p.270)

It is worth noting that the Orestes story is capable of being be utilised for quite other purposes. During the nazi occupation of France, Sartre staged in Paris a play, *The Flies*, modelled, with some amendments, on the middle drama of the trilogy, its classical form being adopted in order to deceive the German censorship. In this case, however, Aegisthus represents the occupier, Clytemnestra the Vichy collaborators, Elektra the intimidated citizenry and Orestes the Resistance forces, who then takes upon himself the responsibility for killing the occupiers and collaborators, that responsibility being represented by the flies (the Erinyes).

Prometheus Bound

The date of this play is uncertain and there are significant doubts as to whether Aeschylus actually wrote it, though ancient writers were unanimous that he did. The myth of Prometheus is well known – he stole fire from the gods and gave it to humankind, and in punishment Zeus chained him to a rock where every day his constantly regenerating liver was devoured by an eagle. Marx regarded him as his patron saint.

However he was not universally treated as a hero. According to Hesiod, technology, for which fire stands as the symbol, had, through the jealousy of the gods, brought only grief and woe upon mankind, social division and endless toil 'instead of enlarging it has diminished the sum of human happiness'. His role is cognate with that of Adam and Eve in the Hebrew myth. Prometheus, in this version is an upstart who well deserved his punishment, an attitude which Thomson regards as typical of the aristocracy, intended to justify their class rule.

In *Prometheus Bound* Zeus is a despotic tyrant (and rapist) who instructs his ministers Might and Violence to take Prometheus to his rock, where the blacksmith god Hephaistos (the Roman Vulcan) reluctantly, for he is sympathetic, chains him up. Throughout most of the play Prometheus constantly and defiantly denounces Zeus, his tyranny and sexual voracity. In the subsequent plays of the trilogy so far as they can be reconstructed, however, Zeus learns justice, mercy and self-control, while Prometheus is persuaded to reveal a secret which will save Zeus from future destruction, so they are reconciled and Prometheus is released.

Thomson sees this outcome as reflecting and endorsing Athens's political evolution towards democracy, and comments that,

> It is essential, however, to remember that [this democracy] owed its completeness to the fact that there was another class which was not free. The slaves were the proletariat of ancient democracy and if they had not been slaves, incapable of organisation and therefore politically powerless, the overthrow of the landed aristocracy would have been followed by a struggle between them and their masters. It was only by excluding this class from his very conception of democracy that Aeschylus was able to regard the democratic revolution as a fusion of opposites symbolised in the reconciliation of Zeus and Prometheus. (p.323)

After Aeschylus

Aeschylus's successor as leading playwright – their writing careers overlapped – was Sophokles, a very wealthy man and holder of both high military and civil appointments as well as a poet, whose life spanned the fifth century almost exactly. He therefore was a witness to Athens's triumph and arrogance as well as its subsequent tragedy. His *Antigone* addresses the conflict between family loyalty and reasons of state, and in Thomson's view, Sophokles's theme, expressed particularly in relation to the Oedipus myth, again reflecting the character of Athenian history in his lifetime, is the manner in which praiseworthy intentions produce their exact opposite via the law of unintended consequences – Oedipus the king for example destroys himself by trying to govern impeccably. 'The Oedipus of Sophokles is a symbol of the deep-seated perplexity engendered in men's minds by the unforeseen and incomprehensible transformation of a social order designed to establish liberty and equality into an instrument for the destruction of liberty and equality'. (p.340)

The third great dramatist is Euripides, a younger contemporary of Sophokles; the latter is reported to have said that he portrayed men as they ought to be and Euripides as they actually were. Thomson contends that, 'Euripides, like Aeschylus, was actively conscious of his relation to society; but for that reason his work was fundamentally different, because society had changed'. His characters are more rounded and human, with greater depth of feeling than those of the other two; they give an insight into the sentiments of women and even slaves. Thomson says of Euripides, an unusually large number of whose plays have survived, that conscious as he was of the widening cleavage in Athenian society due to imperial wealth and the stress of war, 'Euripides was a democrat who saw that democracy was being driven to self-destruction', but could see no way forward. In his later plays he turned to Orphic mysticism.

Thomson concludes that, like the Dionysiac orgy and initiation into the mystery cults before it, tragedy fulfilled the function of *'katharsis* or purification, which renewed the vitality of the participants by relieving emotional stresses due to contradictions generated in the course of social change' (p.359) – but the expressions became less hysterical and violent as society became more complex, coordinated and class divided.

Such was *Aeschylus and Athens.* It is a most thought-provoking work and its virtues greatly outweigh its shortcomings. Harvey Kaye in *The British Marxist Historians* (1984) takes the view that the orientation of the group was towards what he defines as a 'class struggle analysis' in historical interpretation. David Parker (who is rather critical of Kaye) puts it a little differently,

> [Marxism] both insists on a hierarchy of social phenomena that helps systems cohere, whilst simultaneously positing the presence of internal tensions which promote change. For this reason as well as personal inclination, it was entirely to be expected that Communist historians would give prominence to class struggle, as they did from the very beginning; but they did not need to detach it from its structural moorings in order to do so.[21]

Thomson's volume certainly takes that approach, it was the first serious attempt to examine from a Marxist (or indeed any) perspective classical Greek culture in development, taking into account its full social and economic context as well as its political one. Thomson may have sometimes supplied erroneous answers, but he undoubtedly asked the right questions.

Maurice Dobb, *Studies in the Development of Capitalism*

Maurice Dobb was that unusual phenomenon, a communist academic in the twenties, and based in Oxbridge at that. He suffered discrimination and blocked promotion on account of his politics, but at least remained employed. Entering Cambridge as an undergraduate he had intended at first to study history, but switched to economics while remaining conscious that economics is, or ought to be, also a historical science. During the interwar years he had written on various aspects of both capitalist and Soviet economies and in 1943 published *Marx as an Economist*.

Studies appeared in 1946, the same year as the founding of the Group, though the two events were not directly connected. However, with the Communist Party enjoying a higher public profile than ever before, they both reflected the rising significance of Marxism in British intellectual life before that was blighted by the onset of the Cold War. According to Eric Hobsbawm, '... the major historical work which was to influence us crucially was Maurice Dobb's *Studies in the Development of Capitalism* which formulated our main and central problem'.[22]

Studies in the Development of Capitalism is extensive in its scope and profound in its analysis. Its culminating point is, not surprisingly, the Industrial Revolution in Britain. Dobb's purpose was to explain its roots in the course of historical development and the economic and social context of the capitalism in which it occurred. He also examines capitalism's situation in the first half of the twentieth century and ventures some forecasts regarding its future. Throughout he emphasises the central importance of socio-economic class – an indispensable concept for the analysis of exploitation if a poor predictor of political consciousness – to this unique phenomenon in human history.

The opening chapter explores the definition of capitalism, and Dobb examines and rejects interpretations which in one way or another imply that the urge towards capitalism, 'present intermittently throughout most of recorded history', is somehow a permanent component of human nature requiring only favourable circumstances to emerge and flourish. On the very first page he remarks of mainstream economists that ' ... the central concepts of their theory as customarily stated, are modelled on a plane of abstraction that is innocent of these historically relevant factors in terms of which capitalism can alone be defined'. Conceptions such as those of Sombart and Weber, which attribute it to a 'capitalist spirit' emerging in the early modern centuries, have to explain the emergence of that spirit, and their suggested explanations in Judaism or Protestantism are unsatisfactory – there was plenty of 'calculating acquisitiveness' before the Reformation. 'What we clearly need however', Dobb writes, 'is a definition to describe the distinctive institutions of the modern world of recent centuries; and what cannot do this is useless for the purpose that most people intend'. (p.9)

Dobb, writing in 1945, goes on to point out that recent historiography (he cites Ephraim Lipson and William Cunningham) under the pressure of the evidence has moved closer to the definition that Marx pioneered, 'a new type of class differentiation between capitalist and proletarian'. According to Marx capitalism represents a class-divided mode of production in which, overwhelmingly, use-values are produced as commodities for the market and labour power is itself almost universally a commodity – with ownership of the means of production conferring the right, through the wage contract, to extract a surplus from the wage-earning producers.

Furthermore, as an economic system 'characteristic of a distinctive period of history' capitalism presupposes a longer-term history that has been one of *class societies* (Dobb's emphasis), by which is meant dominant and subordinate and mutually antagonistic social and economic classes,

> ... any rising class which that aspires to live without labour is bound to regard its own future career, prosperity and influence as dependent upon the acquisition of some claim upon the surplus of others.(p.15)

Dobb's focus is on England, and for the good reason that it was in that country that industrial revolution first occurred, and it was of course England that Marx cited as his prime example of capital's evolution and functioning. Furthermore he is concerned to argue that capitalism when it came to dominate the British economy was generated through internal processes and that outside influences such as foreign trade were of subordinate importance, though of course not negligible in their effect. He aims to show that it is in production rather than exchange relationships that capital's growth and eventual hegemony lies. By 'capital' of course we are to understand not land or plant and equipment, nor even bank deposits, but specifically money (or, metaphorically, the collective holders of such money) used for the purpose of employing labour.

The following chapter is entitled 'The Decline of Feudalism and the Growth of Towns'. Among historians feudalism is a concept almost as fiercely contested as capitalism. How it is regarded – and it was very different in operation depending on which parts of Europe are being considered – depends on whether it is looked at from the economic, military, judicial or cultural angle. The Marxist understanding includes the notions of a predominantly agricultural economy, with a class of landowners using coercive methods to extract a surplus product, most commonly in the form of labour services but including other obligations, from a dependent peasantry (serfs) bound in one form or another to the service of a particular landowner, and incorporating until a late stage diffused rather than centralised sovereignty.[23] It does not, however, as we will see, exclude substantial market relations in addition to the predominant subsistence production.

English feudalism – later extended to Scotland, Wales and Ireland by assimilation or invasion – is commonly regarded as having originated in the Norman conquest of the eleventh century, though forms of quasi-feudalism are certainly detectable in the earlier Anglo-Saxon period and would doubtless have evolved eventually into the full-blown variety. The feudalism instituted by the appropriately named William the Bastard however included a feature which marked it off from other examples of early feudalism – the state in the person of the monarch was unusually strong vis-à-vis the great feudatories, which included the church and civic governments; and only unusually incompetent ones like Edward II, Richard II and Henry VI could fail to keep them in order. In England the cities never gave any trouble, and except for a couple of occasions neither did the church. Compare that with Frederick Barbarossa, the Holy Roman Emperor, of the twelfth century who squandered his energy and resources warring with the city communes of northern Italy, or his eleventh-century predecessor who lost out in his contest with the Pope. The urban communes of north Italy evolved into independent states such as Florence, Genoa or Milan. The relative strength of the English monarchy was to prove very important.

Dobb contests the importance attributed by such authorities as the great Belgian historian Henri Pirenne to the medieval towns in the decay and undermining of feudalism, but he does not underrate their importance, which was considerable, both as a component of the English feudal structure and in helping to create the conditions for its supersession. Towns were the places where artisan production was carried on, both of necessities, such as coarse cloth, and of luxuries such as high quality cloth, pewter tableware, ornaments and weaponry. They also fulfilled a crucial role as marketplaces for these commodities, and for imported ones like spices, though there existed rural markets as well.

> [Rodney] Hilton shows how at every level urbanization was the consequence of the structure of agricultural activity. In short, the small market towns were determined by 'peasant simple commodity production within the framework and subject to the demands of feudal lordship'. And the large urban centres were the 'consequence of the disbursement of agrarian surpluses by the crown and aristocracy and of the profits from the middleman function of large, middling, and small merchant capitalist'.[24]

The towns were very much part of the feudal structure, and indeed in Scotland there existed a category called 'burghs (the Scottish spelling) of barony', in effect these were towns created by landowners for the commercial advantage they could gain through the dues to be gathered from their markets – the traders of course had to pay a fee for permission to sell their merchandise or buy from the peasantry. Such creations did exist in England too, but better known are the towns which came into being as a result of a royal charter (that naturally had to be paid for as well) conferring the privileges of holding a market, controlling trade and production in the borough (the English spelling), and electing a mayor and corporation to make bye-laws for implementing the regulations.

The evolution of these urban concentrations was very complex, but leaving aside size and importance, tended to follow a standard pattern. The medieval town's citizens (burgesses, bourgeois) typically consisted of wholesale traders on the on the one hand and master craftsmen on the other, employing journeymen (the name means day-workers) and apprentices who did not have the 'freedom of the town' and, like the female population, did not count as citizens. They were frequently at odds with the local baronage or other medieval authority, such as the church – the conflicts between the University of Oxford and the citizens ('town and gown') were notorious. Such strife in England did not however escalate to the level found in Flanders, where the townsmen fought (and bloodily defeated) the nobility in a major pitched battle.

Traders and craftsmen were corporately organised in gilds, and it did not take long for separation into greater and lesser gilds to occur. At first the dominant influence was the merchant gild, which subordinated the craft gilds to its influence and controlled the municipal corporation together with its offices. Many conflicts, accompanied with greater or lesser degrees of violence, resulted from these rivalries. In due course, as production expanded and the towns assumed growing importance, the power of the merchant gild as such tended to diminish in face of the craft gilds – or rather that of some of their members. From the craft gilds, or some of them, evolved a section of master craftsmen who no longer practised their trade, but instead assumed a mercantile role, and employed journeymen and apprentices to do the work, in addition making full status in the gild increasingly difficult to achieve so as to ensure a good supply of subordinate labour.

Whatever sort of urban oligarchy ran the medieval town, privilege, restriction and exclusivity were at the centre of its concerns. 'To acquire political privilege was their first ambition: their second was that as few as possible should enjoy it'. (p.121) To the burgesses of the time the notion of open markets would have struck them as bizarre and akin to madness. Dobb notes that even in England, where all subjects lay under the royal authority, citizens of one town regarded those of neighbouring ones as foreigners. Outsiders, if allowed to trade at all, were only permitted to so under severe restrictions. The underlying concept was that the right to produce or exchange values was a zero-sum game – if one corporation or person had it, someone else was necessarily deprived. A limited market, both in goods and labour (restrictions were set on the number of apprentices which a master might engage) was assumed as a natural phenomenon, and the idea was to grab possession of as much of it as the corporate body was able. Expansion would only depress the market and result in reduced profits. 'To retard this levelling tendency was the essential aim of commercial monopolies in the epoch of merchant capital'. (p.89)

As Dobb points out, in the medieval centuries this was not a wholly unreasonable assumption and programme, and there was a degree of logic behind it. Consequently, neighbouring towns fought and tried to subordinate each other – in England with competition over charter rights rather than with weaponry as in Flanders or Italy.[25] London, being by far the largest as well as the capital and seat of royal government, had a natural big advantage, and provincial towns such as King's Lynn complained bitterly.

Another technique was to reduce the local rural area surrounding the town to virtual colonial status, practised less brazenly in England than on the continent,[26] but nevertheless carried on.

This was the area where there was produced essential raw materials, such as wool, as well as the foodstuffs traded in the town. Every effort was made, frequently in collaboration with the local gentry, to force the peasants to sell any marketable surplus they might produce nowhere else but in the nearby town. The key point so far as Dobb's interpretation is concerned is that during the medieval period the urban centres were wholly integrated into the feudal structure, whose foundation was peasant agriculture with a servile peasantry.

Whatever additional aspects existed, such as the extensive and important wool trade from England to the cloth-producing Flemish cities like Ghent and Bruges, through its tight regulation and monopoly generating a group of very wealthy traders, and whatever the frictions might occur between the two forms of property, aristocratic landowners and urban oligarchies, it all proceeded inside a feudal structure which neither of them questioned. Non-agricultural production and trade did steadily grow in importance, but at a glacial rate with frequent interruptions. It provided no basis at all for a replacement of one mode of production with another, feudalism with capitalism. The ultimate ambition of very wealthy burgesses was to purchase big estates and make themselves landowners so that their descendants might rise into the ranks of the gentry and ultimately aristocracy. A few actually succeeded in that project.

In these circumstances it was foreign trade, particularly in luxuries, or financial relations with the higher aristocracy that was the most attractive form of enterprise,

> ... compared with the glories of spoiling the Levant ... or lending to princes, industrial capital was doomed to occupy the place of a dowerless and unlovely younger sister. At any rate, it is clear that a mature development of merchant and financial capital is not of itself a guarantee that capitalist production will develop under its wing [because of] the need for industrial capital itself to be emancipated from the restrictive monopolies in the sphere of trade in which merchant capital is already entrenched. Without this the scope for any considerable extension of the field for industrial investment will remain limited ... (p.160-1)

The Transition

By the fifteenth century the feudal structure was in crisis throughout Europe. The precipitating circumstance is well known to have been the pandemic of bubonic plague, the Black Death, which swept across the continent in the middle of the previous century and killed at least a third of the European population. However, the severity of the plague was probably not unrelated to the economic circumstances that had gone before. There had been in the thirteenth century expanding population, very modest by modern standards, but discernable, and therefore increasing pressure on good land. This state of affairs suited the landowning aristocracy and gentry (who were also acquiring a taste for more and improved consumer goods) most favourably, for of course it enabled them to strike harder bargains with their peasantry, both serf[27] and free tenants (who did exist), impose harsher conditions and reduce their standard of living and nutrition. In short their health was seriously undermined.

The economic as well as the human consequences were drastic. Previous conditions were reversed. With the enormous death toll there was now a surplus of cultivatable land and a serious labour shortage, and so the balance of power in bargaining had shifted in favour of the working population. The ruling classes were desperate to preserve their advantages and their share of the national income and to continue to enjoy and enhance the lifestyles to which they had become accustomed. Accordingly they used every method at their disposal from legislation to violence to rectify what was from their point of view the intolerable impertinence of upstart demands.

Statutes were issued to bind peasants more securely to their masters and urban workers to their employers. Not content with that, maximum wages were also prescribed. Efforts were made to tighten feudal relations and exactions, and impositions added wherever possible. The resulting pressure-cooker of anger and discontent that was built up over the following three decades exploded in the great Peasants' Revolt of 1381,[28] when the rebels briefly occupied London and executed a number of their most detested tormentors. The rising was suppressed, though more by guile than force, and its leaders hanged, but the institution of serfdom was mortally wounded. By the beginning of the fifteenth century serfs provided a minority of the workforce and by its end serfdom was effectively extinct in England[29] (in Scotland it lasted to the end of the eighteenth century for colliers and saltworkers).

All authorities are agreed that the fifteenth century, therefore, was an era of unprecedented prosperity for the medieval English peasantry and wage workers, despite the civil violence which characterised that century. Lords and gentry, if they wanted to get any income at all from their land, either had to employ labour to cultivate it and employ them on what would have been previously regarded as outrageously generous terms, or else they had to lease their estates out to tenants on whatever terms they could get (and certainly not the hated labour services) at rents which were offered in a buyers' market and very difficult to raise subsequently.

They also borrowed heavily and got themselves into debt to wealthy townsmen, with their estates as security, or else married off their daughters to them, and so infused bourgeois blood into the aristocracy. One way and another it meant that wealth was passing out of the hands of a parasitic class into that of one which would be more likely to use it as working capital whether in agriculture or industry. A final resort of the great ones and their subordinate aristocrats was sheer plunder, either in the shape of attempted foreign conquest or by seizing the property of rival magnates. With possession of the crown as the ultimate prize, rival gangs of noble mafiosi with their hired thugs embarked during the second half of the century in an orgy of mutual murder and dispossession of the losers. This had the welcome outcome of self-decimating the ranks of ennobled gangsters.

What of the major towns with their accumulations of mercantile wealth and centres of industrial production? We have seen that they must not, in Dobb's view, be regarded as the prime originators of capitalism – which does not mean that they were unimportant in that respect. Their career as components of the feudal structure had resulted in the acquisition and concentration in the hands of their oligarchies of mobile assets which were available, once the circumstances became favourable, to be released into the hands of entrepreneurs as industrial capital, and enter directly into production.

In the subsequent century circumstances did change, and change dramatically. With the opening of the Americas to European predation massive quantities of gold and silver bullion entered the European currency system. The exact economic role this metal played is disputed – probably it did not simply increase the quantity of coinage in circulation, but one way or another it certainly generated inflation.

Almost simultaneously, the establishment of the sea route between Europe and Asia round the Cape of Good Hope transformed the commercial map of the world and provoked the collapse of the Venice stock market[30] – what somebody remarked was the most justified crash in history. The historiographical practice of distinguishing particular eras in history is largely fictional, but in this case the sixteenth century can very reasonably be seen as the beginning of early modern times. The world became a unity in a manner that had never previously been. It marked the commencement of globalisation.

A third change was that population growth resumed, and once again labour started to become more plentiful, a situation favourable to employers, though not to labourers. Increased demand for basic commodities stimulated inflationary pressures even further, and, so long as they remained moderate, this too was attractive to the controllers of production, whether agricultural or industrial.

'Enery the eighth I am, I am

To return to England, even in the fifteenth century, which was exceptionally favourable for the small tenant and labourer, there was a cloud on the horizon. This was the practice of enclosure, whereby peasants without legal title to their holdings were dispossessed so that their landlord could create a deer park or more often a sheep run, for wool production was becoming increasingly profitable. The dispossessed were simply thrown out together with their families to survive as best they might – if they were fortunate, to find employment as unskilled labourers. During the fifteenth century this happened on a small scale only, though even so kings were concerned enough about civil disturbance and the loss of military potential to legislate against it – though ineffectually. By the early decades of the sixteenth century however, it was alarming enough to provoke Sir Thomas More's famous remark about sheep eating up men.

That however was only a foretaste of what was to come. King Henry VIII is only mentioned in passing in Dobb's volume, but his reign and his actions were absolutely crucial to the development of capitalism in the English and hence the global context. This Henry Tudor was a tyrant, with a temperament and practices not very dissimilar to those of Stalin – but only the exceptional strength of an English monarch in relation to his great subjects, above all the clerical ones, could have produced the cataclysmic alterations in the economy which set the country on course for industry and empire. Dobb does not underestimate the importance of the changes, indeed they are central to his thesis, but it could be suggested that he does not give all the attention it deserves to the political structures which made them possible.

Henry in the course of his reign from 1509 to 1547 further culled the upper ranks of the English aristocracy, but the crucial development was, following his break with the Papacy, the dissolution of all the monasteries in England, both small and large. There were two momentous consequences. In the first place their estates were sold off, and a colossal quantity of land, amounting, it is estimated, to twenty per cent of English landholdings, were thrown on the market. In the second place, all the monasteries' employees (the monks themselves received a meagre pension) were displaced, to become beggars and vagabonds or available as a cheap, propertyless labour force.

The buyers of the confiscated estates treated them as an investment, either working the land themselves with hired labour, or renting them out to tenants who had similar aims in view. That in itself was an incentive to accelerated enclosure, enormously swelling the ranks of the destitute. During the reign of Henry's daughter Elizabeth these constituted a major social problem; to be healthy and unemployed was treated as a crime and subjected to ferocious punishments including execution. On the continent in France and Germany it was even was even worse. For England in R H Tawney's terse and acerbic comment, 'Villeinage ends, Poor Law begins'. The situation and the reactions of the more fortunate are commemorated in the nursery rhyme, 'Hark, hark, the dogs do bark, beggars are coming to town'.

Dobb describes in detail what happened in one area, Seaton Delavale in Northumberland,

> 'There was in Seaton Delavale township' he quotes a contemporary document, '... twelve tenements whereon there dwelt twelve able men. All the said tenants and their successors saving five the said Robert Delavale either thrust out of their fermholds or so wearied them by taking excessive fines [inheritance payments], increasing their rents ... and withdrawing part of their best land and meadow from their tenements ... he quite thrust them off in one year refusing to repay [money he had extorted from them]', with 720 acres of arable former freeholders land being converted into pasture 'and made into one domaine'

The point was that by means of the upheaval in the English sixteenth century agrarian economy individuals with capital were being brought into association with a class which in Marx's words, 'had nothing to sell but their skins'.

The developments of the sixteenth century marked a crucial and indispensable stage in England's transition towards a capitalist economy and society, but it was as yet by no means firmly established. The majority of landowners still operated on feudal principles and their economic role was as consumers (a dirty word in Tudor times) rather than entrepreneurs. The regime of monopoly still persisted; the gilds strove to maintain theirs, and outside the ambit of the gilds Elizabeth and the early Stuarts were handing out to favoured courtiers monopolies in the manufacture and sale of a wide range of commodities, both luxury and essential, as well as establishing monopoly trading companies for foreign trade.

As Dobb reminds his readers no person or group of persons set out to make capitalism the dominant mode of production. When, over an ostensibly religious quarrel, the Scottish ruling class signed up to the National Covenant in 1638 and went on to invade England in 1639, and the Long Parliament initiated the English Revolution in the following year, none of the movers had the slightest intention of carrying through the political revolution that became Christopher Hill's area of study let alone of entrenching capitalism immovably as the country's future destiny – nevertheless that was what occurred. It happened through the dialectic of unintended consequences – of some seeking profit wherever the market led them and others struggling to survive as best they might in a market-dominated environment.

> While it is true that behind any economic change one has to look for some human action, the action which initiates the crucial change may be inspired by an intention which is quite alien to the final outcome ... (p.9)

Or as summarised by Ellen Meiksins Wood,

> [Capitalism] emerged as an unintended consequence of relations between non-capitalist classes, the outcome of which was the subjection of direct producers to the *imperatives* of competition, as they were *obliged* to enter the market for access to their means of subsistence and reproduction. At the heart of this account is the distinctive 'triad', the nexus of commercial landlord, capitalist tenant and wage-labourer, which marked the most productive regions of the English countryside. (original emphasis)[31]

The revolution was of the deepest consequence, economically, socially and culturally. Possibly things might still have been different if Charles II and his brother, James II, had succeeded in their project of imposing a regime of absolute monarchy, but they failed. The remnants of feudal relations were abolished by the revolution and they were not restored in 1660, unlike the monarchy and certain other elements of the *ancien régime*. Even more important, there were further major land transfers in a capitalist direction. Some cavaliers got back their confiscated estates, but not the ones they had sold to pay the heavy fines imposed by Cromwell's regime. The effect was similar to that which had taken place under Henry VIII – 'improving', enclosing, entrepreneurial landowners multiplied, as did the numbers of a displaced small tenants and cottagers, now become available for labouring work at pittance wages.

The objectionable monopolies also remained abolished. Some still survived for very long distance trade, but general internal manufacture (cloth was still the principal product) and most Atlantic trade became free; the gilds were brushed aside and survived only as ceremonial remnants. Labouring opportunities certainly grew in manufacturing as well as agricultural employments – building, shipbuilding, papermaking, mining of coal and metals, industrial brewing, etc, etc. Samuel Pepys, who was a top bureaucrat running the 'King's Navie' as well as a very revealing diary-keeper, explains in his famous diary how he made his fortune by taking backhanders and enhanced it by cheating seamen out of their miserable wages. Dobb quotes Thorold Rogers,

> From the Reformation till the Revolution the condition of English labour grew darker and darker. From the Revolution to the outbreak of the War of American Independence this lot was a little lightened but only by the plenty of the seasons and the warmth of the sun. (p.237)

The triumph of capitalism in Britain proceeded in two phases – firstly an agrarian and commercial one followed by an industrial stage. The two were of course closely connected, and both significantly influenced, if not determined, by conflict between different types of property on the one hand and between producers and extractors of their surplus labour on the other. By the end of the seventeenth century England and lowland Scotland were market societies, by the end of the eighteenth they were fully capitalist as the final burst of enclosures was wiping out what remained of the independent small cultivators. At that point this capitalist economy was only embryonically machine-driven, a state which had been fully reached a century later.

Mercantilism
In his chapter entitled 'Capital Accumulation and Mercantilism'

Dobb examines the economic ideology, known to historians as 'mercantilism' which prevailed during the transition period. The freedom of English producers and merchants which the Revolution established did not extend to the North American and Caribbean colonies, nor to foreigners. There exclusivity remained the rule. The colonies (which included Ireland) were expected to confine themselves to producing and selling what was needed in England and sell only to England (after 1707 the United Kingdom), and to buy English/British products and no-one else's. Foreigners, who included Scots before the Union, could under the Navigation Acts import to England only in English ships or their own ones, they were forbidden to employ a third party.

> What principally distinguished economic writers prior to the eighteenth century from those who followed after was their belief in economic regulation as the essential condition for the emergence of any profit from trade – for the maintenance of a profit-margin between the price in the market of purchase and the price in the market of sale. This belief was so much part of the texture of their thought as to be assumed rather than demonstrated, and to be regarded as an unquestioned generalization about the economic order with which they were familiar. (p.199)

The system was manifestly an exploitative one, though a pretence of parity was made by prohibiting the cultivation in England of colonial produce such as tobacco. Dobb compares it to the medieval relation of town and adjacent countryside. The best known fact about mercantilist theory (largely following from Adam Smith's denunciation) is that its proponents regarded gold bullion as real wealth rather than as a useful circulating medium for actual values. Dobb points out that the mercantilist theorists were not so daft – their concern with bullion inflow was not because they regarded the metal as some kind of metaphysical economic fetish, but because it measured predominance in the balance of trade with trading partners. Put crudely, the basic idea was to push trading partners as far as possible in the direction of a colonial relationship. It must be remembered that at this time France and Holland were the only countries in the world that were anywhere near the British state of economic development and, with the decline of Dutch power, France was the only serious economic and political rival. The French state was trying to apply the same mercantilist principles as the British one. Trading competition had to be backed up with war, mercantilism was inherently aggressive. One notable success was in 1713 to seize for Britain through war a monopoly of the supply of slaves to the Spanish American colonies.

The East India Company, a survivor of the seventeenth-century cull of monopolies, was of the greatest importance, lasted well into the nineteenth century and was brilliantly successful in implementing these kinds of policies. It monopolised British trade not only with India but with points further east, had its own private army and close links with the British ruling class and succeeded, literally, in turning its main trading partner into a colony, so that it drew revenues not only from commerce but from taxation and governmental functions.

Mercantilism, along with the dispossession of independent producers in town and countryside, was centrally important in the process of what Marx termed 'primitive accumulation'. It generated a concentration of liquid capital which, through various channels, filtered down to lubricate capitalist production in agriculture and industry. Another important source of accumulation was the public debt, which in England was established in the 1690s (through the initiative of a Scottish banker) to meet the financial needs of the state, especially for war. Dobb quotes Marx,

> ...the public debt becomes one of the most powerful levers of primitive accumulation. As with the stroke of an enchanter's wand, it endows barren money with the power of breeding and thus turns it into capital, without the necessity of exposing itself to the troubles and risks inseparable from its employment or even in usury. (p.190)

The key technological breakthroughs of the late eighteenth century, including the most important of them, Watt's development of the existing steam engine so that it became capable of driving a wheel, all have to be understood in this context. The capital was available thanks to dispossession and plunder both at home and abroad, the financial instruments existed for translating it into investment; expanding markets of growing population, overseas consumers, colonists and slaves beckoned the investors; and the workforce composed of individuals with nothing to trade except their labour power was present in sufficient quantity to ensure fierce competition for employment and make it a buyer's market for that labour power. 'The proletariat has the valuable quality, not merely of reproducing itself each generation, but ... of reproducing itself on an ever-expanding scale'. (p.254)

Industrial Revolution
The epochal shift to a capitalist mode of production characterised by power-driven machinery, with influence reaching into every corner of the globe, occurred in the course of the nineteenth century. The Great Exhibition of 1851 in London announced its triumph,[32] and it was celebrated in a different manner in the pages of the *Communist Manifesto* three years earlier.

> The bourgeoisie ... has drawn from under the feet of industry the national ground on which it stood. All old-established national industries have been destroyed or are daily being destroyed. They are dislodged by new industries, whose introduction becomes a life and death question for all civilised nations...
>
> The bourgeoisie, by the rapid improvement of production, by the immensely facilitated means of communication, draws all, even the most barbarian nations, into civilisation. The cheap prices of its commodities are the heavy artillery with which it batters down all Chinese walls ... It compels all nations, on pain of extinction, to adopt the bourgeois mode of production ... In one word, it creates a world after its own image.

It is well understood by historians that the remarkable cluster of technical inventions associated with the Industrial Revolution and pioneered in Britain, could not spring out of nowhere and were made possible only by the existence of an economic climate which encouraged their development; in other words a pre-existing capitalist culture. It is possible to imagine an alternative history in which western capitalism, like the Chinese empire, did not reach beyond the stage of sophisticated technical development of natural power sources and civil engineering – a nineteenth century dominated by water mills, canals and clipper ships rather than coal and steam. Water mill technology could be very advanced – there were textile factories still using it in the early twentieth century.

> Why then do we have instead the actual world we are familiar with? Dobb's answer is that capital was able to accumulate – accumulation being the 'law and the prophets' in Marx's phrase – and capitalism to develop faster than the expansion of the workforce, only on the basis of advancing technology. This was the motive force of the development, not the ingenuity of inventors nor the availability of markets, though of course these also played their part.

> There would seem to be fairly general agreement that ... the technical change of this period had a predominantly labour-

> saving bias ... Capitalism as it expanded was able to economise on the parallel expansion of the proletarian army: capital accumulation was thereby enabled to proceed at a considerably faster rate than the labour-supply was increasing. (p.277)

Dobb argued that the shift towards capitalism in the agricultural economy was predominantly due not to great landowners (though of course their rents benefited and there were exceptions such as the viscount 'Turnip' Townshend) but rather to agricultural entrepreneurs, greedy and hard-driving individuals emerging from the ranks of the better-off peasantry, the equivalent of the Russian kulaks. Similarly the pioneers of industrial capitalism in the era of technical revolution (though again there were exceptions such as the 'Canal Duke' of Bridgewater) were in the main entrepreneurs emerging from the petty bourgeoisie, symbolised by the ruthless and crooked Richard Arkwright, a barber who stole the invention associated with his name and went on to establish himself as the leading cotton-mill owner, the equivalent of a billionaire, and a knight of the realm.

It has often been suggested that the term 'Industrial Revolution' is misleading, as the developments were stretched out over a lengthy period – for example steam technology though available, was not very widely used before the 1830s, and there were hardly any technical advances in the centrally important coal-mining and building industries. The obvious retort is that if the century 1760-1860 did not constitute an industrial revolution what would one look like? Dobb, in using the term, even anticipates E H Carr's point that documentary evidence can be at the same time inadequate and yet too profuse – *'embarras de richesse'* combined with 'a poverty of material' of the kind most needed, so that '... the economic system which emerged from the industrial revolution had so grown in complexity, and moreover was so different in its essence from its appearance as to render the task of interpretation in itself more formidable'. (p.256) He is perfectly conscious that it was a very lengthy and drawn-out process, indeed he emphasises this fact.

Nevertheless, in Lord Macaulay's phrase, which Dobb quotes, economic progress from 1760 became 'portentously rapid', it was 'entirely abnormal judged by the standards of previous centuries' and provoked the cultural shift from a tradition-bound perspective on social reality into 'a conception of progress as a law of life and of continual improvement as the normal state of any healthy society'. (p.256) At the same time,

> The survival into the second half of the nineteenth century of

the conditions of domestic industry ... had an important consideration for industrial life and the industrial population which is too seldom appreciated. It meant that not until the last quarter of the nineteenth century did the working class begin to assume the homogenous character of a factory proletariat. Prior to this the majority of the workers retained the marks of an earlier period of capitalism, alike in their habits and interests, the nature of the employment relation and the circumstances of their exploitation ... the horizon of interest was liable to be the trade, and even the locality, rather than the class ... (p.265)

Both in the above discussion and elsewhere, the *Studies* almost seems to foresee controversies that were to rage among economic historians during the following decades. Dobb also addresses another argument, the one that has been advanced to contest the interpretation of the revolution which stresses its foundations in the dispossession and eviction of agricultural smallholders, as Marx does in the first volume of *Capital*. The contrary view centres on two realities – there was no massive movement of displaced peasants from the southern counties which were the site of the late-eighteenth century enclosures to the northern areas of Lancashire and Yorkshire where the new industries were located. There was also a dramatic rise in the population over the period of industrialisation: could the workforce not therefore have been generated by natural increase?

    These arguments were not central to the interpretation of the revolution at the time Dobb wrote, nonetheless he confronts them, demonstrating that natural increase alone, even with large-scale employment of child labour, could not possibly have proceeded fast enough to supply the growing demand for labour – together with a reserve army of labour sufficient to keep wages at a minimal level. Secondly, the 'natural increase' argument confuses the last phase of enclosure and the industrialisation process with the earlier dispossessions of the sixteenth and seventeenth centuries which established the pre-industrial capitalist economy that was the industrial revolution's foundation. Certainly population increase was very important – without it the industrial revolution could not have taken off; it was needed both in terms of expanding market and labour supply, but it was not the critical variable in the development of capitalism. That was the process of wealth concentration and pauperisation of the wage-earners.

    He deals also with what at the time was known as the Great Depression (to which historians after 1929 added 'of the nineteenth century'), between 1873 and 1896 and how it stimulated, as a response to the squeeze on profit margins, rents and interest the surge in monopoly, imperial conquest and capital export which occurred between then and the outbreak of the First World War. By 1914 the UK, or rather its business classes, possessed £4 billion of foreign assets (around £2 trillion in current values) and drew an annual profit of £200 million from these investments.

Dobb does not deal with the profound changes in the British social culture and political system brought about by the industrial revolution. That is not his remit. What he has done is to trace and explain the processes by which, in the course of several centuries of substantial change in the (predominantly English) economic structure, the propertied classes contrived to extract growing levels of surplus from the basic producers in town and countryside, and in order to do so, kept the latter as near as possible to bare subsistence.

The Twentieth Century
The *Studies* contains a closing chapter, 'The Period between the Two Wars and its Sequel'. To fully understand this chapter it has to be understood that when Dobb completed the volume, against the background of the Attlee government, the total defeat of fascism, social revolution and the advance of Soviet power, he was convinced that capitalism had exhausted its potential and was on the way out. It therefore reads rather like an epitaph.

He explains the financial crash of 1929 and the almost unremitting depression of the interwar period as the predictable outcome of an economic regime dominated by monopoly,

> What seems to be decisive here is that in such a regime the focus of interest is so largely shifted from considerations of production and productive costs to considerations of financial and commercial supremacy: for example to the pyramiding of holding companies ... or of an intimate liaison with banks ... (p.325)

Dobb is not unaware of the consumer impact of new technologies associated with electricity, motor vehicles and chemicals, the expansion of white-collar employment and the improvement in living standards generally in the UK owing to the existence of a huge empire to supply foodstuffs and raw materials cheapened by the depression's impact on their prices. 'Mr Durbin [an inspirer of Gaitskell and Crosland] has even spoken of the "embourgeoisement" of the proletariat, with its Council houses and gardens and radio-sets and hire-purchase furniture, as a twentieth-century development which Marx and his school never foresaw'. (p.348) Here again Dobb is ahead of later revisionist historians who have argued that the interwar depression was really not so bad as historical memory holds it to have been. However, he also emphasises the partial nature of such advances and that they were largely irrelevant to the depressed areas of old industry.

Correctly he attributes the end of the depression not to any turn in the economic cycle or even to the peacetime efforts of government such as the Roosevelt New Deal, but to rearmament and war. He also and at length paints an arresting and horrific picture of the stratagems by which US business strove to obstruct and defy, with armed thugs and heavy weaponry, the National Labor Relations Act, a New Deal measure providing for trade union rights.

> But it is in its dealings with labour that this monstrous regiment of concentrated economic power is most in evidence, and often shows itself as a dominion that operates, not through but independently of the machinery of government ... organized conspiratorial interference with collective bargaining included the mass application of the common anti-union devices such as labour espionage, the use of professional strike breakers, the use of industrial munitions, the blacklist, discriminatory discharge and a host of similar weapons ... cases are also cited where 'police armed by one side of an industrial dispute for the purpose of having them use the arms against the other'. (p.354-5)

And Dobb remarks that in fascism 'we have merely a further and logical stage beyond the measures we have been describing'. (p.357)

Speculating perceptively on the future state of affairs so far as capitalism is concerned, he observes that, 'Any suggestion that State expenditure is to involve investment in lines which compete with existing capital in private hands is likely to evoke strenuous opposition, on the ground that it endangers existing capital values', so that while there is, in order to sustain demand, 'a willingness of industrialists ... to contemplate a new function for the State after the war to replace armament orders: the function of financing an expansionist programme to sustain the market' (p.378) – and he mentions the Beveridge Plan – nevertheless this will never be allowed to encroach too far on private preserves. What Dobb could not predict was that part of the solution would be continuing and increasing postwar expenditure on armaments, consuming an enormous proportion of the state budget, particularly in the USA.

Strengths, weaknesses and impact of the *Studies*
The *Studies* is a work of great depth and insight. It presents a profound analysis that is both coherent and convincing of the manner in which capitalism came to be the dominant mode of production in Britain, while not forgetting that Britain was part of a European and also in due course a world-wide network of economic relations. Nor does it forget, instead it gives priority to, the fact that this was accomplished by means of a cruel and merciless subjection and exploitation of the labour force through all stages of the process. Not the least of its virtues is that it does not moralise, it explains, avoids denunciatory rhetoric and demonstrates how the two developments were inseparably connected. It is a model of its type of approach, and one which Marx himself would surely have applauded.

Nevertheless the volume is not without certain weaknesses. At the time Dobb was writing, the Communist Party was convinced that the capitalist world in general and Britain in particular was headed for a resumption of the great slump, and the closing chapter, on the interwar years reflects this expectation. The Postscript which he added, in the days of 'never had it so good', to the 1963 edition under the title 'After the Second World War' is rather summary and uninformative, unlike the remainder of the volume.

The *Studies* also provoked a famous debate among Marxist theoreticians over the understanding of the transition from feudalism to capitalism, a debate whose echoes are still being heard. It arose from a review of Dobb's volume by the American Marxist Paul Sweezy, and also involved Rodney Hilton, Dobb's colleague as a history group member. It has been well summarised by a Tanzanian blogger as follows,

> In this debate a main point of contention is between Dobb's attempt to demonstrate that capitalism emerged from contradictions internal to feudalism itself; while Sweezy more takes the position that capitalism developed independently of feudalism and overtook it as an external force because of its dynamism in contrast to feudalism's stagnancy.[33]

A further dimension to be added to this is the claim advanced by Sweezy that Dobb was rather too dismissive and insufficiently appreciative of the impact and importance of long-distance trade to the erosion of feudalism and emergence of a capitalist class, in short that more attention should be given to the structure of world economic systems. Dobb himself made some partial concessions on this point.

Harvey Kaye summarises the argument in the following terms,

> In this exchange we recognise the emergence and divergence of two kinds of Marxist analysis of economic history and development. One is decidedly *economic*, focusing on exchange relations, as in Sweezy's critique. The other is politico-economic, focusing on the *social* relations of production and directing us towards class-struggle analysis, as in Dobb's *Studies* and reply.[34]

The argument has been developed further by Immanuel Wallerstein, who writes from a world-systems viewpoint, and his position is contested by Ellen Meiksins Wood and Robert Brenner, who develop Dobb's interpretation from a perspective centred on the English tenant farmer, compelled by market necessity to 'set in train a new dynamic of self-sustaining growth with no historical precedent',[35] (though Brenner also mildly criticises Dobb for not being always sufficiently faithful to his own politico-economic approach). Once again Kaye sums up his achievement, 'Dobb was far from writing "total history" (he never claimed to be doing so) but he pushed economic history beyond economics ... This was significant, for it contributed to the understanding of class as a *historical* phenomenon ...' (emphasis added)[36]

Dobb's *magnum opus* remains, over half a century after its publication, central to our understanding of capitalism's emergence and triumph.

Maurice Dobb

Christopher Hill, *The English Revolution 1640*

Unlike the other two books we are considering, this is a very short volume, 62 small pages in the 1979 edition (the full text, with illustrations, is available on the web).[37] However, as far as historiography is concerned, it was actually of much greater importance than Thomson's and more important even than Dobb's. Written at the CP's instigation to celebrate the tercentenary of the Long Parliament, it marked the beginning of a permanent alteration in the landscape of 'English Civil War' studies and set the agenda for further investigation into the history of the seventeenth century, whether in acclaim and agreement or disdain and rejection. Pretty well everything that has been written since on this theme either endorses and develops Hill's interpretation or challenges and disputes it. As the heading to his *Guardian* obituary puts it, Hill was a 'Marxist historian whose radical interpretation of the 17th century changed the way we think about the English revolution'. The little book of 1940 summed up Hill's approach – his interpretation was not merely political, religious or economic, but integrated all three dimensions in a coherent explanation of what the revolution was and why it occurred. As he put it elsewhere,

> We must widen our view so as to embrace the total activity of society. Any event so complex as a revolution must be seen as a whole. Large numbers of men and women were drawn into political activity by religious and political ideals as well as by economic necessities.[38]

Later he was to write, 'January 1649 [Charles I's execution] was a landmark in human history, a liberation from the tyranny of centuries – not merely the tyranny of kings, but the more powerful and subtle tyranny of superstition'.[39]

Hill, who endured a fair amount of tragedy in his personal life, later said that he wrote it with passion as his testament in the expectation that he would be killed in the war. He was in his late twenties at the time, and had joined the Communist Party as a Balliol undergraduate in the early thirties (and unsuccessfully attempted to join the International Brigade). After his war service he was able to return to academic life, eventually to be elected as Master of Balliol. It is unlikely that *The English Revolution* in itself would have had the influence that Hill's writings were to do, but his subsequent work, published in many volumes over the course of his life, ensured that it did. According to Harvey Kaye, 'In terms both of the quantity and quality of his work, Hill must be considered one of the greatest historians to work in the English language in the twentieth century'.[40] Hill, who was one of the leading dissidents to leave the Communist Party in the wake of the 1956-7 events and did the bulk of his historical work thereafter, nevertheless did not cease to be a Marxist and remarked that the Historians' Group discussions 'were much the greatest stimulus I have ever known'.

In his preface to the 1955 edition Hill acknowledges Dobb's work, remarking that he would need to incorporate its results in a further revised edition of the original text, but, 'this essay must stand as a first approximation, with all its crudities and oversimplifications'. He also appreciates that seventeenth-century developments which he labels 'progressive' because they promoted the expansion of production and potential for the future of 'a more equitable distribution at a new level' (the same can be said of the industrial revolution) were very bad news indeed for those who suffered – 'we do not need to idealise "merrie England" to realise that much was lost by the disruption of the medieval village', whose positive communal features were accompanied by grinding poverty.

> Equality and a communal spirit, combined with a reasonable and rising standard of living, only became attainable after capitalism had performed its historical task of laying the industrial foundation for a socialist society. Hence today [1955] we can at last see our way to realising the dreams of the Levellers and Diggers in 1649. (p.5)

Hill begins with an Introduction in which he sets out his objectives and observes that, 'The Tudors ... were backed by the politically effective classes because the latter did very well out of Tudor rule. Why did the Stuarts ... lose this support'? and goes on to note that the monarchy stood primarily as the representative of that part of the landlord class still attached to feudal relations, but,

> The sharper-witted landowners were grafting themselves as parasites on to the new growth of capitalism, since their own mode of economic existence no longer sufficed to maintain them. It was necessary for the further development of capitalism that this choking parasitism should be ended by the overthrow of the feudal state. (p.9)

In other words, writing in 1940, Hill is stressing that it is not a simplified confrontation between capitalist and feudal elements, nobility against bourgeoisie, but a much more complex form of politico-social development whose outcome is nevertheless the hegemony of bourgeois relationships in economy and society. What in our time we might regard with nostalgia is his footnote comment that, 'The seventeenth-century English Revolution by transferring State power to the bourgeoisie made possible the full development of all the resources of English society in the eighteenth century. A transition to socialism will be necessary to win the same result in England today'. (p.19)

One dimension which does not feature greatly is the British Isles context of the revolutionary years. Scotland and Ireland are mentioned of course in relation to England, but they are not discussed in proportion to their importance in the development of events. Hill cannot be blamed for this however, for at the time he wrote these concerns were largely unexplored historical territory. In the documents printed in David Parker's volume, Scotland receives only passing reference, and always in relation to Calvinist ideology; Ireland not at all. (As far as I can tell there were no inputs to the Group at this time by Scottish communists).

The text of the volume divides onto three sections, respectively titled 'Economic Background of the English Revolution', 'Political Background of the English Revolution' and 'The Revolution' itself, all of which are covered ably and concisely with frequent telling and apposite quotations from the respective combatants. He concludes with a quotation from, Gerard Winstanley, the representative of the Diggers, the most politically advanced section of the radical cause, 'Property divides … the whole world into parties, and is the cause of all wars and bloodshed and contention everywhere. When the earth becomes a common treasury again, as it must … then this enmity will cease'.

Harvey Kaye's view of the Historians' Group is that 'class struggle analysis' was the central theme in their work, and that this applies not least to the question of the English Revolution. Nobody in 1640, it has to be stressed, intended a political revolution, let alone to cut off the king's head and establish a republic. The revolution was initially detonated, as most are, by a quarrel among rival factions of the ruling class, but the 'middling sort', as they were known at the time, who supported the parliamentary faction against the king and his royalists were 'motivated by ideas and values which had developed out of the totality of their class experience' – as were their opponents, and likewise the lower class groupings that came to the fore as the revolution advanced. Hobsbawm himself is at pains to note in his previously quoted chapter on the history of the Group that,

> ... never [reducing] history to a simple economic or 'class interest' determinism ... [and the fact that] the serious concern with plebeian ideology – the theory underlying the actions of social movements – was always ... one of our main preoccupations[41]

was owed largely to Christopher Hill. David Parker, for his part has no difficulty in showing that accusations aimed at Hill of neglecting or downplaying the cultural and ideological dimensions of the revolution – or only adding them as an afterthought in his later work – are absolutely without foundation but only exhibit, 'sloppy scholarship or unrefined preconceptions'.[42] The formulations in *The English Revolution* may be a bit less sophisticated – we recall the 'crudities and oversimplifications' – but they are not essentially different from what he stated later in life, that, '... society must be seen as a whole, that politics, the constitution, religion and literature are in some way (often indirectly) related to the economic structure of society; that there are ruling classes ...'[43]

Hill's subsequent writings throughout his lifetime are nearly all developments of the themes identified in *The English Revolution*. *Lenin and the Russian Revolution* (1947) is an exception. The list is a very long one (Wikipedia cites twenty volumes) and all are extremely informative. If one had to pick out the most important, the main candidates are probably *The Century of Revolution*, an expansion of the 1940 booklet, *Economic Problems of the Church*; *Intellectual Origins of the English Revolution*; *God's Englishman: Oliver Cromwell and the English Revolution* and *The World Turned Upside Down: Radical Ideas During the English Revolution*.

Not surprisingly Hill's work evoked a blizzard of historiographical criticism from commentators who disliked his Marxist approach (I recall being warned about him when I was an undergraduate) most prominently the odious J H Hexter, founder of the Center for the History of Freedom, whose rhetorical style seems to have been copied from some of the more obnoxious polemicists of the early Christian church.[44] Hill was indicted for relying on his unparalleled knowledge of seventeenth century printed sources rather than on handwritten ones, which even Arthur Marwick, no friend to Marxist historians, regarded as a form of snobbery. Hill was not readily forgiven for having revolutionised the interpretation of the revolution, having set the agenda for future study of the seventeenth century and rescued from the condescension of posterity the lower class radicals of the time, previously ignored and disregarded by historians. To be sure, the best of his critics have added greatly to our knowledge and understanding of that century and its central episode, but they have failed to overthrow the framework of interpretation that Hill constructed.

Christopher Hill

Subsequent Debates in the Group

Certainly, and not surprisingly, the discussions which took place in the early days of the Historians' Group gave a great deal of attention to the themes of feudalism, royal absolutism and the seventeenth-century revolution, together with associated ideologies not only in England but also taking into account the work of Soviet historians around this theme (R Palme Dutt too was involved). David Parker's volume reproduces a comprehensive selection of the papers which emerged from these discussions. It demonstrates how central to the Group's concerns were the issues which Hill's booklet had raised. '... it was Hill who drove the agenda of the early modern section, generating debates of remarkable intensity'.[45]

Hill's work had done two things. First he had demonstrated in detail that the events between 1640 and 1660 amounted to a political and social revolution, which, regardless of the conscious and genuine motivations of the participants, was driven by changes in property relationships occurring over the previous 150 years and ended in success with the settlements of 1660 and 1688 – even though these restored a degree of feudal lumber for appearances sake. This was not a new perception – it was evident enough to James Harrington in the seventeenth century itself, let alone to Marx in the nineteenth, though naturally rejected thereafter by mainstream historiography. Hill deepened the interpretation and fleshed it out. What Hill's work also did in addition was to identify a revolution within the revolution, the one which failed, embodying the demands and aspirations of the 'lower orders' and represented by such figures as John Lilburne, spokesman of the Levellers, and the Digger Gerard Winstanley.

His thesis nevertheless provoked brisk and lively debate within the Group, or more particularly its 16th/17th century period section (there were four sections within the Group) less on account of its central postulates as in relation to its details and implications. The documents which David Parker reproduces mostly pertain to arguments in this section, under the two headings 'Absolutism' and 'Ideology'.

An issue of particular contention was the class character of the Tudor monarchy – was it feudal in the Marxist sense or absolutist (and was absolutism itself a means of propping up disintegrating feudal structures or a political development which undermined them) or even proto-capitalist, as Harry Hanson suggested? Hill's own original definition was that the Tudor dynasty was indeed an

English version of continental monarchical absolutism. This was strongly contested by Victor Kiernan, and though he later gave way before the Group's consensus around Hill's definition, David Parker believes that Kiernan's scepticism was justified in the light of later research into the Tudor governmental system. Hill in any case later modified or at least adjusted his position in his 1955 edition to note that this monarchy was 'rooted in feudal society'[46] and thus restricted in its ability to manoeuvre between antagonistic feudal and capitalist proprietors. Elsewhere he wrote that, in contrast to the pre-revolutionary decades, after 1660 the 'landed interest' had become almost as capitalist as the 'money interest'. Back in 1930 Leslie Morton had written that it was a period '… when feudal and capitalist traits jostle one another to form a total world which is neither feudal nor capitalist'.[47]

It was not wholly an argument over historical definitions – there were also twentieth-century political issues at stake. If England had become under Tudor absolutism, already a capitalist society by 1640, despite its surviving monarchical state apparatus, what then was the revolution about – merely brushing off the hangovers of an already dead feudalism? – and what were the implications? Could one mode of production be transformed into another peacefully and without violent revolutionary upheaval? This was a time when the Communist Party was preparing its new programme, *The British Road to Socialism*, which implied exactly that. As the section's document, 'State and Revolution in Tudor and Stuart England', published in the July 1948 number of *Communist Review* phrased it,

> The discussion revealed unclarities about fundamental questions of historical development which are no less important for the present than for the past …The underlying questions of how we determine the class character of a given State and what is the role of the State in the transition from one social order to another are very topical indeed … To understand better what happened in 1649 is to understand better what is happening in Eastern Europe today.

The agreed position of the document was that the monarchy in 1640 was indeed absolutist, was indeed feudal and that the events which followed were indeed the authentic English bourgeois revolution. The views of the Soviet historian M N Pokrovsky, with his posthumous reputation then under a Stalinist cloud (though he was fortunate enough to die before the Great Purges) and who had doubted the feudal character of late Tsarism and regarded it as effectively capitalist, were duly repudiated. Transitions in modes of production *must* have a revolutionary character that was literal, not merely metaphorical (though possibly no longer requiring a great bloodletting).

George Thomson

Conclusion

At the time of their production these three volumes were not written as part of a coordinated project – their appearance at the beginning and end of the war were separate and contingent events, each one had a very different focus, in spite of a degree of overlap between Hill's and Dobb's and acknowledgements to each other – it is said that *Studies* was influenced by discussions with Hill and Rodney Hilton. Taking that into account, and including *Aeschylus and Athens* in spite of its very different theme, all three pointed in a similar direction. As Dobb had remarked a few years before *Studies* was published,

> Marxism ... asserted that the posited harmony of individual interests [referring to Adam Smith et al] did not exist. Consequently reason would not produce harmony but on the contrary reveal contradiction ... it declared that what Comte called 'the essential laws of human nature' were purely abstract; that to search for universal principles on which to found an ideal society was to misunderstand history; and that changes in morality and in ideas in fact followed social change at least as often as they preceded it. For Marx 'history consists precisely in the continuous transformation of human nature' [and] in the opening words of *The Communist Manifesto*, 'the history of all human society, past and present, is the history of class struggles'.[48]

All three of the books discussed in this pamphlet were written in that spirit, and it was the same purpose which animated the History Group in its project to advance what Bill Schwarz terms, in a phrase borrowed from Gramsci, the 'national popular' understanding of English history.

During the seventies and eighties there existed for a time an ambition to write 'total history', producing historical accounts and interpretations which would, for particular periods, incorporate and explain every aspect of human life and interrelationships, from geographical and climatic circumstances to intimate personal activities, via labour and the economy, social institutions, politics, ideology, cultural output and representations, etc. etc. That proved to be an impossible project – reality is simply too inexhaustible. A map as large as the area it represented would be of little use.

However the members of the CP Historians' Group, though without any deliberate aim at such a target, probably got as close to this objective as it was humanly possible to do, though much of that was achieved in the years after the Group's disruption in the mid-fifties. We think in this connection of Hill's subsequent explorations of every dimension of the English Revolution, of E P Thompson's classics, *The Making of the English Working Class* and *Whigs and Hunters*, of Hobsbawm's quartet from *The Age of Revolution* to *Age of Extremes* – not to mention the achievements of Group members such as Rodney Hilton, Victor Kiernan or George Rudé. Harvey Kaye once more sums it up well:

> ... at the same time as they broaden the conception of class experience in historical studies, the British Marxist historians never lose sight of the essential political dimension of that experience. That is, class relations are 'political' in that they always involve domination and subordination, struggle and accommodation ... Moreover their approach does not preclude serious attention being given to elites and ruling classes.[49]

Or in Hobsbawm's own words, 'What I would like to do is not simply ... to save the stockinger and the peasant, but also the nobleman and king of the past, from the condescension of modern historians who think they know better'.[50]

Notes

1. Bill Schwarz, 'The Communist Party Historians' Group', in Richard Johnson et al, eds, *Making Histories: Studies in history-writing and politics*, Hutchinson, 1982, p.44.
2. See Eric Hobsbawm's preface to Joan Allen, Alan Campbell and John McIlroy, *Histories of Labour: National and International Perspectives*, Merlin, 2010.
3. One of them, George Thomson's *Aeschylus and Athens*, was published the following year.
4. Christopher Hill, 'The People's Historian', in Margot Heinemann & Willie Thompson, eds, *History and the Imagination: Selected Writings of A L Morton*, Lawrence & Wishart, 1990, p.11.
5. At the same time, on the 150th anniversary of the French Revolution the French communists made vigorous efforts to present themselves as heirs of the Jacobins.
6. Schwarz, op. cit., pp.55-6.
7. David Parker, *Ideology, Absolutism and the English Revolution: Debates of the British Communist Historians, 1940-1956*, Lawrence & Wishart, 2008, p.246.
8. Alison Ravetz, 'A Note on V G Childe', *New Reasoner* No. 10, Autumn 1959, p.58.
9. de Ste Croix was himself a CP member in the thirties but left the party after its reversal of line following the outbreak of the Second World War.
10. G E M de Ste Croix, *The Class Struggle in the Ancient Greek World*, Duckworth, 1981, p.41.
11. Ellen Meiksins Wood, *Citizens to Lords*, Verso, 2008, p.50.
12. Schwarz, op. cit., p.335.
13. Eric Hobsbawm, 'The Historians' Group of the Communist Party', in Maurice Cornforth, ed., *Rebels and their Causes: Essays in honour of A L Morton*, Lawrence & Wishart, 1978, p.23.
14. George Thomson, 'In Defence of Poetry', *Modern Quarterly*, Vol. 6, No.2, Spring 1951, p.107.
15. *Aeschylus*, 1966 edition, p.15.
16. It also appears in *The Fundamentals of Marxism-Leninism*, published in the early sixties and edited by Otto Kuusinen.
17. Except, of course, for resident foreigners (metics) and slaves.
18. Spartan women despite the militarised and 'totalitarian' nature of their society enjoyed a great deal more freedom than Athenian ones or indeed those elsewhere in Greece.
19. His gravestone refers to his participation at Marathon, but not to the success of his dramas.
20. A parallel legend features in the book of Joshua, where the Israelite commander Jephtha promises God that if given victory he will sacrifice the first living thing which comes out of his house on his return – which turns out to be his daughter.
21. Parker, op. cit., pp.18-19.

22. Hobsbawm, op. cit.
23. See Perry Anderson, *Passages from Antiquity to Feudalism*, NLB, 1974.
24. Harvey J Kaye, *The British Marxist Historians*, Polity Press, 1984, p.61.
25. The medieval federation of mainly German commercial ports, Hanseatic League, regularly employed such violent methods to enforce their commercial monopolies.
26. In Norway, the Hanse cut off the imported grain supply until the king accepted its terms.
27. Serfs were bound to their lords and had few rights, but tradition, which was an important ideological consideration, provided an obstruction to their total helplessness, and therefore bargaining could occur.
28. The immediate occasion for the uprising was the imposition of a poll tax, but that came as the final straw on top of a multitude of impositions and assaults on traditional rights.
29. In Elizabeth's reign a landowner tried to get the courts to declare that his tenants were also his 'bondsmen' or serfs. He failed.
30. Venice had been until then the European entrepot for the trade in Asian products.
31. Ellen Meiksins Wood, *The Pristine Culture of Capitalism*, Verso, 1991, p.10.
32. It should not be forgotten however that even into the following century there remained plenty of intense exploitation of hand labour – hence the investigations and legislation connected with the sweated trades.
33. http://dvdjvalle.blogspot.com/2008/12/paul-sweezy-and-maurice-dobb-debate-on.html (accessed 07.11.2011)
34. Harvey J Kaye, op. cit., p.46.
35. Wood, *Pristine Culture of Capitalism*, p.11.
36. Kaye, op. cit., pp.67-8.
37. http://www.marxists.org/archive/hill-christopher/english-revolution/
38. Christopher Hill, *Puritanism and Revolution: Studies in Interpretation of the English Revolution of the 17th Century*, Secker & Warburg, 1958, p.31.
39. Christopher Hill, 'The English Revolution and the State', *The Modern Quarterly*, Spring 1949, p.117.
40. Kaye, op. cit., p. 99.
41. Hobsbawm, op. cit., pp.38, 44.
42. Parker, op. cit., p.20.
43. Christopher Hill, 'The end of History? Premature Obsequies?', *History Today*, April 1991, p.44, quoted in David Parker, 'The Communist Party and its Historians 1946-89', *Socialist History* 12, p.35.
44. For example (there are plenty of others) Hexter was fond of describing historians he disliked as 'lumpers'. 'Lump' was also a favourite metaphor of Augustine of Hippo.
45. Parker, op. cit., p.10.
46. See Perry Anderson *Lineages of the Absolutist State*, NLB, 1974, for an extended argument that this state formation was feudal in its essential character.

47. A L Morton, *A People's History of England*, Lawrence & Wishart, 1965 edition, p.165.
48. Maurice Dobb, 'Marxism and the Social Sciences', first delivered as a contribution to a symposium in 1942 and subsequently republished in *Modern Quarterly*, Winter 1947-48. Available as a web page at http://www.monthlyreview.org/0901dobb.htm
49. Kaye, op. cit., p.228.
50. Quoted in ibid., pp.228-9.

Bibliography and further reading

George Thomson
Marxism and Poetry (1945)
Aeschylus and Athens (1941, republished 1969)
The Prehistoric Aegean (1949; republished 1978)
The First Philosophers (1955; republished 1973)
The Greek Language (1960; republished 1972)
The Oresteia Trilogy and Prometheus Bound, English verse translation (1965)
From Marx to Mao Tse-Tung: A Study in Revolutionary Dialectics (1971)
Capitalism and After: The Rise and Fall of Commodity Production (1973)
The Human Essence: The Sources of Science and Art (1977)

Christopher Hill
The English Revolution, 1640 (1940, frequently republished)
Lenin and the Russian Revolution (1947, republished 1993)
Economic Problems of the Church: From Archbishop Whitgift to the Long Parliament (1956)
Puritanism and Revolution: Studies in Interpretation of the English Revolution of the 17th Century (1958)
The Century of Revolution, 1603–1714 (1961, frequently republished)
Society and Puritanism in Pre-Revolutionary England (1964)
Intellectual Origins of the English Revolution (1965)
God's Englishman: Oliver Cromwell and the English Revolution (1970)
Antichrist in Seventeenth-Century England (1971, revised 1990)
The World Turned Upside Down: Radical Ideas During the English Revolution (1972)
Change and Continuity in Seventeenth-Century England (1974, revised 1991)
Milton and the English Revolution (1977)
The Religion of Gerrard Winstanley (1978)
Some Intellectual Consequences of the English Revolution (1980)
The World of the Muggletonians, Hill, Barry Reay and William Lamont (1983)
The Experience of Defeat: Milton and Some Contemporaries (1984)
John Bunyan and His Church: A Turbulent, Seditious and Factious People (1988)

A Nation of Change and Novelty: Radical Politics, Religion and Literature in Seventeenth-Century England (1990)
The English Bible and the Seventeenth-Century Revolution (1992)
Liberty Against The Law: Some Seventeenth-Century Controversies (1996)

Maurice Dobb
Capitalist Enterprise and Social Progress (1925)
Russian Economic Development since the Revolution (1928)
Wages (1928)
Marx as an Economist (1943)
Studies in the Development of Capitalism (1946, republished 1963, 1981)
Soviet Economic Development Since 1917 (1948, republished 1966)
Papers on Capitalism, Development and Planning (1967)
Welfare Economics and the Economics of Socialism (1969)
Socialist Planning: Some Problems (1970)

The Author
The Good Old Cause: British Communism 1920-1991 (1992)
The Left in History: Revolution and Reform in Twentieth Century Politics (1997)
The Communist Movement since 1945 (1998)
What Happened to History? (2000)
Postmodernism and History (2004)
Ideologies in the Age of Extremes: Liberalism, Conservatism, Communism, Fascism (2011)

Other works
Geoff Eley and William Hunt, eds, *Reviving the English Revolution: Reflections and Elaborations on the Work of Christopher Hill* (1988)
Harvey J Kaye, *The British Marxist Historians: An Introductory Analysis* (1984)

THE SOCIALIST HISTORY SOCIETY

The Socialist History Society was founded in 1992 and includes many leading Socialist and labour historians, both academic and amateur, in Britain and overseas. The SHS holds regular events, public meetings and one-off conferences, and contributes to current historical debates and controversies. The society produces a range of publications, including the journal *Socialist History*.

The SHS is the successor to the Communist Party History Group, established in 1946. The society is now independent of all political parties and groups. We are engaged in and seek to encourage historical studies from a Marxist and broadly-defined left perspective. We are concerned with every aspect of human history from early social formations to the present day and aim for a global reach.

We are particularly interested in the struggles of labour, women, progressive and peace movements throughout the world, as well as the movements and achievements of colonial peoples, black people, and other oppressed communities seeking justice, human dignity and liberation.

Each year we produce two issues of our journal *Socialist History*, one or two historical pamphlets in our *Occasional Papers* series, and members' newsletters. We hold a public lecture and debate in London five times per year. In addition, we organise occasional conferences, book-launch meetings, and joint events with other sympathetic groups.

Join the Socialist History Society!
Members receive all our serial publications for the year at no extra cost and regular mailings about our activities. Members can vote at our AGM and seek election to positions on the committee, and are encouraged to participate in other society activities.

Annual membership fees (renewable every January):
Full UK   £25.00
Concessionary UK   £18.00
Europe full   £30.00
Europe concessionary   £24.00
Rest of world full   £35.00
Rest of world concessionary   £29.00

For details of institutional subscriptions, please e-mail the treasurer on francis@socialisthistorysociety.co.uk .

To join the society for 2012, please send your name and address plus a cheque/PO payable to **Socialist History Society** to: SHS, 50 Elmfield Road, Balham, London SW17 8AL. Subscriptions can also be paid online. Visit our websites on www.socialisthistorysociety.co.uk and www.socialist-history-journal.org.uk.